JUST FAMILY NIGHTS

Susan Vogt, Editor

faithQuest

Copyright © 1994 by *faithQuest*. Published by Brethren Press, 1451 Dundee Ave., Elgin, IL 60120

Unless otherwise noted, scripture quotations are from the New Revised Standard Version of the Bible, copyright 1989 by the National Council of Churches of Christ in the USA, Division of Education and Ministry.

Illustrated by Beth Gallo

98 97 96 95 94   5   4   3   2   1

Library of Congress Cataloging-in-Publication Data

Just family nights / Susan Vogt, editor.
        p.   cm.
      Includes bibliographical references and index.
      ISBN 0-87178-473-4 (pbk.)
      1. Family—Religious life. 2. Family recreation. I. Vogt, Susan.
BV4526.2.J85   1994
249—dc20   94-8570

Printed in the United States of America

DEDICATION

To my husband, Jim, and children, Brian, Heidi, Dacian, and Aaron. They have been the inspiration, refiners, and guinea pigs for this project (long before there was any talk of a book).

To all the families who have been doing family nights in their own way for many years.

—*Susan Vogt*

CONTENTS

JUST FAMILY NIGHTS

in Calendar Order

MARCH

APRIL

MAY

JUNE

JULY

AUGUST

SEPTEMBER

OCTOBER

November

December

FAMILY NIGHTS

by Categories

PEACEMAKING

RACISM

SEXISM

Stewardship

Media

Family Unity

Justice/Social Action

The Environment

The World

ETHNIC/CULTURAL DIVERSITY

FAITH

RELIGIOUS SEASONS

Lent

Advent/Christmas

Judaism

Nature's Seasons

Spring

Summer

Fall

Winter

Equinox

ACKNOWLEDGMENTS

In addition to the authors of *Just Family Nights*, many people contributed to its development. Jim and Kathy McGinnis, founders of Parenting for Peace and Justice Network (P.P.J.N.), had the initial idea for the work and encouraged it through its long evolution. Along the way, the following people contributed their original wisdom:

Readers: Jim and Kathy McGinnis, Beth Worland, Ann Marie Hansen, Rudy Anderson, Julie Procter, Rochelle Lewis, Gloria Morgenstern, Stuart Falk, Carol Hirt, Colleen Aalsburg Wiessner, Therese Shuler.

Testers (families who reality-tested the family nights): John and Kathy Bookser-Fiester family, Dave and Mary Repaske family, Jean Baublitz family, Jim and Linda Young family, Jim and Debra Chinworth family, Nancy Peirce family, Rich and Sue Burns family, Lita Sharone and Ken Palisin family, and members of the Greater Cincinnati Family Support Group.

A special word of thanks to Jane Bohman, our volunteer typist and sounding board who spent numerous hours typing (and retyping) the manuscript.

INTRODUCTION

What is a **FAMILY NIGHT**?

A time for your family to grow together in unity, faith, and justice. Having a family night is a custom that a number of religious traditions have encouraged over the past decade or two. The goals are usually to promote family unity and to foster healthy values consistent with the family's faith tradition. The Parenting for Peace and Justice Network (P.P.J.N.) undertakes this book to combine the concept of family nights with the family values identified in the founding of P.P.J.N.:

1. Stewardship/Simplicity
   How do we deal with the influence of consumerism and T.V. on our families? How can we best care for the environment?

2. Nonviolence in the Family
   How can we improve communication, cooperation, and peacemaking within our families?

3. Helping Children Deal with Violence in the World
   How can we contribute to world peace?

4. Appreciating Cultural Diversity
   How can we be enriched by the racial, ethnic, and cultural differences among people?

5. Sex-Role Stereotyping
   How can we respect both sexes and help each other reach our full potential?

6. Family Involvement in Social Action
   How can a family make a dent in the needs of our society?

7. Prayer/Spirituality
   How can our faith tradition guide and support our values?

Just Family Nights uses these themes as a basis for developing activities that a family can use at home to nurture stewardship, nonviolence, tolerance, action, and spirituality. They're different from family meetings that are aimed at problem solving. *Just Family Nights* focuses on two fundamental aspects of family: understanding and growth.

Why have a **FAMILY NIGHT**?

It's hard to take the time to grow purposefully. You're busy! But you're also committed! You care about your family and the world. At times you may feel guilty that you are neglecting one of these priorities for the good of the other. *Just Family Nights* is a way to balance both values without guilt or insanity.

Having a regular time, consciously set aside to be together, is a way you can stay faithful to your values and share them with your children. Most families value togetherness, but the fast pace of our society often means that unless a family intentionally saves some time (puts it on the calendar like an important meeting or birthday), it gets squeezed out.

In addition, P.P.J.N. has always tried to avoid burdening already busy families with numerous meetings outside the home. Indeed, when families meet together for mutual support, it is generally very meaningful and enriching, but let's face it—getting together takes a lot of time, scheduling, finesse, organization, and space. Besides, some families just do not have the luxury of living close to other families who are willing to join them in strengthening their values. In response to these needs, an in-home resource like *Just Family Nights* provides flexibility and ease.

How does a **FAMILY NIGHT** actually work?

Just Family Nights follows a simple format:
1. Opening
2. Presentation of Theme
3. Family Response
4. Treat

In addition, you are alerted to any supplies or preparation that you might need ahead of time. Many sessions also offer ideas to adapt the theme for use with toddlers or teens.

OPENING

An opening ritual is helpful to set the family night apart from the rest of the day. It helps calm minds, bodies, and spirits and says, "Be alert, something special is about to happen." Certainly there are many meaningful and life-giving casual times that healthy families share during the course of their life together, but a family night is meant to be a special time, a focused time.

The opening might include the lighting of a candle, singing a song, or just holding hands for a moment of quiet. Candles are effective not just because they're pretty, but they also help focus the attention of young children. (Hint: A long fireplace match works well since it allows plenty of time to light the candle safely.)

A note of caution to parents anytime fire is used: Fire is a fascinating and riveting thing, especially for children. That is why lighting a candle is often used as part of an opening to focus attention. Parents should be clear with children, however, that lighting matches and candles is *only* to be done with a parent present. Make sure the children know that if they would like to recapture the feeling they had when the candle was lit, you will be happy to light one for them and to sit quietly with them as they enjoy it.

The opening needn't be long or involved, but it is important for it to be done with a sense of reverence. Once you've found a ritual that feels comfortable to your family, stick with it. The repetition of a familiar opening helps children move into this special time more smoothly and quickly.

PRESENTATION OF THEME

Each activity provides a description of the event. In a sentence or two, the leader restates in his or her own words what the focus of the evening will be. Generally, this is then followed by some input—a story, a scripture reading, perhaps a dramatization. The point is to understand the scope of the theme.

FAMILY RESPONSE

Although family discussion is certainly encouraged, learning is most effective and enjoyable when many senses are involved—not just mouths and ears. Thus, art, pantomiming, and physical activity help bring the themes to life and deepen understanding. This is especially true when young children are involved. Adult discussion usually loses the children, but hands-on activities enable everyone to participate more fully. Creativity, humor, and simplicity are also key ingredients.

Read the activity instructions sometime in the week before to make sure you have the necessary materials for an activity.

TREAT

Usually the treat will take the form of a dessert, but it could also be an excursion to a favorite place or another fun activity. Suggested treats are listed for each family night, especially if there is a natural connection with the theme. Don't panic if you don't have the time or ingredients to provide the specified treat. These are meant to give you ideas when your mind is on pause and you just don't feel like thinking up something yourself.

Our own children often enjoyed helping with preparing a special dessert, and the older ones made it by themselves. Don't hesitate to ask your children to help! Although we try to avoid spending a lot of money on treats, sometimes it's a "treat" for the parent to go out to an ice cream parlor instead of having to make something.

A final note

Please feel free to improvise and change things to suit your family's style. The sessions in this book all originated from different families' experiences. There is no incorrect way to do it. If an alternative works for you, so much the better.

Who are **FAMILY NIGHTS** for?

The whole family. This usually means everyone living in a particular household is welcome to attend. For some families this might include grandparents, exchange students, boarders, or friends who are "just like family to us." *Just Family Nights* can also be used by a group of several families who want to come together around the themes.

That's the ideal, but families are diverse and don't always come in neat packages. So here are some additional guidelines.

Are my kids too young or too old?

Although *Just Family Nights* can be used by people of all ages, the sessions are primarily geared to families with children between the ages of three and twelve.

Children younger than three obviously don't have the verbal skills to join in discussions. (If they are not a distraction to the rest of the family, however, there's no reason they shouldn't be included.)

It is not uncommon for teenagers to protest (at least publicly) that their families are "boring." It's generally not "cool" to spend organized time with parents and younger siblings (unless the family is out of town and no one they know can see them). They especially don't want to do anything that might appear childish. If you are lucky and your teenagers want to be involved, we have provided more in-depth adaptations for teens. If, however, your family is of mixed ages and the older ones opt out, just go with the family members who are interested. Alternative activities with their peers are often more attractive to teens anyway. *Helping Teens Care* is a resource more directly geared to families with teenagers. (See Appendix D, Resources.)

Does everyone have to come?

No, but … it is most effective initially to enlist the whole family's commitment to try the family nights as a way of being closer and growing together. Carefully schedule the night so that it does not conflict with other commitments. Once scheduled, it has priority. The expectation then is that everyone would be present.

Suppose, however, that one or two family members are not "in the mood" when the time comes. When this happens, gently remind the child that you would enjoy their presence, but if they choose not to be part of the family night, that means not being part of the entire night—including the fantastically exciting activity that is planned and the treat that is his or her favorite dessert.

Of course, this presumes that the reputation of the family nights is a positive one more often than not. Is this a bribe? Yes! But it generally works. In the corporate world this is called an "incentive." In human services it's called "understanding motivation."

Does the **FAMILY NIGHT** require both parents?

No, but it helps! Of course, single-parent households will not have a choice in this matter. The experience of single parents who have authored and tried some of the family nights, however, indicates that it can work very well. The main challenge is that, over time, the single parent becomes the sole initiator and organizer. The bigger problem occurs in a two-parent household when one parent is not interested in participating. This undercuts the goal of family unity and makes it difficult for the children to believe it's an important time if one parent does not participate.

How frequently should **FAMILY NIGHTS** happen?

Ideally, once a week. The consistency of having it weekly and on the same night makes it easy to remember and builds in a rhythm of expectation. Just because it is referred to as a family night, however, doesn't mean that it has to be in the evening. It could be on a Sunday afternoon or whatever works best for you.

Now for the real world! It's hard to do anything once a week for a long period of time. Schedules change. Unexpected meetings or trips come up. We get tired. When our family started having family nights, we made a big effort to be faithful to the same night every week and to have them weekly. We made family night a priority and for the most part scheduled other commitments around it. Now that the children are older and we don't have as much control over their schedules (or our own), we've become more flexible on the day and may go several weeks without having a family night. It seems to work fine because the children have the rhythm ingrained in them. They get back in the groove very easily. It did help, though, in the beginning, to have the nights regularly.

It also helps to respect both adults' and children's priorities so the family night doesn't conflict with a favorite TV program or special activities with friends.

Where's the best place to have a **FAMILY NIGHT**?

Most families prefer gathering around a kitchen or dining room table. Our own family started out sitting on the floor in the living room. We soon learned, however, that although this seemed like a comfortable setting for the parents, the young children had a hard time staying still and paying attention. The dining room table was the next experiment and has lasted for about fifteen years. The advantage of a table is that everyone has a chair, which helps keep wriggling little bodies in place. Also, there is a ready surface for any craft or art project.

In addition to choosing a room in which to hold the family night, make sure the table is uncluttered to avoid distractions (even if this means putting all the clutter under a cloth in the corner).

Also take the phone off the hook so you won't be interrupted.

Who should plan and lead the **FAMILY NIGHT**?

At the beginning a parent would probably take the initiative. After a parent models the leadership style a few times, most older children would feel honored to be a leader. This has the added advantage of investing a child in the process personally. Even when a parent is the primary leader, different roles in the session should be rotated as much as possible. As mentioned earlier, children can help prepare the treat. Older children can do readings. Sometimes one of the children might work with a parent to prepare the session and then co-lead it or do it themselves.

Are **FAMILY NIGHTS** connected with any particular faith?

No, but there is a religious or spiritual dimension to doing something like a family night. It certainly is not religious in the sense of teaching any particular church's doctrine or having a connection with a specific faith tradition. It is religious, however, in the broader sense of deepening the values that undergird the family's life—values that most organized religions and people of good will support.

Whenever we search to better understand life and our fellow human beings or strive to grow in peace, justice, and goodness, we are undertaking a profoundly sacred and religious endeavor. Although certain family nights are connected with a specific faith tradition, this is done in the spirit of exposing the family to the variety and richness of different religious heritages. The goal has not been to present one style of spirituality that fits all, but rather to include a variety of faith traditions. Each of these brings different insights to the search for truth and meaning in life. It is the quest for the Holy, the Other or, if you prefer, simply—God.

Since we anticipate that *Just Family Nights* will be used by many Christian and Jewish congregations, we have generally connected a biblical reading with each theme. Readings from the NRSV have been provided, but families may use the translation of their choice. In addition, a nonbiblical reading is offered for expansion and as an option for families of other faiths or no formal faith.

What if I don't have the recommended supplies?

Not to worry. Improvise or substitute. In the spirit of simplicity, stewardship, and easing family life, families certainly aren't expected to go out and buy materials for the family nights. An effort has been made to limit essential supplies to things often found around a home. Generally, the family nights are not dependent on a specific reading, song, activity, or recipe. The value of the suggestions is to give you a place to start.

In regard to the readings:

It is assumed that families using a scriptural reading have a Bible and, therefore, this is not listed under "You will need...."

Secular readings not included in the text can be found at most public libraries or in your local bookstore.

In regard to music:

An attempt has been made to pick songs that are widely known. Occasionally, however, a less common song is suggested because it fits the theme so well. These special songs are included in Appendix A, Music, when possible. If your family likes to sing, an all purpose family songbook would be a good investment. See Appendix A for suggestions.

In regard to treats and food:

Treats and foods that tie in with the theme have been suggested. Often these are rather arbitrary decisions, however. What your family likes and what is handy are more important criteria. Special recipes are included in Appendix B, Recipes.

Since a candle is used so frequently as part of the Opening, it is assumed that the family has one and is not mentioned under "You will need ...."

Helpful hints for **FAMILY NIGHTS**

1. It must be fun and attractive, or else.

Although this is well understood by anyone who works with children, sometimes we parents get so focused on making a point or doing something that another family raved about that the family night can become a chore or merely a soapbox for the parent(s). It won't stand the test of time. This doesn't mean that every family night has to be a peak experience or equal to a trip to the amusement park, but it's better when everybody generally looks forward to the time.

If interest begins to lag, why not throw in a night of games or splurge on an activity that is rarely allowed, like going out for a fast-food binge. In other words, sharing important values *can* be accomplished by lightening up, throwing in a little humor, and letting go. The family harmony, or "shalom," you are trying to foster is more important than any one evening's theme.

2. Give it time.

Perhaps you will have a wonderful experience the first time you try one of the family nights, perhaps not. It is helpful to ask the family for a commitment to participate in about five family nights before making any firm evaluation. Sometimes everyone is in a good mood, the theme fits the family well, and it clicks. Sometimes there just seems to be a black cloud over the home and everything is a struggle. You might wonder if this is really worth the trouble. After five family nights, most families have experienced both and can make a fair evaluation.

3. Use props and activity as much as possible.

Although many props and activities are suggested for the family nights printed in this book, use your imagination to include other things you have around the home or activities you enjoy. For example, when our family is talking about a certain part of the world, we will often have a map or globe on display. Or, if we are talking about the environment, we might have a bowl of dirt displayed on the table. We have found pantomiming situations and using puppets to be favorite activities in our family. The important thing is to look for symbols that are naturally found in or around *your* house and to adapt activities to skills, knowledge, and supplies that your unique family has.

4. Be positive.

Don't get in the habit of family night becoming primarily a gripe session. Although it is appropriate to sometimes work on solving family problems, you will lose interest if this is the norm. Even the family meeting, which is more of a decision-making, problem-solving forum, started to get a bad rap around our house when the children began to associate it primarily with getting more responsibilities. (See *Parenting for*

Peace and Justice: Ten Years Later, Appendix D, Resources, for tips on how to hold a family meeting.)

5. Have gentle but clear ground rules.

Everyone needs to be clear about what will be acceptable behavior, especially for young children. For example, how much fidgeting will be tolerated? Does hanging your head on the table and playing with the candle wax qualify as lack of interest and, therefore, grounds for being excused? How reverent an attitude or environment will we insist on? Does humming the theme from *Star Wars* really interfere with the family's meditation on peace? These, of course, are all judgment calls.

The family should mutually agree on guidelines for family night behavior. Ones that worked for us when the children were young were:

- The leader recognizes people who want to talk.
- We keep our hands still.
- We rotate who lights the candle and who blows it out.

If someone doesn't "feel" like participating, that's okay, but they have to be part of the *whole* family night to be included in the treat.

If the children are too young to help *develop* the guidelines, parents need to be sensitive to making this an enjoyable time, therefore, minimizing preaching and heavy-handed discipline.

6. Tap your own talents and interests.

Just Family Nights should give you lots of ideas on how to have some interesting family nights at home, without having to create them all from scratch. Each family, however, has a wealth of unique interests, hobbies, and skills to tap. Therefore, consider interests you or your children have and build on them. If someone in your family is very musical, singing might be a common ingredient in your sessions. Other families like arts and crafts and will frequently incorporate these kinds of projects. Our family is neither of these, but we love to ride bikes. So we find ways to weave riding bikes and exploring the neighborhood into some of the themes and activities.

Whatever your special interests, there's probably a unique family night lurking in your subconscious just waiting to be activated. All it takes is a little advance planning.

7. Don't feel you have to do everything printed in the session.

Use only what is comfortable and convenient for your family. Most of *Just Family Nights* has been written to provide structure for families new to the family night notion, plus plenty of options to suit a variety of families. Because of this, some family nights may seem complicated or elaborate. Over time, our own family nights have become progressively simpler and shorter. Often our notes could be written on paper the size of your palm.

Tips for responding to resistance

As wonderful and meaningful as we have found our own weekly family nights to be, we would be doing you a disservice to imply that our times are always peaks of family harmony and insight. Sometimes one or more of us is in a bad mood. Sometimes we're just too tired to plan the family night, or our lives have been so busy and crowded that we've decided that the healthiest choice is to skip a week. Sometimes we've very recently been on vacation together and have had all the togetherness we can take for awhile.

Whatever the reason, any family that holds family nights for awhile is bound to have some failures. Here's a troubleshooting guide for when this happens.

1. *Is this an isolated negative experience or two, or does it look like a trend?*
Wait. If the feedback continues to be negative, check the next points.

2. *Are we having fun yet?*
As mentioned earlier, family night probably can't compete with Disneyland for excitement, but if it doesn't include a dimension of fun, it won't last long. Lighten up and be creative.

3. *Does the time conflict with other prime activities like a favorite TV program, sporting event, time with friends?*
Find a better time.

4. *Are the children involved enough in the evening?*
Perhaps children need to be asked to help plan the evening or facilitate it. Maybe the parents can take a break and let the kids take a turn planning whatever they think would be interesting. (In the long run, one night of watching sitcoms or playing video games is not going to destroy the whole concept.)

5. *Are the children squabbling?*
Agree on a system of taking turns and upholding standards of general politeness.

6. *Do some family members enjoy family night while others don't?*
You may be experiencing the "I'm too old for this" phenomenon. Although the teen adaptations are meant to address the needs of older youth, you may decide it's more prudent to excuse them from family nights and find alternative ways to encourage their developing values. You may have more success if these alternatives include their peers and pizza. (For other teen related tips, see *Helping Teens Care*, Appendix D, Resources.)

7. *"I just don't want to even try this stupid idea."*
    The most important suggestion we can give in response
to this complaint is to *start* young before the child gets to
this stage of development. (Hopefully, it's not your spouse
who's saying it.) Usually children under eight are happy
and eager to join in these special times.

If you're reading this too late for the *start young* approach, you may
need to be very creative or make tradeoffs to give the family nights a
chance. Here's where you may want to negotiate something like:
"Let's try it five times and if you genuinely still don't like it we'll
pursue other means of family togetherness."

Ways to use this book

Just Family Nights has sixty different sessions that correspond roughly to
the calendar year. One way to proceed would be to start in January and
work your way through the book week by week, but you may certainly
start anywhere. There are five sessions offered per month. Not every
family will find weekly family nights workable, however. You also want
to be flexible enough to take advantage of the rhythms and interests of
your unique family. Therefore, we have also provided a categorical listing
in case you are looking for particular topics. You will also find that many
themes are optional in relation to the calendar year and when you use
them. Please feel free to jump around in the book.
    Four appendices follow the sixty family nights. They include songs,
recipes, family night activities, and related resources, including
Parenting for Peace and Justice Network publications.

What do I do when I'm done with the book?

Although it would be convenient to be able to move directly to a
follow-up edition of *Just Family Nights*, this doesn't currently exist. The
hidden blessing in this is that once a family has gotten into the habit of
having a regular family night and has an intuitive sense of the
ingredients, it becomes relatively easy to make up your own. This
personalizes the theme and insures that the family night is always
relevant.
    Here are some ideas for themes to help you get started on your own:
- Current local or world news events
- Seasons of the year (summer, fall, winter, spring)
- Holidays, birthdays
- Issues (justice, truth, poverty, peace, hunger…)
- Nature, the environment

- ◆ Our bodies and senses (appreciating our talents, eyes, ears, feet, hands…)
- ◆ Our emotions (understanding our fears, joys, anger, sadness…)
- ◆ Home issues (jobs, allowances, vacations, safety…)
- ◆ Whatever has come up recently (starting school, death, sickness…)

Enjoy!

PEACE RESOLUTIONS

New Year's Eve or New Year's Day—January 1

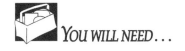 **YOU WILL NEED...**

☐ 2 half sheets of construction paper for each family member (light colors)

☐ pens, pencils, crayons, or markers

**Option 1:
Book of Resolutions**

☐ stapler or punch

☐ 4 half sheets of construction paper for each family member (light colors)

**Option 2:
Countdown to Midnight**

☐ 12 slips of paper with a different month on each (use self-stick notes if you have them)

☐ noisemakers (bells, whistles, pans)

**Option 3:
Game-a-Rama**

☐ Games or activities for the family

NOTE: By the time New Year's Eve comes, many families welcome the opportunity to stay at home and relax from hectic holiday activities. This family night may take place on New Year's Eve as an alternative to going out to parties. Also, allowing the children to stay up later, in itself, can be a treat. New Year's Eve also provides a longer stretch of time to use the "game-a-rama" option. Depending on the ages of your children or your family tradition, however, scheduling this activity for New Year's Eve may not be practical. New Year's Day or a vacation day near the holiday would certainly be an appropriate alternative.

 **OPENING**

Gather the family around a table. Light a candle as a reminder of God's presence and to emphasize the specialness of the time together. Then pass out two half sheets of construction paper to each family member, along with pens, pencils, crayons, or markers. The following incomplete statements may be written on the sheets (one per sheet) beforehand, or family members may write them down as they are read aloud.

> The happiest time for me during this past year was ...
> The thing I regret most about last year is ...

As you read each question, the family members are to think silently for a moment about how they would answer these questions. Allow about thirty seconds to one minute for young children, a little longer for older ones.

Ask each person to write or draw his or her response on the appropriate sheet. Then discuss all the responses briefly, and keep the sheets of paper to include if you choose the book option below.

 **PRESENTATION OF THEME**

We've just finished remembering some good and difficult things about the year we are leaving behind. Now we turn to greet the new year. Often at this time of year people make promises (resolutions) to become better people. Frequently, however, these

 **READING**

Colossians 4:12-15

Epaphras, who is one of you, a servant of Christ Jesus, greets you. He is always wrestling in his prayers on your behalf, so that you may stand mature and fully assured in everything that God wills. For I testify for him that he has worked hard for you and for those in Laodicea and in Hierapolis. Luke, the beloved physician, and Demas greet you. Give my greetings to the brothers and sisters in Laodicea, and to Nympha and the church in her house.

——

Colossians 3:10

[You] have clothed yourselves with the new self, which is being renewed in knowledge according to the image of its creator.

——

A Young People's Vision— A Junior High's Peace Treaty

We children of the world
    declare peace on the
    future!
We want a planet free of
    war and weapons.
We want an end to all

(cont.)

promises are quickly forgotten because change is hard. Since New Year's Day is also widely celebrated as a day of prayer for world peace, let's focus on promises or resolutions to be peacemakers.

Reading:

Colossians 4:12-15 *or*
Colossians 3:10 *or*
"A Young People's Vision—A Junior High's Peace Treaty" *or*
Baha'i selection

FAMILY RESPONSE

Choose one or more of the following options.

1. Book of Resolutions

Tonight we are each going to make our own book of personal resolutions for the new year. Having something on paper will help us remember our promises. Some of the resolutions may be actions that our family will do together so we'll be able to help each other.

On two half sheets of paper for each family member, print the following statements ahead of time, one to a page, or have each person write down the statement as you read it:

> One way I could be more at peace with myself during this next year is …

> One way I could be more at peace with my family during this next year is …

Have a brief discussion about ways each person might make peace with themselves and the family.

Examples of ways to make peace with myself:

◆ I will forgive myself when I make a mistake or do something dumb.

◆ I will save time to do things I enjoy, such as reading, coloring, sports.

◆ I will have some quiet time each day to relax and be calm.

◆ I will remind myself of something I'm good at.

Examples of ways to make peace with my family:

- ◆ I will try to avoid teasing or fighting with the person in the family who's the most difficult for me.

- ◆ When a quarrel is over, I will say "I'm sorry" or forgive the family member quickly.

- ◆ I won't complain about food.

- ◆ I won't scream (or hit or pout).

When everyone has an idea of a resolution they want to make relating to the statements, write or draw it on the appropriate sheets.

Now pass out two more half sheets of paper to each family member. Either print the following statements on each sheet, or have each person write the statement as you read each one.

One way our family could make peace in our neighborhood this next year is …

One way our family could contribute to world peace this next year is …

Discuss what the family might do to promote peace in your neighborhood and in the world.

Examples of ways to make peace in the neighborhood:

- ◆ If there is a person who is not liked or is an outcast in the neighborhood, consider doing something kind for him or her.

- ◆ Make peace with the environment by picking up litter around your neighborhood.

Examples of ways to contribute to world peace:

- ◆ Choose another country and learn more about it during the next year. Perhaps become pen pals with someone from that country.

- ◆ Donate money to causes that help people in other parts of the world, i.e., the United Nations, C.R.O.P., Church World Service, Catholic Relief Services.

- ◆ Study a foreign language.

- ◆ Pray for peace.

After discussing these and other possibilities, hopefully the family can decide on a joint action for promoting peace in the neighborhood or in the world. (Combine them if you wish.)

disease, death and destruction.
Hatred and anger make no sense to us.
We want them done away with!
Our earth gives us food enough for all—we will share it.
Our skies give us rainbows everywhere—we will safeguard them.
Our waters give us life eternal—we will keep them clean.
We want to laugh together, play together, work together,
learn from each other, explore and improve life for everyone!
Grown-up of the world, join us; grab hold of our smiles and imagine …
Together peace is possible!

—7th Grade of Palms Junior High, West Los Angeles, California

———

Now is the beginning of a cycle of Reality, a New Cycle, a New Age, a New Century, a New Time, and a New Year. Therefore, it is very blessed.

—Selected readings of Abdu'l-Baha (Baha'i faith)

Write or draw your resolutions on the appropriate sheets. While preparing your sheets, determine what steps it will take to carry out your decision and when you can do it.

Combine these four sheets with the two from the opening to make a book of resolutions for each person. Make a cover and decorate it with symbols of peace (i.e., doves, rainbows, holding hands). Put a copyright symbol © and your name on your book for authenticity. Then staple the pages or punch holes and tie them with a piece of ribbon. Agree on a place in your home to display the books so that they can be a reminder of your resolutions.

> **NOTE:** Since resolutions, by their nature, are often well intentioned but easy to forget, followup is helpful. Perhaps a family meal on the first day of each month would be a convenient time to check in with each other about how the family is moving toward fulfilling the resolutions.

2. Countdown to Midnight

Tonight we're going to use *noise* as a way to help us remember important events that happened to our family during this past year. Noise is often seen as the opposite of *peace*; for example, we say, "I want some peace and quiet." Noise need not always be negative, however. Noise gets our attention; noise will help us remember our resolutions. Tonight we'll make some joyful and happy noises of remembering.

This option requires that the family night last from three to twelve hours before midnight. Put a piece of paper marking the twelve months of the year next to each hour on a clock. (If you are spending six hours or three hours, every thirty or fifteen minutes respectively could equal a month.) Choose a family member for each month. At the appointed time on the clock, the "January person" makes a noisy racket and interrupts whatever the others are doing, calling them to a central spot. The family then remembers significant things that happened to them during that month. (It might be helpful to have the family calendar handy to prompt memories.) When this reminiscing has run its course, family members return to whatever they were doing until the next

month's noisemaker calls them back. If the family will be staying up late, plan the intervals so that December's noisemaker rings just before midnight.

3. Game-a-Rama

Since this family night closely follows a time when many families traditionally give holiday gifts, sampling new games and toys can be fun. The value, however, is greater than just play, as family members learn to take turns, negotiate, and work together in a common activity. This is the foundation of living peaceably with each other.

Decide how much time the family wants to spend playing together. Divide this time by the number of people in the family. Each person then gets to choose a game or activity for the family to do during their portion of the time. Agree that no request is too silly or dumb and that everyone at home will participate. If this "game-a-rama" goes until midnight on New Year's Eve, celebrate the new year at the stroke of midnight with noisemakers.

TREAT

Since this may be a more festive time than many family nights, you may want several treats, one chosen by each member of the family. Hot mulled cider and eggnog are delicious beverages in keeping with the season. Sing "Auld Lang Syne" if your family is the nostalgic kind. (See Appendix A, Music.)

AGE ADAPTATION

Families with very young children may want to skip the book making and just have fun playing holiday games together. Families with children of mixed ages may play the games first with all the children, then put younger ones to bed and make books of resolutions with the older children.

RELATED READING

Educating for Peace and Justice: Religious Dimensions (Grades K-6 and Grades 7-12) by Jim McGinnis. For New Year's, see units two and three in grades K-6 or unit five in grades 7-12.

—Susan Vogt

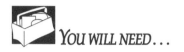 YOU WILL NEED . . .

❑ A candle and clear jar, large enough to fit over the candle

❑ *The Great Kapok Tree,* Lynne Cherry, Harcourt Brace Jovanovich, 1990, optional

❑ National Geographic's video or magazine on Costa Rica (January 1983)

❑ slips of paper with names of rain forest animals for charades

❑ paper and bright paints, crayons, markers, pencils, OR brightly colored clay or modeling compound

❑ shorts and t-shirts for all

❑ heat turned up to the comfort level

 READING

Psalm 8

O LORD, our Sovereign, how majestic is your name in all the earth!

You have set your glory above the heavens. Out of the mouths of babes and infants you have founded a bulwark because of your foes, to silence the enemy and the avenger.

(cont.)

 OPENING

Light the candle and sing "Solar Carol" (Appendix A, Music). Slowly lower a jar over the candle until the flame flickers and dies. Then everyone changes into shorts!

 PRESENTATION OF THEME

While our life goes on relatively smoothly each day, there is something dying far away from us. It may take a long time to die, and we may never see it completely dead in our lifetime, but *eventually* this death will affect our earth, and it may make life harder for our children and grandchildren. Tonight we want to learn what is dying, where it is, and what we can do to save it.

Reading:

Psalm 8 *and/or*
The Great Kapok Tree

> **NOTE:** If you read *The Great Kapok Tree,* use a different voice for each animal. To allow listeners to think about what might happen, pause as the human is awakening. Older listeners may know Chico Mendes to whom the book is dedicated. He gave his life in order to preserve a part of the rain forest.

Show the video or share the issue of *National Geographic* featuring Costa Rica. All but the last five minutes of the video are simply the wonder of the plants and animals in one rain forest. You'll see the "Jesus Christ lizard," which can walk on water. The last five minutes describe the rate of destruction of the rain forest and the ramifications. For very young children, you may want to stop the video early.

FAMILY RESPONSE

Paint, draw, or sculpt real or imaginary plants and animals from the rain forest. Discuss their unique abilities and adaptations. Play charades using animals from the rain forest as subjects.

Light the candle and sing "Solar Carol" again; cover the candle, but this time remove the jar before the flame dies to demonstrate that it's not too late to save the rain forest.

Extend the activity:

To extend this session, consider writing a family letter to a program called The Child-Forester Education Fund, founded by Fr. Bernard A. Survil. This program sponsors a rural parish school in Guatemala. Families must pay $1.00 per child per month to attend, which is hard or impossible for most families. But you can pay these children to do a job. The money they earn planting and tending trees next to their homes will be used as scholarships for schooling. The $5.00 you send will pay for the care of three firewood cypresses, two hardwoods, and one broadleafed, oxygen-producing tree. Send your contribution to:

> The Child-Forester Educational Fund
> c/o The Thomas Merton Center
> 5125 Penn Ave.
> Pittsburgh, PA 15224
> 412-361-3022

If you want to know the name of the child you have sponsored and the location of the grove, write to Director Escuela San Antonio, Senahu, A.V., Guatemala.

 **TREAT**

Serve tropical fruits (pineapple, bananas, coconuts) and nuts (peanuts, Brazil nuts) with pineapple juice, pina colada mix, or coffee. Also look for Rain Forest Crunch ice cream, nut brittle, popcorn, candy chews.

 **AGE ADAPTATION**

For older children, include the last five minutes of the National Geographic video. Discuss the political steps that Costa Rica is taking and whether they might be tried elsewhere. How can we support those attempts? To express concern write letters to Rainforest Action Network, 300 Broadway, #28, San Francisco, CA 94133.

When I look at your heavens, the work of your fingers, the moon and the stars that you have established; what are human beings that you are mindful of them, mortals that you care for them?

Yet you have made them a little lower than God, and crowned them with glory and honor. You have given them dominion over the works of your hands; you have put all things under their feet, all sheep and oxen, and also the beasts of the field, the birds of the air, and the fish of the sea, whatever passes along the paths of the seas.

O LORD, our Sovereign, how majestic is your name in all the earth!

RELATED READING

Journey Through a Tropical Jungle by Adrian Forsyth. S. & S., 1989.

One Day in the Tropical Rainforest by Jean Craighead George. HarperCollins Children's Books, 1990.

Panther Dream by Bob Weir and Wendy Weir. Hyperion Paperbacks for Children, 1993.

—Patricia Higgins and Nancy Corindia

3 CELEBRATING THE DREAM

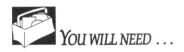

YOU WILL NEED ...

☐ a book or summary of Martin Luther King's life (Many good books for all ages are available at the library. You may want to start reading excerpts from one a few days before the family night.)

☐ strips of red, green, and black paper, ribbon, or yarn (cut in 4- to 6-inch lengths, 2-4 per family member) in a basket or container

☐ a Kwanzaa kinara (candle-holder) with a red, a green, and a black candle, *or* place three white candles in candleholders, designated as red, green, and black by tying ribbon or yarn around the bottom (See Family Night 60 for background on Kwanzaa.)

☐ a single candle for the opening and to light the other candles

OPENING

Light a candle and turn off a few lights. Enjoy the glow and discuss briefly what candlelight does to darkness. With young children, sing a few verses of "This Little Light" (Appendix A, Music).

PRESENTATION OF THEME

During this family night we will use the symbols of Kwanzaa, an African-American celebration, to commemorate the life of Dr. Martin Luther King, Jr., a great African-American who taught people of all races about freedom and equality. Dr. King's birthday is observed on the third Monday of January. We honor Dr. King annually so that we will remember the important things he taught us through his life.

Kwanzaa is observed from December 26 to January 1 each year. In celebrating Kwanzaa, African-Americans and others are reminded of their history and struggle. Kwanzaa is a time to keep African-American families strong, to encourage people to work together for the good of all African-American people, and to picture a prosperous future for African-American children. All of these things were also important to Dr. King.

Reading:

Read a storybook or a part of a biography of Dr. King. As you read about some of his experiences, tell how you may have felt or what you might have wanted to do in his place.

Also read Matthew 5:9-12, 14-16. Talk about how these verses relate to the life of Dr. King. In what ways did he bring light into his world? How did he let his light and the light of God shine? What happened to him as a peacemaker?

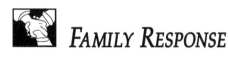 **FAMILY RESPONSE**

Prepare to light the three kinara candles and read the explanations provided below. Family members can participate by doing a reading, lighting a candle, or distributing an equal number of paper, yarn, or ribbon strips to each person. After each candle is lit and the reading given, participants can take turns telling a way in which Dr. King lived the words that were read. For younger children, placing a strip of paper, ribbon, or yarn at the base of a candle when they comment will emphasize the importance of each person's contribution and encourage an orderly and fair distribution of comments.

Reader 1: We light the black Kwanzaa candle to remember that Dr. King worked to create *umoja*—unity in the family, community, nation, and race. *(Take turns naming things that Dr. King was able to change for people, such as desegregation of buses.)*

Reader 2: We light the red Kwanzaa candle to celebrate the *kuumba*—creativity with which Dr. King worked to make his community and the world a better place. *(Tell unique ways in which Dr. King helped people do that, such as finding ways of protesting without using violence.)*

Reader 3: We light the green Kwanzaa candle to remind us to keep our *imani*—faith— holding onto our dream for ourselves and for our future, as Dr. King encouraged us. *(Name some rights and values that Dr. King believed belonged to all people.)*

These are only three of the seven principles of Kwanzaa. If time and interest warrant, you may give the other four principles in a like fashion. (See Family Night 60 on Kwanzaa.)

Conclude this time with each person choosing a colored strip of paper, ribbon, or yarn and telling how they will follow the

 **READING**

Matthew 5:9-12, 14-16

Blessed are the peacemakers, for they will be called children of God. Blessed are those who are persecuted for righteousness' sake, for theirs is the kingdom of heaven. Blessed are you when people revile you and persecute you and utter all kinds of evil against you falsely on my account. Rejoice and be glad, for your reward is great in heaven, for in the same way they persecuted the prophets who were before you.... You are the light of the world. A city built on a hill cannot be hid. No one after lighting a lamp puts it under the bushel basket, but on the lampstand, and it gives light to all in the house. In the same way, let your light shine before others, so that they may see your good works and give glory to your Father in heaven.

example set by Dr. King. Keep the piece to remind you to follow through on your commitment.

Close by holding hands and singing "We Shall Overcome."

TREAT

Share red, green, and brown M&M's candy. Red, green, and black fruit or vegetable pieces could be served as an alternative (for example, red and green apple slices, raisins, cherry tomatoes, broccoli flowerettes, ripe olives.) Mixing all the colors of the M&M's candy together would signify how Dr. King felt the people of the world should be able to live together in harmony. Some of Dr. King's attributes could be renamed as the participants pick out the red, green, and brown pieces of candy. The taste of the candy could also emphasize the sweetness of achieving King's goals. Another analogy can also be drawn: Although each piece of candy is a different color on the outside, inside they are all the same. Color should not determine the core value of a person.

AGE ADAPTATION

For preschoolers, focus more simply on the concept of light. Light can help us see in the darkness. Light the candles and talk about some of the ways Dr. King shone as a light, helping us to see the way. Dr. King helped many people to see that everyone should be treated equally and fairly, regardless of the color of his or her skin.

Deepen this experience with teenagers by discussing a few more questions:

- ◆ In what ways did Dr. King die for an important cause?

- ◆ In what ways did Dr. King die in vain?

- ◆ How would your school be different if everyone practiced what Dr. King taught?

- ◆ In what way would *you* be different if you acted on Dr. King's beliefs?

—Colleen Aalsburg Wiessner

MANY FAITHS

OPENING

If the weather is pleasant, gather outside in a circle and invite the family to gaze at the sky and contemplate how all of this came to be. If the weather is not so comfortable, remain inside, light a candle, and focus on creation as the family ponders the source of life and power in our world. Do either of these activities reverently, in silence, for about one minute.

PRESENTATION OF THEME

One's religion is a very personal and deeply held belief. While we may be very committed to our own religion and see it as a positive force in our lives, others are equally committed to their religion. Sadly, throughout history, people have fought wars over whose religion was right. In our society today, it is important to respect the rights of others to have deeply held religious beliefs even if these beliefs are different from our own.

Each of the world's major religions began with a person who believed he or she had been given a divine revelation. The founder took the message to a few people and they started telling other people. Now each of these religions has millions of people in the world who seek the Divine and use the Holy Book of that religion to guide their lives.

Each religious tradition seeks to help its members understand the human experience and the nature of God. Learning about religions other than our own can help us recognize that some beliefs are universal to all people who seek God. It also helps us see which beliefs are unique and essential to our own faith. Maybe as we learn to understand and respect each other, our differences will seem less important than the care we have for each other.

FAMILY RESPONSE

Tie eight knots in a rope at regular intervals, at least six inches apart. Each knot represents 500 years with the first knot being 2000 B.C.E., and the eighth knot being 2000 C.E. The middle of the rope is year 0 C.E. This activity works best with the rope suspended between two chairs or doorknobs, but it can also be done with the rope laid on the floor.

YOU WILL NEED . . .

☐ rope or string, at least five feet long

☐ clothespins or paper clips

☐ tape, staples, or string

☐ photocopy of world religion cards (Appendix C, Activities)

NOTE: Instead of dividing history between the years before and after Christ, which means little to people of non-Christian faiths, scholars are dividing history into "Before the Common Era" (B.C.E.), which is the formative period of Judaism, Buddhism, and Hinduism, and the "Common Era" (C.E.), which is the period that all the major religions share, including Christianity and Islam. The numbering of years remains the same.

Cut out the Religion Cards for each world religion—founders, Holy Books, and symbols. (See Appendix C, Activities.) Count back by centuries (knots) on the rope, and, using a clothespin, attach each symbol to the approximate founding date of the religion. Take turns matching the founder cards and the Holy Book cards to their religions with tape, staples, or string.

Extending the activity:

1. The Gregorian calendar starts with the birth of Christ. There are other calendars used in the world. Find out what year this is in the Jewish, Muslim, Hindu, and Baha'i calendars. (Dates can be found in an encyclopedia or on the "Multifaith Calendar" available from Canadian Ecumenical Action, 33 Arrowwood Place, Port Moody, BC, Canada V3H 4J1, 604-469-1164.)

2. Increase your understanding and celebration of religious holidays beyond those of your own family. Ask people of other faiths about their holy days, such as Hanukkah, Ramadan, and Ridvan, and make plans to share their traditions with them.

TREAT

Fill a squeezable margarine bottle or cake frosting tube with pancake batter. Squeeze out the batter into a hot skillet in shapes of religious symbols. With each member of the family representing a religion, hold hands and pray for the coming together of the religions to do God's will. Then enjoy the pancakes.

AGE ADAPTATION

Very young children may be happy just to color the symbols while older children play the matching game.

—Sue Blythe

 # GUNG HAY FAT CHOY!

 ## OPENING

Light a candle and listen to Chinese music to set the mood.

 ## PRESENTATION OF THEME

The Chinese New Year, which has been celebrated for about five thousand years, is the most festive and important holiday on the Chinese calendar. It falls on the first day of the new moon after the sun enters Aquarius, which is somewhere between January 21 and February 20 on the Western Gregorian calendar. It signals the end of winter and the coming of spring. The Mien (Laotian hill tribe) and Vietnamese New Year are on the same day. In China the celebration of the new year continues for five days.

Reading

Start out by reading a book to the children about the Chinese New Year (see Related Reading at the end of the session). Also play some tapes of Chinese folk music. You may also wish to observe the tradition of giving each child a small red envelope called *lei-cee* with a little money in it.

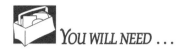 ## YOU WILL NEED ...

- ☐ a book on the Chinese New Year

- ☐ Chinese music on tape from the library

- ☐ construction paper and scissors for lanterns

- ☐ little red envelopes called *lei-cee*

FAMILY RESPONSE

Choose from the following activities.

1. Paper Lanterns

Decorate the house with paper lanterns. Simple ones can be fashioned from construction paper. More elaborate lanterns can be bought in specialty or party stores.

2. The Dragon Dance

The Dragon dance is a traditional part of the New Year celebration. In this spirit the family could play the game called Dragon. A dragon is formed by having each person wrap their arms around the waist of the person in front of them. The head of the

dragon (the first person in line) attempts to catch the tail by tagging the last person in the line. When the tail is caught, the last person then goes to the front of the dragon to become the new head, and the game begins again. (This works best with five or more people. Invite friends or neighbors to join you, if you'd like.)

3. The Chinese Zodiac

The Chinese zodiac has a twelve-year cycle and each year is named after an animal. The animal that represents the year of a person's birth becomes his or her animal sign. The Chinese traditionally believed that one's animal sign determined much of one's character and destiny. From the listing below, have each person find out his or her animal sign and draw a picture of it. Chinese restaurants often have these animals displayed on colorful placemats. Discuss the attributes that might be associated with each family member's sign.

Dragon	1940	1952	1964	1976	1988
Snake	1941	1953	1965	1977	1989
Horse	1942	1954	1966	1978	1990
Sheep	1943	1955	1967	1979	1991
Monkey	1944	1956	1968	1980	1992
Cock	1945	1957	1969	1981	1993
Dog	1946	1958	1970	1982	1994
Boar	1947	1959	1971	1983	1995
Rat	1948	1960	1972	1984	1996
Ox	1949	1961	1973	1985	1997
Tiger	1950	1962	1974	1986	1998
Rabbit	1951	1963	1975	1987	1999

RELATED READING

Gung Hay Fat Choy by June Behrens. Children's Press, 1982.

Mei Li by Thomas Hanforth. Doubleday, 1955.

Twelve Years, Twelve Animals: A Japanese Folk Tale by Yoshiko Samuel. Abingdon, 1972.

TREAT

This celebration could start with a typical Chinese-style meal, such as a stir fry with rice. If a meal is not planned, treat the family to fortune cookies. You might try writing fortunes. End your activities by learning to say Happy New Year in Chinese: *Gung Hay Fat Choy.*

—Karen Schneider-Chen

Do You Know That...

Black History Month—February

It would be ideal to center this family night around a meal at which one or two traditional African-American foods are served, for example: red beans, black beans, or black-eyed peas and rice, greens, sweet potatoes, okra, or peanut butter. (See Appendix B, Recipes.)

Also, if you are African-American, consider inviting a family of a different race to join you and vice versa.

Both suggestions will take a fair amount of planning ahead, but will make the experience more fulfilling.

 ## Opening

Have a meal together as an opening. In your dinner discussion, include the importance of traditions, rituals, customs, and celebrations. Tell stories and reminisce rather than teach or preach.

 ## Presentation of Theme

Of course, it is important for each of us to know our heritage, but until recently, history taught in our schools was almost entirely the history of white people. For this reason, it is important for all of us to supplement our knowledge of Black history. Non-Blacks may not have the same personal investment in this subject as Blacks, but everyone benefits from appreciating the history and culture of neighbors, classmates, or friends who have a different heritage.

Children often are not aware that they are a part of history in the making. This family night will provide an opportunity for people to recognize heroes and heroines of the past and the present. As they appreciate the contributions of Blacks in history, the family can dream about how their own lives will affect history.

 ## Family Response

Choose to do one or more of the following activities.

1. Remembering the Past

Divide into two teams of mixed ages and races (if you have invited a family of another race to participate in this family night). Each team receives half of the hero/heroine index cards that were

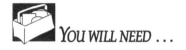 ## You Will Need ...

**Option 1:
Remembering the Past**

☐ ten index cards, each with the name of an African-American hero (Below each name, print several historical facts about the person; see Biographical Sketches in Appendix C.)

**Option 3:
Dreaming the Future**

☐ 1 half sheet of construction paper for each person

☐ crayons or markers and pins

prepared ahead of time. A spokesperson for team A picks one of the cards and states one of the facts. Team B huddles and tries to identify the person on the card. When the correct person is guessed, both teams applaud to celebrate the life of this hero/heroine. Teams alternate, asking the questions until each index card has been used at least once. The point of this game is not to win but to learn. The prize is dessert for everyone!

2. History in the Making

Establish a Frederick Douglass Award honoring African-American people who are making history today. Brainstorm possibilities and list their names and contributions on newsprint or poster board. Save this list and add to it each time you celebrate this family night. Include the names of people in the news, community leaders, teachers, people who help children, and others—well-known or little-known people who touch your family. As each name is written, celebrate the person by applauding heartily.

3. Dreaming the Future

Ask family members to think about how they would like to be remembered in history. Have each person print his or her name and dream on a half sheet of construction paper and tape or pin it to their back. Then mingle and read each other's dreams. Each time someone reads another's dream, pat that person on the back and say something like, "You really might be able to do that!"

After five minutes gather in a circle. Share one-word feelings about the evening.

Extending the activity:

To develop a library of African-American resources...

- ◆ Make a family plan for gathering a library of resources.

- ◆ Scout used-book sales and thrift shops for books by and about Blacks.

- ◆ Create files of articles from newspapers and magazines. Categorize by topic.

- ◆ Borrow books from the public library.

- ◆ Collect books of African folktales.

- ◆ Collect treasures: African-American art, music, sculpture, fabrics.

TREAT

Serve sweet potato pie for dessert, and close by singing "Lift Ev'ry Voice and Sing" (see Appendix A, Music) or chant the following:

We celebrate your being here,
Your being here in history.
We celebrate your being here,
Your being here in history.
Amen, Amen, Amen!

AGE ADAPTATION

Include very young children into the family groupings, because they will enjoy the camaraderie. In dreaming of the future, however, you could encourage them to dream of something they would like to be able to do in a year, such as tie their shoes, ride a bike, or whistle.

—Louise Bates Evans

 **YOU WILL NEED ...**

Option 1:
Sweet Talk

☐ one sheet of red or pink construction paper for each person

☐ markers

Option 2:
Valentines or Letters to Prisoners

☐ address of a person in prison (see option 2)

☐ pens and stationery

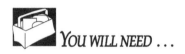 **READING**

Luke 6:27-36

But I say to you that listen, Love your enemies, do good to those who hate you, bless those who curse you, pray for those who abuse you. If anyone strikes you on the cheek, offer the other also; and from anyone who takes away your coat do not withhold even your shirt. Give to everyone who begs from you; and if anyone takes away your goods, do not ask for them again. Do to others as

(cont.)

 **OPENING**

Light a candle and think of people you love.

 PRESENTATION OF THEME

There are several stories about how Valentine's Day started. One common story is that in the third century there was a priest named Valentine who was put in prison for aiding persecuted Christians. While he was in prison, legend has it that he cured the blindness of his jailkeeper's daughter. The night before Valentine was to be executed, he gave a note of friendship to the daughter and signed it "Your Valentine." So Valentine's Day is not only about loving and caring for each other, it is also about caring for prisoners—a group of people who often don't get enough love.

Reading:
Luke 6:27-36 *or*
Luke 10:25-28 *or*
"A Feast for Friends and Sweethearts"

FAMILY RESPONSE

Choose one or both of the following options.

1. Sweet Talk

Have everyone cut out a big valentine shape from a piece of construction paper and put his or her name at the top. (If the children are very young or you want to minimize hassle, you could prepare these ahead of time.) Then, starting with the youngest, the rest of the family calls out all the things they like about this person. For example: "You've got pretty hair." "You're smart." "You're kind." "You're a good cook." As each quality or talent is called out, write it on that person's valentine. Everyone in turn gets a chance to receive this "sweet talk." Decorate the valentines (glitter-glue pens could add variety), and place them in a prominent spot in your home for a few days before returning them to each person to keep as a private reminder that he or she is good.

2. Valentines or Letters to Prisoners

It's nice to love people who are like us and live with us, but it's important that our love also go beyond our cozy family. God's love doesn't depend upon "perfect" goodness, and neither should ours. None of us would qualify. Prisoners in jail sometimes have done very bad things and hurt people. Sometimes they are poor people who don't have the advantages of money or education that we may have, and so they have done something dishonest to get what we have. Sometimes their mother or father may not have been able to love them like we love each other. These prisoners may never have gotten any "sweet talk." If you don't know anyone in prison, you can obtain names and addresses of inmates who are willing to correspond by writing to:

Prison Pen Pals
P.O. Box 1217
Cincinnati, OH 45202

Prison Fellowship
c/o "Mail Call—Pen Pal Match Program"
P.O. Box 17500
Washington, D.C. 20041-0500
703-478-0100

If the family wants to send an anonymous letter or card to a prisoner, you could send it to a nearby prison, jail, or juvenile facility in care of the chaplain.

you would have them do to you.

If you love those who love you, what credit is that to you? For even sinners love those who love them. If you do good to those who do good to you, what credit is that to you? For even sinners do the same. If you lend to those from whom you hope to receive, what credit is that to you? Even sinners lend to sinners, to receive as much again. But love your enemies, do good, and lend, expecting nothing in return. Your reward will be great, and you will be children of the Most High; for he is kind to the ungrateful and the wicked. Be merciful, just as your Father is merciful.

———

Luke 10:25-28

Just then a lawyer stood up to test Jesus. "Teacher," he said, "what must I do to inherit eternal life?" He said to him, "What is written in the law? What do you read there?" He answered, "You shall love the LORD your God with all your heart, and with all your soul, and with all your strength, and with all your mind; and your neighbor as yourself." And he said to him, "You have given the right answer; do this, and you will live."

A Feast for Friends
and Sweethearts

The middle day of February
was special even before the
birth of Christ. In ancient
Rome it was the feast of
Lupercalia, god of flocks and
fertility. It was also a day that
people remembered Juno,
women's protectress in
marriage and childbirth.

   Romans celebrated the
February 14 festival in a sacred
cave called Lupercal.
Unmarried men drew names of
young women from a box.
Each young man was expected
to protect and befriend the
woman who's name he picked
for the next year. Some say
this ritual was in honor of
Cupid, the god of love.

—Armandine Kelly, *Seasonal Stories for
   Family Festivals*

 ***TREAT***

Serve red finger gelatin, cut into heart shapes. (See Appendix B,
Recipes.) The recipe is also on the back of most large gelatin
packages.

—Mary Joan Park and Susan Vogt

DON'T STAND STILL

Lent, Rosh Hashanah to Yom Kippur, Time of Family Transition

  OPENING

Make the room as dark as possible. Light a candle and ask the family to carefully and silently watch the flame flicker for about one minute. Notice how it moves and changes shape. If the flame did not move and change, it would be dead.

Reading

Genesis 1:1-30 (Shorten or use a children's Bible for young children.) *or*

Romans 8:19-23 (Paraphrase for young children; adjust Presentation of Theme as needed.) *or*

Ancient Chinese Proverb

PRESENTATION OF THEME

Just as our planet was not created instantly (God created it in steps we call "days"), so we humans develop in stages too. We grow from baby, to child, to teen, to adult. Sometimes these changes are quick and easy to see. Sometimes they are more gradual like the changes in the seasons. Sometimes a major change may occur that makes us feel like we're almost beginning a new life, such as when we move, start a new job, lose a job, have a baby, change schools.

Decide as a family what change you are going to focus on tonight.

 FAMILY RESPONSE

Choose one of the following activities.

1. For the Penitential Season

This holy season is a time when we especially try to look inside ourselves and change whatever may be keeping us from being the most loving person we can be. Taking a hard look at our faults or imperfections, however, is not always a pleasant experience. It is like dying to oneself to become a new and better person.

Pass out a small piece of paper to each family member. Ask each person to write or draw one thing that they would be willing to try to change about themselves to become a more loving person. Family members take their small piece of paper to

 YOU WILL NEED . . .

**Option 1:
For the Penitential Season**

☐ metal container

☐ one small piece of paper for each family member

☐ matches or lighter

**Option 2:
Coping with a Family Transition**

☐ yin yang symbol for each family member

☐ small pieces of paper and pencils

Planting Activity:

☐ clay pot with garden soil (or pebbles for Paperwhites)

☐ seeds or a bulb: daffodil bulbs or indoor narcissus called "Paperwhites"

Alternative planting activity:

☐ three sheets of green construction paper for each person

☐ pencils

☐ scissors

☐ a tree branch

8 FAMILY NIGHT

 READING

Be not afraid of growing slowly, be more afraid of standing still.

—Ancient Chinese Proverb

____

Genesis 1:1-30

(see Bible for full text)

In the beginning when God created the heavens and the earth, ... [Then] God said, "See, I have given you every plant yielding seed that is upon the face of all the earth, and every tree with seed in its fruit; you shall have them for food. And to every beast of the earth, and to every bird of the air, and to everything that creeps on the earth, everything that has the breath of life, I have given every green plant for food." And it was so.

____

Romans 8:19-23

For the creation waits with eager longing for the revealing of the children of God; for the creation was subjected to futility, not of its own will but by the will of the one who subjected it, in hope that the creation itself will be set free from its bondage to decay and

(cont.)

the fireplace or a safe metal container. The leader invites (and helps) them to burn the paper as a symbol of something they are willing to let go of in order to grow. (If you use a metal container, let the ashes cool, but save them for later.)

2. Coping with a Family Transition

Focus on a specific family transition (a move, change or loss of job, change of schools, divorce, etc.). When we face big changes in our lives, it can be exciting and frightening at the same time. The Chinese yin yang aptly symbolizes the simultaneous existence of both crisis and opportunity.

Pass out a prepared yin yang symbol to each member of the family. Ask everyone to list on one side of the curved *S* line, the things that they don't like about the change that has just occurred (or will occur). On the other side list all of the things that might be good about the change. Invite family members to share their lists and their feelings about the change without comments or criticism from anyone present. While each person shares, the rest of the family tries hard to listen and understand. At the end of the sharing, pass out a small piece of paper to everyone and have them write or draw one thing that might be hard for them because of the change.

> **NOTE:** Depending on the intensity of the discussion, the family may want to spend additional time hearing each other's concerns or fears. You might want to plan a special meal for this purpose.

Whether you have chosen option 1 or 2 above, continue with the following activity. Bring out the pot of soil and seeds or a bulb. Let everyone feel the dirt and mix it around. Comment that in order for things to grow it is necessary for the ground to be plowed or dug up. Sometimes it is messy. Sometimes it is difficult, but this is the *work* of growth. Tonight we will start new growth, both for a plant and for ourselves.

Planting Activity:

Plant the seeds or bulbs according to directions. If you have the cooled ashes from the note-burning activity, mix a few in with the soil to remind the family that growth can come out of pain and difficulty. If this family night is done on Ash Wednesday, Christians may want to use the ashes to bless each other with a sign of the cross.

As a family, water the pot of soil and put it in a sunny location where the family can watch the plant grow and be reminded of the ongoing growth and change in the family.

Alternative planting activity:

If it is not convenient to obtain supplies for planting, you may grow a paper tree. Pass out green paper to each family member. Ask each person to trace around his or her hand on the green paper and cut it out. Put your name on the palm of the paper hand. On the paper fingers, each person writes something he or she will do either to become more loving or to help the family deal with the change they face.

Attach the hands to a branch of a tree or tape them to a window, wall, or poster. To create a pine tree shape, point the fingers down. The first person to tape up a hand, can begin the top of the "tree shape," with the next two hands placed below, then three, etc. More hands may be added during the next few days.

TREAT

In keeping with the theme, perhaps the family would like to try a new treat that no one has ever had before. You could make a game of thinking of new possibilities, such as trying a new flavor of ice cream. Don't let the treat become a burden or obstacle, however. Old family favorites are always appropriate.

AGE ADAPTATION

Very young children may not be able to make the lists for the yin yang symbol, but they should be able to talk about the things they like or don't like about the change.

will obtain the freedom of the glory of the children of God. We know that the whole creation has been groaning in labor pains until now; and not only the creation, but we ourselves, who have the first fruits of the Spirit, groan inwardly while we wait for adoption, the redemption of our bodies.

—Linda Lapp Young

THE HONESTY POLICY

 YOU WILL NEED . . .

❑ blindfolds (long dark socks and large safety pins will do)

❑ *The Boy Who Cried Wolf*, Tony Ross, 1985, optional

 READING

John 13:4-5, 12-17

[Jesus] got up from the table, took off his outer robe, and tied a towel around himself. Then he poured water into a basin and began to wash the disciples' feet and to wipe them with the towel that was tied around him.... After he had washed their feet, had put on his robe, and had returned to the table, he said to them, "Do you know what I have done to you? You call me Teacher and Lord—and you are right, for that is what I am. So if I, your Lord and Teacher, have washed your feet, you also ought to wash one

(cont.)

OPENING

Light a candle and quietly ponder the flame as a symbol of the "Light of Truth." Light helps us to see, both in the sense of visualizing what is real and in the sense of understanding what is true.

PRESENTATION OF THEME

Both George Washington and Abraham Lincoln, great U.S. presidents, were known for their honesty. There is the well-known story of how George Washington cut down one of his father's favorite cherry trees and when asked about it replied, "I cannot tell a lie. I did it." Abraham Lincoln was known as "Honest Abe" due to his reputation for fairness and honesty as a lawyer. Tonight we're going to explore what it really means to be *honest*—the costs and rewards of this virtue.

Reading:
John 13:4-5, 12-17 *or*
The Boy Who Cried Wolf

FAMILY RESPONSE

To take a trust walk the family divides into pairs (oldest person with youngest, next oldest with next youngest, etc.). If there is an uneven number, one group may include three people. Partners choose one to be the leader and one to be the follower. The follower puts on a blindfold and sits down.

   Common instructions: In a minute, the leader will *gently* pull the blindfolded follower to his or her feet and *carefully* lead the follower around the house or yard. The leader's job is to introduce the follower to many interesting and varied objects and sensations in the environment.

   Secret instructions: While the followers are still seated and blindfolded, call aside the partners who will lead and instruct them to incorrectly identify about half of the objects they ask their partner to touch, for instance: "This [rock] is a ball." Or "This [apple] is an orange."

another's feet. For I have set you an example, that you also should do as I have done to you. Very truly, I tell you, servants are not greater than their master, nor are messengers greater than the one who sent them. If you know these things, you are blessed if you do them."

After the trust walk, discuss the following questions:

◆ What did it *feel* like being blind? Did you feel safe? Did you trust your leader?

◆ What did it *feel* like to be the leader and to have the responsibility for your partner's safety?

◆ If you were blindfolded, were you aware that your partner was lying? If you were, how did that make you feel about your partner?

◆ If you were the leader, how did you feel about knowingly telling an untruth? Was it hard?

   NOTE: Make sure that very young children are told that the only reason the leader was allowed to lie was that we are pretending in order to learn the difference between truth and lies. In real life, lies and dishonesty are wrong.

Say something like: Lies are wrong not only because they are untrue, but also because they hurt people and relationships. It's hard to trust a person who has lied to us. Has that ever happened to any of us?

Even though lying is hurtful and wrong, most people have been tempted not to tell *the whole truth* at least once. Usually that's because we're afraid. We're afraid that we'll be punished or someone won't like us if we tell the truth. The truth is that in the long run we will get into bigger trouble and people will like

us even less if they know they can't trust us to tell the truth. For example, if I lied about stealing some money from my boss, not only would I have to pay the money back, but I would probably lose my job too.

Close the session by asking each leader to briefly take his or her partner back to the objects that were not identified correctly and correct the lies.

TREAT

Serve cherry pie (or anything with cherries) in honor of George Washington.

AGE ADAPTATION

For very young children, use puppets to act out the legend of George Washington's honesty.

Teenagers can delve into the finer points of honesty, such as *integrity*. Lying doesn't always require words. It can be done by acting contrary to our beliefs or by omitting information. Discuss the following questions:

How do you feel about "socially convenient lies"?

Do you agree that "the truth is always friendly"? Can you think of any situations in which not telling the truth would be permissible?

How "clean" (totally truthful) do we expect our leaders, elected officials, executives, to be?

Is cheating on taxes okay if you're poor but not okay if you're rich?

Should a terminally ill person be told the truth about how long she or he has to live?

Should a president lie to an enemy about the strength of his or her army or plans for an invasion?

Have you ever been untrue to yourself? Have you gone against something in which you believed, perhaps to be popular or to avoid embarrassment?

RELATED READING

Lizzie Lies a Lot by Elizabeth Levy (junior novel). Delacorte, 1976.

The True Francine by Marc Brown. Little, Brown and Co., 1981.

—Susan Vogt

Trophies for Tightwads

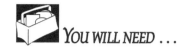

 ## Opening

Invite the family to gather around the kitchen table or other gathering place. Light a candle and sing "Simple Gifts." (See Appendix A, Music.)

 ## Presentation of Theme

Living simply is not a simple task. It takes more creativity and more of our physical and spiritual energy than "buying into" our fast-paced, convenient, throw-away society.

In her book *Living More with Less*, Doris Janzen Longacre suggests a change in "life standards ... characterized by timeless values and commitments." The life standards she suggests are to do acts of justice, learn from the world community, nurture people, cherish the natural order, and "nonconform" freely.

Although these steps may seem overwhelming, one way to begin this process is to look at our living environment and let go of some of what clutters our lives.

Reading:
Matthew 6:25-34 *or*
Basil the Great quotation

 ## Family Response

Family members find two or three items in their bedrooms or around the house they can't live without (i.e., a teddy bear, Walkman portable stereo, Nintendo video game). Examine the use of each item and discuss if these are wants or needs. Discuss what your family actually needs for survival.

Then choose one or both of the following activities.

1. Treasure Hunt

Take a tour of your home together. In each room look at what is scattered on the floor (clutter) and ask: How do we take care of our belongings? What furnishings, knickknacks, and other things unnecessarily "clutter" our lives?

 ## You Will Need ...

☐ boxes or bags for collecting excess clutter, clothes, and other items to give away

Reading

Matthew 6:25-34

Therefore I tell you, do not worry about your life, what you will eat or what you will drink, or about your body, what you will wear. Is not life more than food, and the body more than clothing? Look at the birds of the air; they neither sow nor reap nor gather into barns, and yet your heavenly Father feeds them. Are you not of more value than they? And can any of you by worrying add a single hour to your span of life? And why do you worry about clothing? Consider the lilies of the field, how they grow; they neither toil nor spin, yet I tell you, even Solomon in all his glory was not clothed like one of these. But if God so clothes the grass of the field, which is alive today and tomorrow is thrown into the oven, will he not much more clothe you—you of little faith? Therefore do not worry, saying,

(cont.)

"What will we eat?" or "What will we drink?" or "What will we wear?" For it is the Gentiles who strive for all these things; and indeed your heavenly Father knows that you need all these things. But strive first for the kingdom of God and his righteousness, and all these things will be given to you as well.

So do not worry about tomorrow, for tomorrow will bring worries of its own. Today's trouble is enough for today.

When someone steals
    another's clothes we call
    him a thief.
Should we not give the
    same name to one who
    could clothe the naked
    and does not?
The bread in your cupboard
    belongs to the hungry;
The coat hanging unused in
    your closet belongs to
    the person who needs it;
The shoes rotting in your
    closet belong to the
    person who has no shoes;
The money which you hoard
    up belongs to the poor.

—Basil the Great
  Bishop of Caesarea, c. 365

Look at the clothes in your closets and drawers. Do you have clothing or accessories you don't use anymore that someone else may be able to use?

Collect in boxes or bags clothing and other items you can give away. Determine if there are families you know who need clothes, appliances, or furniture, and arrange to give your excess to these families in a dignified fashion. If this is not feasible, donate the items to a charitable organization.

2. Repair Night

Ask each member of the family to find clothes, toys, electronics, or housewares that need to be mended. Teach the children how to sew on a button or mend a tear. Try to fix all the items collected. For those items you are unable to repair yourselves, look in the Yellow Pages for businesses that repair small appliances.

 **TREAT**

Serve popcorn and apple juice.

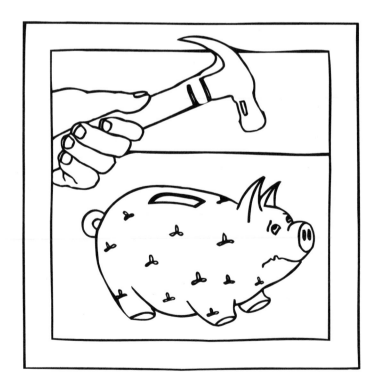

AGE ADAPTATION

Teens as well as adults are often cynical about this "simple lifestyle stuff": What I really want is to become sinfully rich and lead a life of conspicuous consumption. Sometimes this might be a reaction to fanatical parents, teens think, who make a career out of "taking all the fun out of life." As a balance, and to bring in some humor, share the following with your teens.

Several years ago *The Oakland Tribune* held a contest called "How Cheap Are You?" Some of the winners were:

"Top Tightwad Award" for separating two-ply toilet paper to make it go further.

"Tacky Award" for the couple who used two-for-one dinner coupons when taking guests out for dinner.

"Gross Award" for the couple who saved dental floss on a hook for use again.

"Incredible Award" for the person who cut open vacuum bags, emptied them, and then resewed them.

"Dishonest Award" for the person who carried an "Out of Order" bag along to avoid feeding parking meters.

The moral: It's possible to go overboard! Have fun giving each other tightwad awards, complete with homemade certificates and acceptance speeches.

RELATED READING

For children:

The Biggest House in the World by Leo Lionni. Random House, 1968.

For teens and adults:

99 Ways to a Simple Lifestyle by the Center for Science in the Public Interest. Anchor Press, 1977.

Beyond the Rat Race by Arthur G. Gish. Herald Press, 1973.

The Heart Has Its Own Reasons by Mary Ann Cahil. La Leche League International, 1983.

The Simple People by Tedd Arnold. Dial Books for Young Readers, 1992.

Small Is Beautiful by E. F. Schumacher. Harper & Row, 1973.

Staying Home Instead by Christine Davidson. D. C. Heath & Co., 1986.

The Tightwad Gazette. Order this monthly newsletter by writing to: The Tightwad Gazette, R. R. #1, Box 3570, Leeds, ME 04263.

—Ann Marie Witchger Hansen

Why Is There Hunger?

Fasting has a significant role to play in deepening our relationship to God as well as deepening our willingness to sacrifice and take risks for peace and justice and our sense of solidarity with others.

Fast days should be special days of prayer. The tiny moments of wanting to eat during the day can be a reminder to pray and a motivator to work for relief of hunger.

—Jim McGinnis, *Journey into Compassion*

Myth 1:
There is not enough food and not enough land.

Measured globally, there is enough to feed everyone, but the world's food supply is not evenly distributed.

Myth 2:
There are too many people to feed.

Contrary to popular belief, overpopulation is not the cause of hunger. It's usually the other way around: hunger is one of the real causes of overpopulation. The more children a poor family has, the more likely it is that some will survive to help support the family and to care for the parents in their old age.

Myth 3:
Growing more food will mean less hunger in poor countries.

Excess food from production in developed countries does not always get to the people who need it. When land is in the hands of the people who live and work on it, they are more likely to be motivated to make the land more productive and distribution of food more equitable, thus benefiting all peoples.

Myth 4:
Hunger is a contest between rich countries and poor countries.

Hunger will never be eliminated until we recognize the poor of Bangladesh, Colombia, or Senegal as our neighbors. Rich or poor, we are all part of the same global food system, which is gradually coming under the control of a few huge corporations.

Myth 5:
Hunger can be solved by redistributing the food to the hungry.

The rich world's overconsumption and wastefulness are endlessly compared with the misery of the poor. True, adapting a simpler lifestyle helps us to understand our interrelatedness with all people, and less wastefulness is better stewardship. But people will only cease to be poor when they control the means of providing and producing food for themselves. We must face up to the real questions: Who controls the land? Who cultivates it?

Myth 6:
A strong military defense provides a secure environment in which people can prosper.

The security of countries, both great and small, depends first of all on a population that has enough food, enough jobs, adequate energy, and safe, comfortable housing. When a society cannot provide these basics, all the guns and bombs in the world cannot maintain peace.

Adapted from *Make a World of Difference:
Creative Activities for Global Learning*, revised edition.
Copyright © 1989 Office on Global Education,
Church World Service. Used by permission
of Friendship Press.

"Where there is too much ... something is missing."

—Jewish proverb

Related Resources

Hunger Activities for Children, Brethren House, 6301 56th Ave. N., St. Petersburg, FL 33709.

NOTE: Ask the family a day ahead if they would be willing to fast in some way the day of the family night. (The fast could mean skipping a meal or it might just mean not eating between meals.)

OPENING

Gather the family in the living room or other family meeting place other than where the dinner table has been set. Light a candle. Ask everyone to close their eyes and listen to the quiet. Then ask them to reflect on how it feels to be hungry. If possible, while their eyes are still closed and their bodies quieted, present the theme for this evening's family night.

PRESENTATION OF THEME

Lent is a time Christians pause to reflect on their relationship with God through the Lenten traditions of praying, fasting, and sacrificial giving. Jewish people address this same theme in conjunction with Sukkot or Yom Kippur. During this family night, we will remember those who are hungry and poor and whose sacrifice is not a choice. In particular, we will look at the imbalance in world food distribution, one cause of world hunger. (See background.)

Reading:
John 21:4-15 *or*
Daniel Berrigan quotation

FAMILY RESPONSE

Ahead of time, set different types of place settings for your dinner table:

1. An elegant setting for six percent of your family, representing the United States (six percent of the world's population). Certainly there is poverty and hunger in the United States but, taken as a whole, this country is wealthy and privileged.

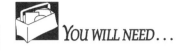

YOU WILL NEED...

- your family's favorite one-dish meal

- different types of place settings for your table

  - an elegant setting for six percent of your family

  - a simple setting for nineteen percent of your family

  - one bowl on newspaper for seventy-five percent of your family

- place cards

READING

John 21:4-15

Just after daybreak, Jesus stood on the beach; but the disciples did not know that it was Jesus. Jesus said to them, "Children, you have no fish, have you?" They answered him, "No." He said to them, "Cast the net to the right side of the boat, and you will find some." So they cast it, and now they were not able to haul it in because there were so many fish. That disciple

(cont.)

whom Jesus loved said to Peter, "It is the Lord!" When Simon Peter heard that it was the Lord, he put on some clothes, for he was naked, and jumped into the sea. But the other disciples came in the boat, dragging the net full of fish, for they were not far from the land, only about a hundred yards off.

When they had gone ashore, they saw a charcoal fire there, with fish on it, and bread. Jesus said to them, "Bring some of the fish that you have just caught." So Simon Peter went aboard and hauled the net ashore, full of large fish, a hundred fifty-three of them; and though there were so many, the net was not torn. Jesus said to them, "Come and have breakfast." Now none of the disciples dared to ask him, "Who are you?" because they knew it was the Lord. Jesus came and took the bread and gave it to them, and did the same with the fish. This was now the third time that Jesus appeared to the disciples after he was raised from the dead.

When they had finished breakfast, Jesus said to Simon Peter, "Simon son of John, do you love me more than these?" He said to him, "Yes, Lord; you know that I love you." Jesus said to him, "Feed my lambs."

2. A simple place setting with utensils, a plate, and cup for nineteen percent of your family, representing other "developed countries" (Europe, Canada, Japan, Austria, Russia, etc.). Many families in these countries enjoy just as high a standard of living as the United States, but they often have a stronger tendency to conserve resources.

3. Only one bowl set on top of newspaper for seventy-five percent of your family, representing the hungry Third World countries (Africa, Asia, and Latin America).

NOTE: Adjust the percentages as needed. For example, a family of six may be divided by 1-2-3, whereas a smaller family may contrast only the U.S. with the developing countries.

Write the names of Third World countries, developing countries, and the United States on place cards so your family can identify with the countries representing the world's imbalance of food distribution.

Now gather the family at your dinner table, which has been set according to the instructions above. Have each family member pick a country "from the hat" and sit at the appropriate place. An adult serves portions of the one dish to each family member according to the world's imbalanced food distribution. The person with the fancy place setting gets the largest portion. The people with the bowls get the least.

Pause before eating to say your family grace or a special prayer invoking God's help for the many hungry families around the world.

Listen to the responses to the size of the portions. Allow family members time to express their feelings about the imbalance. Process this experience with them and try to explain the dilemma. (Kids may decide on their own to share their meal with others who do not have as much. Note the emotions, particularly as they see someone they care about not getting enough to eat.)

After processing this experience completely, adjust food portions as necessary and proceed with your family meal.

Extending the activity:

During penitential seasons, many families make donations to others in need. This experience may motivate the family to contribute to food funds such as CROP, Bread for the World, or Operation Rice Bowl.

 ## TREAT

Serving dessert may seem extravagant since the focus is on lack of food. Perhaps the family could treat themselves to a favorite game together or have a song fest.

 ## AGE ADAPTATION

For younger children who may become confused by the complexity of the problem and the way it is dramatized, adapt the activity for a snack time, and demonstrate the unequal distribution at their level of understanding. Try serving popcorn, animal crackers, or dry cereal.

Sometime in your life, hope that you might see one starved man, the look on his face when the bread finally arrives. Hope that you might have baked it or bought or even kneaded it yourself. For that look on his face, for your meeting his eyes across a piece of bread, you might be willing to lose a lot, or suffer a lot, or die a little even.

—Daniel Berrigan, S. J., *Peacemaking: Day by Day*

—Ann Marie Witchger Hansen

Homelessness has been a much discussed and much misunderstood problem confronting our urban and rural communities throughout America as well as many other parts of the world. Estimates of the number of homeless people in the United States range from a low of 300,000 to several million. The problem increased dramatically in the United States during the 1980s as nearly seventy-five percent of the resources allocated by the federal government for low- and moderate-income housing were slashed.

Other factors cause homelessness too. Floods, fires, tornadoes, earthquakes, and hurricanes, which are clearly beyond our control, also put people out of their homes. The *way* we respond to the homeless is well within our control, however. Other causes of homelessness, such as displacement as a result of war, redevelopment, zoning, code enforcement, highway and airport construction, are well within our control from their inception.

The largest and fastest growing segment of the homeless population is single-parent families with children. Another primary factor affecting low- and moderate-income families with children is the failure of state and local governments and the private sector to adopt policies and priorities that would insure maintenance of an adequate supply of decent, affordable housing for those who need it.

A related dimension of homelessness is the condition of substandard housing. Although people in this situation technically have a home, the quality of their housing is often unsafe or unhealthy.

Interacting with people who are actually homeless will probably not be feasible for most families unless you visit a shelter at night or make some guesses about individuals you see along the street. For this reason, the focus of this family night is to notice substandard housing and imagine what life must be like for the people who live in it.

 **YOU WILL NEED...**

☐ a square outlined on the floor with tape or string according to size of your family: family of 3 (2'x2'); family of 4 (3'x3'); family of 5 (4'x4'); family of 6 (5'x5'), etc.

☐ *Benjamin Brody's Backyard Bag,* Phyllis Vos Wezeman and Colleen Aalsburg Wiessner, Brethren Press, 1991, optional

Option 3: Visit a Different Neighborhood

☐ a neighborhood to visit that is of lower socio-economic status than your own

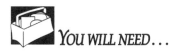 **READING**

Isaiah 58:6-7

Is not this the fast that I choose: to loose the bonds of injustice, to undo the thongs of the yoke, to let the oppressed go free, and to break every yoke?

(cont.)

 **OPENING**

Have the family stand in the square space you have outlined. Ask everyone to stoop, turn around, and try to lie down without putting any part of their bodies outside the square. Experiment with this for about one minute, then try to do the reading while still in the square.

Reading:

Isaiah 58:6-7 *or*
Benjamin Brody's Backyard Bag

Now move to the family's usual gathering place, light a candle, and think about what kind of space each person needs to feel comfortable.

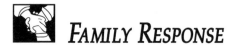 **PRESENTATION OF THEME**

Everybody needs a certain amount of personal space to feel comfortable. Ask: How did the amount we had a moment ago feel to each of us? What would it be like if our whole home was only as big as that space? Tonight we're going to learn about the difficulties some people have who either live in a very crowded, unhealthy space or have no home at all.

FAMILY RESPONSE

Choose one or more of the following activities.

1. Tour Your Own Home

Paying particular attention to the kind of home you live in, take a slow walk around the house. Count the number of rooms, the windows, and how many major repairs are needed (e.g., roof leaks, door won't shut tight, appliance is broken, wood is rotting). Walk around the outside of the house too, noting the size of the yard (if you have one) and repairs needed there also.

2. Draw a Picture of Your Home

The drawing of your home could be of a particular room or the whole house, inside or outside. Family members may want to make individual pictures or draw a common one.

3. Visit a Different Neighborhood

Select a neighborhood to observe the kinds of houses that are there. The ideal way to make this visit is by bicycle, depending on the weather and the ages of the family members. Bikes allow you to go slowly enough to actually notice things but fast enough to avoid gawking.

> **NOTE:** If the family chooses to walk, be sensitive to the reality that you are visiting another family's neighborhood. Be aware that you are an intruder. Avoid staring.

If it is not practical to ride bicycles or walk, take your car or ride the bus to an appropriate destination such as a public playground.

If time and interest permit, the family may also want to tour another neighborhood that is of a much higher socio-economic status than your own for contrast.

Return home for discussion:

This experience naturally leads to comments or questions from children about why some houses are so run down and some places very littered and unattractive. Be prepared for questions like these:

Why don't these families fix up their homes?
Because they don't have enough money. They may not have a job or they may have a very low-paying job.

Why can't they get a good job?
Often it's because they haven't had a good education or their family didn't know how to help them learn.

Why can't they get a good education?
Often schools in poor neighborhoods don't have as much money as schools in richer neighborhoods. Or perhaps their parents were uneducated or sick or had other problems and couldn't help their kids with their school work.

Build on the children's natural curiosity and help them see the complexity of why some people live the way they do. Generally, it's not a matter of laziness as some may think, but rather a combination of generations of hardship, discrimination, poor health, lack of equal education, or lack of jobs paying adequate wages.

If you noticed anyone who seemed to be living on the street on your neighborhood tour, weave homelessness into the conversation too.

Is it not to share your bread with the hungry, and bring the homeless poor into your house; when you see the naked, to cover them, and not to hide yourself from your own kin?

NOTE: If the children don't raise questions, parents may wish to bring up the concerns themselves. With young children it's preferable for this to be a subtle learning experience without formal teaching. Older children can be challenged to look behind the problem of homelessness and substandard housing to seek its root causes.

Extend the activity:

Go as far with this topic as you choose. If you want more information about housing and homelessness in your area, contact your state's housing development agency because every state is required now to have a Comprehensive Housing Affordability Strategy (CHAS). They can tell you if there is a local housing development agency handling homelessness in your community. For more information on homelessness at a national level, contact:

National Low Income Housing Coalition
1012 14th St. NW
Washington, DC 20005
202-662-1530

Habitat for Humanity
419 W. Church St.
Americus, GA 31709
912-924-6935

It's easy to become overwhelmed by the extent of the housing problem. To avoid this helpless feeling, pick one or more practical actions the family can do for people without homes and those who live in substandard housing:

- ◆ Donate food, clothing, or toys to a pantry, shelter, or service organization helping homeless people.

- ◆ Write letters to elected officials, business leaders, and religious leaders, encouraging them to act.

- ◆ Donate to or get involved with organizations such as Habitat for Humanity that are building or renovating housing.

TREAT

Perhaps you are able to buy a treat at a bakery, convenience store, or other place that sells food in the neighborhood you have visited. You might mention to your family that homeless people often salvage food thrown away by grocery stores and restaurants.

RELATED READING

The Biggest House in the World by Leo Lionni. Knopf, 1987.

—Mike Magrath and Susan Vogt

NOTE: Although this family night is scheduled for St. Patrick's Day (perhaps the most widely celebrated nationality day in North America), we hope you will take this occasion to explore your own ethnic heritage, whatever it might be.

Some families or family members may not be aware of their national origins because of adoption, slavery, or a mixed background. In this case, choose a likely or favorite country to adopt and explore its culture.

You may also want to consider inviting your oldest relatives living near you to join you.

OPENING

Light a candle. Ask family members to think quietly of their own grandparents (or, if they can, remember their great-grandparents). Try to picture what they look like and think of any typical sayings that are associated with them.

Reading:
Matthew 1:2-16 (Summarize if the genealogy is too long to keep the attention of the children.) *or*
The Relatives Came or *The Keeping Quilt*

PRESENTATION OF THEME

Tonight we're going to take a step back in time and try to get a taste of what it might have been like to live a hundred or more years ago—about the time when "my grandma's grandma" was a child. To get back to that time, we're going to work our way back generation by generation. We will not only experience what life was like in a more primitive time, but we will also learn about some of the unique heritage and customs of the countries from which our ancestors came.

FAMILY RESPONSE

If you don't already have a family tree, make a simple one (see the example in Appendix C). Talk about each individual as you put his or her name down. Do you know any interesting family stories about their lives, idiosyncrasies, sayings, values, or personalities?

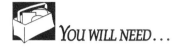
YOU WILL NEED...

☐ several candles

☐ mementos of your family's heritage (i.e., songs, clothes, pictures, artifacts, food)

☐ family tree form (make your own or photocopy the one in Appendix C, Activities)

☐ *The Relatives Came,* Cynthia Rylant, Bradbury Press, 1985 (for ages 3-9), optional

☐ *The Keeping Quilt,* Patricia Polacco, Silver Burdett Press, 1992 (for ages 5-10), optional

READING

Matthew 1:2-16

Abraham was the father of Isaac, and Isaac the father of Jacob, and Jacob the father of Judah and his brothers, and Judah the father of Perez and Zerah by Tamar, and Perez the father of Hezron, and Hezron the father of Aram, and Aram the father of Aminadab, and

(cont.)

Aminadab the father of Nahshon, and Nahshon the father of Salmon, and Salmon the father of Boaz by Rahab, and Boaz the father of Obed by Ruth, and Obed the father of Jesse, and Jesse the father of King David.

And David was the father of Solomon by the wife of Uriah, and Solomon the father of Rehoboam, and Rehoboam the father of Abijah, and Abijah the father of Asaph, and Asaph the father of Jehoshaphat, and Jehoshaphat the father of Joram, and Joram the father of Uzziah, and Uzziah the father of Jotham, and Jotham the father of Ahaz, and Ahaz the father of Hezekiah, and Hezekiah the father of Manasseh, and Manasseh the father of Amos, and Amos the father of Josiah, and Josiah the father of Jechoniah and his brothers, at the time of the deportation to Babylon.

And after the deportation to Babylon: Jechoniah was the father of Salathiel, and Salathiel the father of Zerubbabel, and Zerubbabel the father of Abiud, and Abiud the father of Eliakim, and Eliakim the father of Azor, and Azor the father of Zadok, and Zadok the father of Achim, and Achim the father of Eliud, and Eliud the father of Eleazar,

(cont.)

Are there any physical resemblances to members of your immediate family?

Your direct recollections may be limited to the parents' grandparents. Generations with whom you are unfamiliar can be noted simply by a family name or relationship. This exercise will probably take you back to somewhere between 1850 and 1900.

To complete your travel backward through time, transform your home into a typical late nineteenth-century dwelling. If you know the kind of lifestyle particular ancestors were living at that time (rural, urban, homestead, etc.), try to approximate it. If not, use the following guidelines:

- No computers or compact discs (not common until 1990s)
- No VCRs, microwaves, or video games (not common until 1980s)
- No cassette tape recorders (not common until 1970s)
- No TVs (not common until 1950s)

Now it gets a little harder:

- No talking movies (not common until 1930s)
- No automobiles (not common until 1920s)
- No refrigerators (not common until 1920s)
- No electric stoves (not common until 1910s)
- No indoor plumbing (not common until 1910s)
- No electric lights, telephone, phonograph, or anything run by electricity (not common until 1900s)

  NOTE: Dates of inventions are geared to when an item came into common use and may vary (give or take a decade) depending on (a) socio-economic status or whether one lived (b) in a rural or urban setting, (c) in the East, Midwest, or West. A list of inventions with dates are listed in *The World Almanac* under "Science and Technology."

Decide as a family how far you would like to go back in time. (We recommend a pre-light bulb decade for greatest effect.) Then take a slow walk together through every room in your home. At each room pause and take stock of what would be different in the decade you have selected. What items weren't invented yet? What items would look different? As you leave each room, turn off anything that would not have been a common possession or fixture. When you get to the final room (probably the living room), settle in for an evening in your time warp. Assuming you have chosen a time before 1900 (when electric lighting was not common), you will need to place candles and oil or kerosene

lamps in several secure places. If you have a fireplace, think about what it would be like for this to be your primary means for heating and cooking.

> **NOTE:** If you are lighting only by candles or oil lamps, be sure to make a rule that no one is to leave candles burning in unoccupied rooms.

Spend the remainder of the evening exploring your ethnic heritage, being as faithful as possible to the lifestyle of your decade.

- ◆ Parents or grandparents may describe ethnic artifacts and talk about their use or meaning, for example: Irish lace, German beer steins, Ukrainian Easter eggs, African ivory.

- ◆ Tell stories about what life was like in the "old country" or at least a generation or two ago in your own country.

- ◆ Sing ethnic songs. (Remember that tapes and CDs were not invented yet.)

TREAT

Of course, a traditional ethnic dessert is appropriate. Make it ahead of time, or just eat something fresh, like fruit. If you feel energetic or want to be "pure," try cooking over a wood fire or making ice cream in an old-fashioned ice cream maker.

AGE ADAPTATION

Teens may want to create a more involved family tree that includes geneagram-type information (marking divorces, deaths, close or distant relationships, family crises).

In exploring the family's heritage, teens may also enjoy delving into the following issues:

- ◆ What are some stereotypes of people from your ancestral country (for example: Latin lovers, stubborn Germans, stoic Slavs, alcoholic Irish, dumb Dutchman, Polish bowlers, sly Chinese, shrewd Jews)?

- ◆ How do you feel about these generalizations?

- ◆ Is there any truth to them?

- ◆ What are some positive characteristics for which your nationality is known?

and Eleazar the father of Matthan, and Matthan the father of Jacob, and Jacob the father of Joseph the husband of Mary, of whom Jesus was born, who is called the Messiah.

—Nina Phipps and Susan Vogt

14 BALANCING ACT

Spring Equinox—March 21

 **YOU WILL NEED...**

☐ *One Day at a Time*, P. K. Hallinan, Hazelden, 1990, optional

Option 3: Roles

☐ one piece of light-colored construction paper

READING

Ecclesiastes 3:1-8

For everything there is a season, and a time for every matter under heaven:
a time to be born, and a time to die;
a time to plant, and a time to pluck up what is planted;
a time to kill, and a time to heal;
a time to break down, and a time to build up;
a time to weep, and a time to laugh;
a time to mourn, and a time to dance;
a time to throw away stones, and a time to gather stones together;
a time to embrace, and a time to refrain from embracing;

(cont.)

 **OPENING**

The family stands in a large circle with lots of space on either side. Close your eyes. Lift one leg and try to stay balanced for one minute. (Everyone can count slowly together.) Half way through, open your eyes to see if it's any easier to balance with eyes open. After the silliness dies down, gather the family around a table and light a candle. Ask each person to think silently about "all the different activities I'm doing in my life right now."

PRESENTATION OF THEME

The Spring Equinox (around March 21) and the Fall Equinox (around September 23) are the two days of the year when daylight and darkness are most equally balanced. Let's take some time to check out how balanced our lives are too. Life can be out of balance in many ways. Families sometimes need to balance ...

time—we're too busy to relax and have fun.

jobs—Mom and Dad or older siblings spend too much time at work, *or* the jobs around our house are not distributed fairly.

roles—activities, jobs, or privileges are allotted according to typical male or female roles instead of allowing family members to try a range of experiences.

Reading:
Ecclesiastes 3:1-8 *or*
One Day at a Time

 **FAMILY RESPONSE**

Pick one of the three suggested areas in which to bring the family's life into better balance.

1. Time—Are We Too Busy?
a. Everyone makes a list of how he or she spends discretionary time (time *not* spent sleeping, eating, at school or work). If anyone has more than two outside activities (sports, lessons,

44

clubs, committees), evaluate the amount of stress the activities are putting on the family system and whether they should be put on hold. If the family feels very stressed, consider pruning unnecessary activities to allow relaxed "empty" time at home.

b. Ask each person to name an activity they enjoy doing by themselves and one they enjoy doing with the family. If it has been awhile since the family has had some fun together, talk about favorite or enjoyable family activities and decide on one you'd like to do. Schedule it for today or soon. Do it!

2. Jobs

a. Poll the family about jobs. Ask each if he or she feels someone in the family is working too much at a job. If so, have an honest discussion about whether it is a temporary situation and if there is any way to change it.

b. Then poll family members about household jobs. Ask if everyone is happy with his or her jobs around the house. If anyone is dissatisfied, list on paper large enough for everyone to see all the possible household jobs (grocery shopping, meal preparation, table setting, meal cleanup, laundry, pet care, inside cleaning, outside cleaning, car maintenance, yard care, etc.). Put the name of the person who currently does each job after each one.

Evaluate the job distribution. After considering age, skill, and time available, does the job distribution seem balanced and fair? If not, ask people to switch or add jobs. If this doesn't work voluntarily, and if the parents are courageous, try living for a period of time with the job undone and see what this experience teaches.

> **NOTE:** Although this process is meant to be as democratic as possible, exert your role as leader and set up minimum expectations to ensure fairness.

3. Roles—Masculine and Feminine

For all ages:
Take the job list from the exercise above. Check if there are any jobs that only males or only females do. If so, why? Could it be different? Are there any physical reasons why certain jobs can be done only by males or vice versa?

For older children or teens:
Make a drawing of a yin yang symbol (see page 22) on construction paper. The yin yang is the Chinese symbol of

a time to seek, and a time
  to lose;
a time to keep, and a time
  to throw away;
a time to tear, and a time
  to sew;
a time to keep silence, and
  a time to speak;
a time to love, and a time
  to hate;
a time for war, and a time
  for peace.

complementarity. The yin stands for female, the earth, passive qualities. Yang stands for male, the heavens, active qualities. The philosophy of the yin yang is that the whole is made up of both yin and yang though in different proportions at different times or in different people. List typical feminine characteristics on the yin side and typical masculine characteristics on the yang side.

♦ Is it possible for one person to have some of both characteristics (intuitive/logical, compassionate/strong, physical/intellectual, passive/aggressive)?

♦ Are there any qualities on the list connected with your gender that you don't think fit you?

♦ Are there any qualities on the list of the opposite gender that you would like to develop to become a fuller person? For example, females might want to develop assertiveness. Males might want to develop sensitivity.

♦ Does anyone in the family want to try out a new job or activity based on this exercise?

TREAT

If you are familiar with the song, sing "Day by Day" from *Godspell*, and serve anything that comes in two equal parts or can be divided in half and shared (sandwiches, cookies, popsicles). That's almost anything.

AGE ADAPTATION

This family night, especially the activity on masculine and feminine roles, is geared more to the middle-aged child and older. Jobs for younger children will, of course, need to be simplified and often done with a parent. In the roles option, it would probably be enough just to introduce the young child to gender-neutral language such as *firefighter, police officer, letter carrier, flight attendant*. Also in this option teens might want to discuss what masculine or feminine qualities they imagine God has.

RELATED RESOURCES

Free to Be You and Me by Marlo Thomas. This audiocassette has delightful songs and stories for young children that break down sex stereotypes.

—Susan Vogt

 ## OPENING

Before we start tonight, we're going to have a humdinger of an argument—just to get it out of our systems. Divide into pairs: Person A and Person B. (If there is an uneven number, the leader doesn't play.)

How to Start an Argument

Person A chooses a word that has an opposite (for example: hot/cold, yes/no, hard/soft, high/low). Stand and face each other. Person A says the word softly and person B responds softly with the opposite. Person A then continues to repeat his or her word, gradually escalating volume and intensity. Person B responds in kind. When person A has gotten as loud as possible, he or she then gradually de-escalates the word back to a whisper and person B responds in kind. (It usually helps for the leader to demonstrate this process briefly with a partner before the whole group does it.)

Once the words are chosen, the whole family (all sets of pairs) does this exercise at the same time. It gets pretty loud. Then have A switch with B and repeat the "argument."

Now light the candle as each member silently thinks about, What do I generally get most mad about in our family? With whom do I fight the most?

 ## PRESENTATION OF THEME

Now that we know how to start an argument, we want to get better at stopping them. It's not a horrible thing to get mad at each other and sometimes fight. Anytime people live closely together and lead a common life, there are going to be differences—different personalities, different opinions, and different ways of doing things. If there aren't differences in a family, it probably means people are hiding their true feelings and are not being individuals. The problem comes when we let a fight or argument cause hurt—either physical hurt or hurt feelings. We're going to try to get better at fighting and forgiving tonight.

Reading:

Matthew 18:21-35 *or*
Matthew 6:12-14 *or*
Genesis 27 (the story of the conflict between Jacob and Esau) *or*
Bhagavadgita quotation

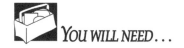 ## YOU WILL NEED...

☐ a hand puppet for each person in the family (socks with buttons for eyes can be used)

 ## READING

Matthew 18:21-35

Then Peter came and said to him, "Lord, if another member of the church sins against me, how often should I forgive? As many as seven times?" Jesus said to him, "Not seven times, but, I tell you, seventy-seven times.

"For this reason the kingdom of heaven may be compared to a king who wished to settle accounts with his slaves. When he began the reckoning, one who owed him ten thousand talents was brought to him; and, as he could not pay, his lord ordered him to be sold, together with his wife and children and all his possessions, and payment to be made. So the slave fell on his knees before him, saying, 'Have patience with me, and I will pay you everything.' And out of pity for him, the lord of

(cont.)

that slave released him and forgave him the debt. But that same slave, as he went out, came upon one of his fellow slaves who owed him a hundred denarii; and seizing him by the throat, he said, 'Pay what you owe.' Then his fellow slave fell down and pleaded with him, 'Have patience with me, and I will pay you.' But he refused; then he went and threw him into prison until he would pay the debt. When his fellow slaves saw what had happened, they were greatly distressed, and they went and reported to their lord all that had taken place. Then his lord summoned him and said to him, 'You wicked slave! I forgave you all that debt because you pleaded with me. Should you not have had mercy on your fellow slave, as I had mercy on you?' And in anger his lord handed him over to be tortured until he would pay his entire debt. So my heavenly Father will also do to every one of you, if you do not forgive your brother or sister from your heart."

––––

Matthew 6:12-14

And forgive us our debts, as we also have forgiven our debtors. And do not bring us

(cont.)

FAMILY RESPONSE

What's the beef?

Reflecting on the opening meditation time, each person thinks of a recent time when they felt angry with another member of the family and maybe got into a fight. Invite two family members to act out the situation using puppets. It's okay to exaggerate the conflict a little for drama and humor's sake.

Solving the beef

After each member has had a chance to act out his or her "beef," it's time to solve the problem. Ask for suggestions for the family's "rules for fighting" and list them on a large sheet of paper. The list may include such things as ...

- ◆ No name calling.

- ◆ No hitting.

- ◆ Name your feeling. Own it. "*I feel* mad when you ... " instead of "*You* make me so mad when ... "

- ◆ If two people want the same thing and only one can have it, toss a coin or pick numbers. (The person closer to the parent's number gets it.)

What are some agreed upon consequences when familiar fights erupt (time out, no TV, go to different rooms, no one gets it, etc.)?

Don't just complain. Suggest alternative solutions to the problem.

Add your own rules.

Decide on a prominent place to display the list for a while.

Finishing the beef

Invite family members to use their puppets to replay their fight of a few minutes ago, using the rules for fighting hopefully to get to a satisfactory resolution.

Forgiving the beef

At the end of each skit, have the two members put aside their puppets and ask them if they feel they can ask for and offer forgiveness. Conclude by hugging one another.

> **NOTE:** Practice saying "I'm sorry that you feel hurt." It is a statement that does not incite a comeback, nor does it admit blame. A simple "I'm sorry" should not be forced or required, but only encouraged, since it must be genuine to be believed and effective. If a member is not ready to ask or offer forgiveness, merely accept the reality that

someone is hurt and express the hope that time will heal the wound.

In closing ask the whole family to stand in a circle; take two steps toward the middle of the circle and have a "family hug."

Extend the activity:

If there is anyone outside your immediate family from whom you feel alienated, summon up your courage and write a letter of reconciliation. It's never too late!

 **TREAT**

Try "eating your words." Take an alphabet-shaped cereal, spell out any angry feelings you might have, and "eat" them to get rid of them.

to the time of trial, but rescue us from the evil one. For if you forgive others their trespasses, your heavenly Father will also forgive you.

———

Genesis 27

(see Bible for text)

———

If you want to see the brave, look at those who can forgive. If you want to see the heroic, look at those who can love in return for hatred.

—*The Bhagavadgita* (holy book of Hinduism)

 **RELATED READING**

The Forgiving Family by Carol Luebering. St. Anthony Messenger Press, 1983.

How to Talk So Kids Will Listen and Listen So Kids Will Talk by Adele Faber and Elaine Mazlish. Avon, 1982.

The Pain and the Great One by Judy Blume. Dell, 1985.

Traits of a Healthy Family by Dolores Curran. Harper San Francisco, 1985.

—Susan Vogt

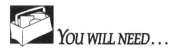 *YOU WILL NEED...*

Option 1: Sunrise Worship

☐ the time of sunrise in your area

☐ a place where you can see the sunrise (Hills and parks are good for this, but a backyard would do if you can see any part of the sunrise.)

☐ a picnic breakfast, optional

Option 2: Easter Egg Hunt

☐ Easter eggs

☐ 1 plastic egg that separates (one for each child with their name on it)

☐ a note in each egg that says "Surprise! I have risen. I'm not here anymore. Look for me in ─────" (clue to a special hiding place)

☐ Special prizes symbolizing resurrection (bubbles, balloons, kites)

Easter, like Christmas, already holds many family and religious customs for Christians. Our goal is not to add another layer of activity to already busy families at this holiday, but rather to help families deepen their understanding of this feast. For this reason we suggest activities that can be used in the course of your usual celebration of Easter: the sunrise worship and the traditional Easter egg hunt.

If your family is not Christian, you can focus on the more general theme of transformation. Just as nature goes through seasons of birth, death, rebirth, so too humans experience cycles like this. The family could use the symbols of sunrise or the egg to prompt a discussion of "What has died or changed in each of us so that we might grow to a new stage of maturity?"

1. SUNRISE WORSHIP

 PRESENTATION OF THEME

A day or two before Easter, ask the family if they would like to celebrate Easter in a simple but really unique way. Remind the family that the central mystery of Easter revolves around Jesus' death and his resurrection three days later. The daily setting of the sun can be a symbol of his death. Likewise, the rising of the sun symbolizes his resurrection. If people are willing and able to get up very early, we can let the sunrise teach us about resurrection.

Reading:
When the leader notices the first rays of the sun, he or she invites the family to turn to the east with hands stretched out to the sun. "As the sun comes alive to us again today, we remember, O Jesus, that you arose from the dead."
  or
Mark 16:1-8

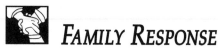 *FAMILY RESPONSE*

A Litany of Courage and Praise

Pause and ponder the changing sky. Each member thinks of their fears. If they wish to voice them, the family can respond together by praying something like: "God, protect us and give us courage." Then each member of the family looks around and thinks of the

wonders of God's creation. As things come to mind, they are voiced and the family can respond, "We praise you, God of Wonder, God of Life."

TREAT

Enjoy a picnic breakfast or return home to juice, breakfast, or bed, whichever you prefer.

2. EASTER EGG HUNT

PRESENTATION OF THEME

Egg hunts originated as a springtime ritual to celebrate the return of life to the world after the long winter. Eggs, themselves containers of new life, symbolized all rebirth and renewal. Over time, the Easter celebration adopted the egg as one of its traditions because it expresses so well the new life promised in the resurrection. The empty eggshell is an apt symbol of the empty tomb and the triumph over death. Today we're going to have a special egg hunt.

Reading:
Mark 16:1-8

FAMILY RESPONSE

Ahead of time, prepare a "resurrection egg" for each child. Inside a two-piece plastic egg, put a clue pointing the child to the hiding place where a special resurrection prize such as balloons, bubbles, or kite is hidden. On the outside write the child's name. Then hide the resurrection eggs and dyed eggs according to family custom.

Announce before the family starts the traditional Easter egg hunt that there is a special egg for each child that is different from the real eggs. They are resurrection eggs and there is one for each child. Tell them that theirs will have their name on it. When they find their own, instruct them to look inside. They will find a clue for a special prize. If they find another child's egg, they should pass it by without revealing its hiding place.

READING

Mark 16:1-8

When the sabbath was over, Mary Magdalene, and Mary the mother of James, and Salome bought spices, so that they might go and anoint him. And very early on the first day of the week, when the sun had risen, they went to the tomb. They had been saying to one another, "Who will roll away the stone for us from the entrance to the tomb?" When they looked up, they saw that the stone, which was very large, had already been rolled back. As they entered the tomb, they saw a young man, dressed in a white robe, sitting on the right side; and they were alarmed. But he said to them, "Do not be alarmed; you are looking for Jesus of Nazareth, who was crucified. He has been raised; he is not here. Look, there is the place they laid him. But go, tell his disciples and Peter that he is going ahead of you to Galilee; there you will see him, just as he told you." So they went out and fled from the tomb, for terror and amazement had seized them; and they said nothing to anyone, for they were afraid.

The Easter egg hunt proceeds as is customary. Wait until all the special eggs are found before allowing the children to pursue the special clue. When all the resurrection prizes are found, ask the children if they can figure out why this toy is a symbol of resurrection.

 **TREAT**

Easter candy—what else! And Easter eggs. If you like the old-fashioned brown eggs, save the outer brown layers from onions and put the skins in a large pot of boiling water for the length of time it takes to hard boil the eggs. Voila! They're stained brown.

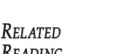 **RELATED READING**

Hope for the Flowers by Trini Paulus. Paulist Press, 1972.

—Susan Vogt

SPRING AHEAD

Change to Daylight-Saving Time

FAMILY NIGHT 17

 ## OPENING

Have a puzzle ready that the family will find challenging but not too difficult. Set a timer and let the children work on the puzzle for three to five minutes. When the timer goes off, stop work on the puzzle.

PRESENTATION OF THEME

Tonight we will talk about how we use time. Ask: Were you frustrated when I interrupted your work on the puzzle? What other timed events cause anxiety? Do you get frustrated when time is too short to accomplish something? Describe situations when time seems to last forever, such as waiting for Christmas or a birthday.

Daylight-saving time originated when farmers wanted more time to work in their fields during the busy summer months. The nation decided to change the clocks so that there would be one more hour of daylight for work. We were "saving" daylight!

During this time of "saving" daylight, it is good to talk about how we waste or save time. Time, for young children, seems to stretch forever. It's only we old folks who really appreciate how it speeds by!

> **NOTE:** By focusing on situations in which children don't have enough time to do what they want, you might be able to get them to see how important time is.

If you have a large kitchen clock with a second hand, you can demonstrate the passing of time. Have the children watch the second hand moving around the clock. Explain that as it moves, those seconds are gone forever and we can never get them back.

 ## FAMILY RESPONSE

Have each family member think of one thing they can do to make better use of time, since it is so precious. For example, most adults have had the experience of intending to say something nice to someone, letting the occasion pass, and then never getting the opportunity again. To focus on the good use of time, make a large clock on poster paper and, instead of putting numbers on the face of the clock, put the things the family members have resolved to do to use time better.

 ## YOU WILL NEED...

❏ a puzzle

❏ a timer with buzzer or bell

❏ a large piece of poster paper and magic markers

❏ *It's a Wonderful Life* video, optional

Ask the children to think of something that happened to them because they were at the right place at the right time. For example: "What if you left your homework on the dining room table and Mom happened to see it and gave it to you just before you left for school?" "What if you were walking home from school just as the neighborhood kids were choosing up sides for a big game and you got in and made a big play?" The events don't have to be momentous, but they might illustrate how important every minute is and how things would be different if we ignored time.

On the other hand, think about ways we enjoy "wasting time" that are really refreshing, such as taking naps, daydreaming, taking time to "smell the roses."

If you have enough time, rent *It's a Wonderful Life* and watch the movie together. This movie (usually a Christmas favorite) demonstrates how one person's presence in the world can change everything. If you don't have time to watch the video, but your children are familiar with it, you can discuss it a little.

Conclude the activity by singing "Grandfather's Clock." (See Appendix A, Music.)

TREAT

Choose a treat that takes a while to eat, like a hard caramel sucker, something chewy, or pieces of hard candy (no biting). As you enjoy the treat, go back to the puzzle that you started earlier and complete it in a fun, leisurely manner.

RELATED READING

Clocks and More Clocks by Pat Hutchins. Aladdin, 1994.

Sunshine by Jan Ormerod. Mulberry Books, 1990.

—Wendy Bauers Northup

OPENING

Begin by burning some play money.

PRESENTATION OF THEME

NOTE: This session works best when there is an element of surprise, so we recommend announcing the theme merely as "money." In this way, the experience itself is the teacher. Say to the family, "Let's play a game using pretend money, since most of us don't have money to burn. People sometimes use poker chips as a substitute for money in games, so that's how we'll do it."

Prepare to play a poker chip game like Tripoli or a cash game like Monopoly. If the family is not familiar with these games, teach the game first. It may be helpful to play a practice round under the normal rules.

Once everyone understands the game, unevenly distribute the poker chips or play money to everyone. For example, the youngest child may get the most. Make sure there are obvious inequalities.

It is unlikely that the game will get very far before you have reactions from those who were dealt fewer chips or given less money. At this point, stop the game to debrief the feelings of the different players:

◆ Why is it unfair that you didn't get as many chips/money?

◆ If you got more than the others, how do you feel?

◆ Did you do anything special to deserve more chips/money?

◆ Who wants to keep playing?

Then explain that unfortunately this unfair distribution of money actually happens in the real world. In fact, six percent of the world's population (the equivalent of the population of the U.S.) uses forty percent of the world's resources. Many people are born poor and haven't done anything to deserve poverty; but they have a hard time getting money because they have poor health, inadequate education, or a family who can't help them succeed.

Reading:
Matthew 19:23-26 *or*
Alexander, Who Used to Be Rich Last Sunday

YOU WILL NEED...

☐ play money

☐ matches or lighter

☐ a safe way to burn money: in a metal bucket, roasting pan, or 4-quart pan

☐ poker chips (or buttons or pebbles)

☐ Tripoli (or similar game that uses poker chips) or Monopoly board game

☐ paper and crayons for younger children

☐ *Alexander, Who Used to Be Rich Last Sunday,* Judith Viorst, Aladdin, 1987, optional

READING

Matthew 19:23-26

Then Jesus said to his disciples, "Truly I tell you, it will be hard for a rich person to enter the kingdom of heaven. Again I tell you, it is easier for a camel to go through the eye of a needle than for someone who is rich to enter the kingdom of God." When the disciples heard this, they were greatly astounded and said, "Then who can be

(cont.)

saved?" But Jesus looked at them and said, "For mortals it is impossible, but for God all things are possible."

FAMILY RESPONSE

Continue to discuss why inequities of wealth exist in our country and in our world. Do we know anyone who has fewer material goods than we have? Is there a discreet way to help someone who currently has a legitimate need for more money? Should our family consider tithing of our time and resources?

When discussion has run its course, start a new game of Tripoli or Monopoly. This time everyone gets an equal amount of chips or money.

TREAT

Anything green like currency or round like coins would be a fitting treat, perhaps green cookies or thin mints.

AGE ADAPTATION

For preschoolers, simplify the poker chip game, or make up your own. Perhaps an adaptation of the Uno card game would be more appropriate. If the discussion of money is too advanced for younger children, they could draw pictures of something that money can't buy or something they would buy if they had all the money in the world.

To expand the discussion for teens, explore the public assistance system.

- What barriers do people on welfare face in trying to "pull themselves up by their bootstraps"? (Inadequate education, poor health, mental illness are a few examples.)

- Why are some countries poorer than others?

- Does our country play any role in causing another country's poverty?

- How does our country help poorer countries?

- How can our family help?

Also, to hold the interest of teenagers, plan an outing in which each person is given an envelope with money to spend on recreation for the family, such as a movie, miniature golf, shopping at the mall. Distribute unequal amounts of the money. Family members will have to decide whether to let someone stay home for lack of money or to share their resources.

—Susan Vogt

WE'RE ALL IN THIS TOGETHER

Earth Day—April 22

 ## OPENING

Light a candle and sing "This Land Is Your Land" (Appendix A, Music).

 ## PRESENTATION OF THEME

The earth we live on is like a giant organism. Sometimes this is called an ecosystem, which means that everything in, on, and above the earth is dependent on everything else. When one part of the system changes or is hurt, other parts are affected. Even parts of the environment that are not generally thought of as having life, like the sun, water, or soil, affect each other and all life.

 ## FAMILY RESPONSE

Play the Web of Life game.

Instructions:

Form a circle. Place one nature name card on each player (in smaller families, some people will have more than one name card, or invite another family to join you). The leader (the spider) stands in the middle of the circle and weaves a magical web, "the web of life." Tell the story of ecology below, weaving or passing string from sun to plant to food to water, and so forth, as you come to those words in the story.

Read:

All things on earth, living and nonliving, are in some way depending on each other. This relationship is called the balance of nature. It is the web of life.

- ◆ All life depends upon the *sun.*

- ◆ The *sun* is needed by green *plants* to make their own *food,*

- ◆ But *water, soil,* and *air* are also necessary.

- ◆ Some *animals* eat *plants,*

- ◆ And *people* depend upon *plants* and *animals* for food.

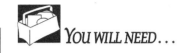 ## YOU WILL NEED...

- ☐ a globe or picture of Earth

- ☐ ball of string or yarn

- ☐ 8 nature name cards on strings to go around the neck (sun, plants, food, water, soil, air, animals, and people)

- ☐ *50 Simple Things Kids Can Do to Save the Earth,* John Javna, Andrews and McMeel, 1990, optional

- ☐ *Helping Families Care,* James McGinnis, 1989, optional

READING

Romans 12:5-6

[Just as nature is inter-connected, so also is the human community.] So we, who are many, are one body in Christ, and individually we are members one of another. We have gifts that differ according to the grace given to us: prophecy, in proportion to faith.

RELATED READING

Brother Eagle, Sister Sky: a Message from Chief Seattle by Susan Jeffers, Illus. Dial Books for Young Readers, 1991.

The Great Trash Bash by Loreen Leedy. Holiday House, 1991.

Hawk, I'm Your Brother by Byrd Baylor. Aladdin, 1986.

The Lorax by Dr. Seuss. Random House Books for Young Readers, 1971.

Professor Noah's Spaceship by Brian Wildsmith. Oxford University Press, 1980.

50 Simple Things Kids Can Do to Save the Earth by John Javna. Andrews and McMeel (4900 Main Street, Kansas City, MO 64112), 1990.

—Karen Schneider-Chen

People must be aware of this balance of nature and do their best to protect and preserve it.

Reading:

Romans 12:5-6

Optional Activities:

Look through *50 Simple Things Kids Can Do to Save the Earth* and choose one the family can do.

The family could do Worksheet 20 or 21 on stewardship from *Helping Families Care*.

Closing:

To the well-known tune of "He's Got the Whole World in His Hands," sing "God's put the whole world in our hands" as you pass the globe from person to person. For additional verses, substitute words like "water and the air" or "flora and the fauna" or the name of a favorite animal in place of "whole world."

Finally, recite the Earth Pledge. As a family, make a collage of beautiful nature scenes and write the Earth Pledge on it. Hang the picture in a prominent place as a reminder of our responsibility to the earth.

> **Earth Pledge**
> I promise to care for all the earth
> Because of its life and awesome worth.
> For land and water and plants and air,
> For animals and people everywhere,
> For all that lives, and all that gives
> Me LIFE, I give my word.
> —Susan Vogt

TREAT

Serve vegetables and dip or fresh fruit to represent produce from the earth.

Some TV Facts

The National Association for the Education of Young Children (NAEYC) reports that children who watch television frequently ...

♦ may become less sensitive to other people's pain and suffering.

♦ may become more fearful of the world around them.

♦ may behave aggressively toward others.

Children exposed to media violence may see violence as a normal response to stress and an acceptable way to resolve conflict.

A recent survey done by the Center for Science in the Public Interest showed that during four hours of Saturday morning cartoons, 202 of the 222 food ads were for junk food.

According to "Sex and Violence on TV" from the Cooperative Extension Service of Kentucky State University:

♦ The average child has watched more than 200,000 commercials by the time she or he graduates from high school.

♦ In a typical American household, a television set is on for seven hours per day. By the time a young person finishes high school, he or she will have spent more time watching TV (15,000 hours plus) than sitting in a classroom (11,000 hours).

♦ A typical American will spend nine years of his or her entire life in front of a TV by the age of 65.

♦ Children now think in seven-minute time frames (the amount of time between commercials).

♦ By the age of fourteen, a devoted viewer will have witnessed 11,000 TV murders. (There are an average of five violent acts per hour on prime time and eighteen acts per hour on children's weekend programs.)

Family TV Tips

1. Parents, "walk the talk." Make sure your own TV viewing habits are moderate and wise.

2. Become a one-TV family. In addition to limiting the total TV hours, deciding which programs to watch can be a valuable learning experience.

3. Set time limits. Establish a maximum time that each person can watch TV, perhaps one hour per day or ten hours per week.

4. Select programs ahead of time. To avoid random flipping through channels, have each family member decide at the beginning of the week which programs they will view.

5. Plan alternatives to TV. Play a game, take a walk, bake a cake, reminisce, fly a kite, visit a neighbor, plant some flowers, laugh, read, write, enjoy quiet time.

6. Watch questionable shows together and discuss them. If your child wishes to watch a particularly violent show, or one with race or gender stereotypes, or one with promiscuity, make a deal to watch it together and discuss concerns that you have about the program.

7. Reclaim the evening. Allocate time for homework. Plan interesting out-of-door or away-from-home activities. Encourage hobbies, sports, music, reading, and other active pursuits.

8. Start your own television network. Record the best shows around and/or rent quality videotapes. Then set up your own television schedule.

9. Adopt a TV station. After monitoring the shows of a station, write to or meet with station officials to share compliments and discuss concerns.

—Adapted from "Watch What You Watch"
by the Cooperative Extension Service
of the University of Kentucky.

MEDIA MADNESS

NOTE: This family night presumes the family has access to a TV and videocassette recorder. If you don't have a VCR, gear the session to common TV programs the family watches. If you don't have TV, you obviously have already made a significant decision about the place of media in your family life. More power to you! As alternatives:

- ◆ Focus on other media, such as magazine and newspaper ads, billboards, *or*

- ◆ Join with a family that has a TV. Since children will inevitably be exposed to this medium at the homes of friends and relatives, help them distinguish between truth and manipulation on TV.

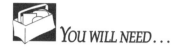

YOU WILL NEED...

- ☐ popular teen and adult magazines

- ☐ a TV and videocassette recorder

- ☐ videocassette tape of a music video program featuring the week's top ten hits or a collection of videos from various programs

- ☐ Videos and Values worksheets for each member of the family (Appendix C, Activities)

OPENING

Ask each family member to skim through the magazines provided and find three ads he or she likes. Have family members take turns showing the ads and telling why they like them (no negative comments allowed).

PRESENTATION OF THEME

During this session we are going to look at media—the good and the bad. We will try to recognize what the media creators are trying to get us to feel, think, and buy. We will judge how much our behavior is influenced by the media and whether that is good or bad. Although this family night will focus primarily on music videos, which are a combination of movie images and music shows on TV, the same approach can be used with other media such as TV programs, videos, music, newspapers, magazines, and movies.

A lot of the videos on MTV are not extremely negative. In fact some of the videos are actually filled with positive images and values. However, you probably will find some material that bothers you.

Go over some basic communication rules that both parents and children agree to follow in the discussion:

- ◆ No judgments on people's feelings (feelings are not good or bad).

- ◆ One person speaks at a time.

◆ Be open to what another person is saying (you don't have to agree).

◆ Are there other rules participants want to establish?

FAMILY RESPONSE

Everyone gets a Videos and Values worksheet. After watching the video, check off the appropriate responses on part 1 of the worksheet. Do this work in silence. When everyone is finished, share your answers. Then respond to the questions on part 2 of the worksheet. Discuss your responses to these questions.

> **NOTE:** This is only a suggested format. Go with the flow at the moment. Maybe the first worksheet will erupt into a heated discussion on sexism. Go with it. Use these sheets in a way that will best help your family.

You may want to view another video and go through the process again.

> **NOTE:** You can use this process to look at TV and print ads, even using the ads you looked at to start off this activity. This process will also work well with TV shows and movies. Decide how much time you have to view the media. An alternative is to have someone tape sections of shows or movies to use in this session.

For additional discussion, ask these questions:

◆ What were the creators trying to sell with this piece?

◆ Was I being manipulated in any way?

◆ Can I see how my child (my parent) sees this media piece now?

◆ Using the statistics from the background on this activity, talk about how media (TV, for example) can have an impact on young and old just by the amount of time we spend with the media.

◆ Which do I think happens more?

a. The media *mold* our attitudes and view of life.

b. The media merely *reflect* the reality of our society.

◆ Are there any values I hold that differ from those commonly seen on TV or in movies?

Extending the activity:

1. As a family, make a video with music that reflects the positive values of your family.

2. Invite another family with similar values to a Media Madness night.

3. As a family, write letters to TV station managers, editors of the local newspaper, and others with some of the conclusions the family came to concerning media.

 **TREAT**

Select a movie that the entire family likes, put away all the Videos and Values worksheets, make a gigantic bowl of popcorn, break out the root beer, and have a "good ole time" watching a movie together.

 **AGE ADAPTATION**

This activity with videos works well with teenagers and children who are in middle elementary school and up. For the younger children, spend a Saturday morning watching some cartoons and ask questions based on the worksheets that would be appropriate for younger children. Tallying each act of violence that you and your child see would be a fun game as well as an eye-opener for both of you.

Share with your child your feelings and concerns about violence (hitting) being the main way to solve problems. Make a game out of creating new nonviolent endings for the programs you have watched.

 **RELATED READING**

The Bionic Bunny Show by Marc Brown. Joy Street Books, 1985.

The Family Guide to Movies on Video by Henry Herx and Tony Zaza, eds. Crossroad, 1988.

Parenting in a TV Age (workbook). The Center for Media and Values, 1991.

Ralph Proves the Pudding by Winifred Rosen.

The TV Smart Book for Kids by Peggy Charren and Carol Hulsizer. Dutton Children's Books, 1986.

What to Do After You Turn Off the TV by Frances Moore Lappe. Family Ballantine Books, 1985.

Your Children and TV: A Practical Guide for Making Television a Positive Influence in Children's Lives by Ellen B. DeFranco. Mar Co Products, Inc.

—Jim Ford

21 PUNCH A PILLOW!

 YOU WILL NEED...

☐ a set of the "Animal Cards"
(Appendix C, Activities)

 READING

Genesis 4:1-8

Now the man knew his wife Eve, and she conceived and bore Cain, saying, "I have produced a man with the help of the LORD." Next she bore his brother Abel. Now Abel was a keeper of sheep, and Cain a tiller of the ground. In the course of time Cain brought to the LORD an offering of the fruit of the ground, and Abel for his part brought of the firstlings of his flock, their fat portions. And the LORD had regard for Abel and his offering, but for Cain and his offering he had no regard. So Cain was very angry, and his countenance fell. The LORD said to Cain, "Why are you angry, and why has your countenance fallen? If you do well, will you not be accepted? And if you do not do well, sin is lurking at the door; its desire is for you, but you must master it."

Cain said to his brother Abel, "Let us go out to the field." And when they were in

(cont.)

 OPENING

Light a candle and ask the family members to look at each other and make the meanest, nastiest faces they can muster for thirty seconds. This may result in a lot of giggling and laughter, or it could reveal some genuine feelings of resentment or anger that have been lurking within some individuals. Either reaction is okay, but it is essential to honor the thirty-second time limit so this exercise doesn't get out of hand.

Pause for a moment, and then ask the family to switch moods and gently and kindly hold hands or give each other loving hugs. For some it may be difficult to make this transition quickly. Give it time. The point of this experience is primarily to get in touch with how our bodies feel when we are angry versus when we feel loved. We can't change our underlying feelings, but we do have some choice over how we *act* when we are angry.

Reading:
Genesis 4:1-8 *and/or*
Philippians 2:1-5

 PRESENTATION OF THEME

Conflict is a part of life. People have different objectives, or they see the same situation differently because of their beliefs or experiences. Therefore, people handle conflicts differently. Some people get mean and attack—like sharks. Others try to hide or pretend a conflict isn't happening—they withdraw into a shell, just like turtles.

The animal cards in Appendix C (Activities) suggest different ways of handling conflict. Photocopy the page and cut out the cards. Then talk about each one for a minute. Can you remember a time when you acted like a teddy bear? or a fox? There are probably times when you've acted like a wise old owl, too! Make sure to talk about your own mistakes or shortcomings rather than pointing out someone else's.

We know about these different styles of handling conflict because we've all used most of them at one time or another. Tonight we'll practice some of the choices we have in any conflict situation.

> **NOTE:** If the family is unfamiliar with ground rules for "fighting fair," see Family Night 15 for additional tips (p. 47).

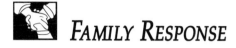

FAMILY RESPONSE

Pass out the animal cards so each family member has one. If there are more than five people in your family, you can team up or make more than one copy of the cards.

Let someone read one of the conflict situations on page 221 in Appendix C. Then take turns acting out responses to the situation, using the style of the animal on the card in your hand. Brief discussion is fine, but keep activity moving.

When everyone has had a turn, rotate cards and read a new situation.

Close by discussing what family members have learned from this activity. It helps to remember that we always have choices in dealing with conflict situations. We're never locked into one style of handling conflict.

Mount the animal cards on the refrigerator or some other central location as a reminder that we have choices in dealing with conflict situations. You may even choose to use the cards the next time an actual conflict arises.

TREAT

Decorate and serve a cake with the picture of an owl as a reminder that we all want to be wise in the way we handle conflicts.

AGE ADAPTATION

Younger children can color pictures of the animals for the family. Teens might enjoy helping younger children make puppets or posters of the animals. Teens could also make up words of a song about the animals' styles of resolving conflicts and set them to a familiar tune such as "Row, Row, Row Your Boat" or "Mary Had a Little Lamb."

---

the field, Cain rose up against his brother Abel, and killed him.

———

Philippians 2:1-5

If then there is any encouragement in Christ, any consolation from love, any sharing in the Spirit, any compassion and sympathy, make my joy complete: be of the same mind, having the same love, being in full accord and of one mind. Do nothing from selfish ambition or conceit, but in humility regard others as better than yourselves. Let each of you look not to your own interests, but to the interests of others. Let the same mind be in you that was in Christ Jesus.

RELATED READING

C Is for Curious: An ABC of Feelings by Woodleigh Hubbard. Chronicle Books, 1990.

Easy Does It by P. K. Hallinan. Hazelden, n.d.

Mrs. Pig Gets Cross and Other Stories by Mary Rayner. Puffin Books, 1991.

Rosie and the Yellow Ribbon by Paula DePaola. Little, Brown, and Co., 1992.

—Sue Blythe

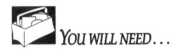 **YOU WILL NEED...**

☐ paper and crayons or markers

☐ garden tools

☐ paper for mapping out the garden

☐ calendar

☐ *The Tiny Seed*, 2nd ed., Eric Carle, Picture Book Studio, 1991, optional

**Option 1:
Plant a Garden**

☐ tilled garden space near your home or small containers to put outside

☐ vegetable seeds (beans are fast-growing)

**Option 2:
Gardening with Immediate Results**

☐ seedlings or bedding plants

 **READING**

Mark 4:3-9

"Listen! A sower went out to sow. And as he sowed, some seed fell on the path, and the birds came and ate it up.

(cont.)

NOTE: The primary activity for this family night is a long-range project of watching a garden grow. For those who just can't wait, option 2 provides more immediate results.

 **OPENING**

As a family, make a mini "pilgrimage" to the garden space. Spend a few moments quietly looking over the area and imagining what you want to plant, where to plant it, and how it might look as it grows. Sing "Garden Song" (Appendix A, Music). Return to the gathering place in your home.

 **PRESENTATION OF THEME**

We're going to start an experiment to find out how things grow best. It'll take quite a while for our study to be finished and it'll take some work. But growth is frequently like that—slow and often difficult.

Reading:
Mark 4:3-9 *or*
The Tiny Seed

 **FAMILY RESPONSE**

Begin by doing one or more of the following:

♦ Draw a picture. It's always fun for young children to depict spring with drawings of flowers, trees, the sun, and birds. This can be fun for children of almost any age, even if they're too young to make the flowers look like flowers.

♦ While the little children are drawing, parents and older children can make maps of the garden. Each person can plot out on a piece of paper where things will be planted in the garden, even if there is space for only a few things. Allot three rows for the special experiment. The maps help everyone understand the importance of planning, making choices, seeing how things fit in relation to each other, and

the reasons why. Young children can decorate the borders of the maps or glue on pictures of what will be planted. The maps make colorful wall hangings for the kitchen or the bedroom.

♦ Make a calendar to record the garden's growth day by day, or simply use a monthly calendar format to keep a running log of the progress. The calendar can be made on the family night. Keeping the log and maintaining the garden will serve as extended activities.

1. Plant a Garden

Now go to the garden space and plant your experimental seeds according to the following directions:

Rows 1 and 2: Plant according to directions on package.

Row 3: Plant the seeds simply by scattering them on top of the soil in this row and covering a few seeds lightly with soil.

> **NOTE:** If you do not have an outside garden, plant seeds in styrofoam cups or other small containers. In the first two containers, plant seeds according to the package directions. In the third container, just cover the seeds lightly with soil. Then place these containers outside on a porch or to the side of a doorstep.

When the planting is complete, take some time, perhaps while enjoying your treat, to discuss the following plans for the rest of the experiment:

Let the seeds grow. Check them daily.

If there is not enough rainfall, see that the first two rows (or containers) are watered according to the directions.

Do not water the third row (or container). It should depend solely on rainfall.

Monitor and record when and how the seeds begin to grow.

After the seeds have grown two or three inches, do the following to the plants in the second row (or container):

Other seed fell on rocky ground, where it did not have much soil, and it sprang up quickly, since it had no depth of soil. And when the sun rose, it was scorched; and since it had no root, it withered away. Other seed fell among thorns, and the thorns grew up and choked it, and it yielded no grain. Other seed fell into good soil and brought forth grain, growing up and increasing and yielding thirty and sixty and a hundredfold." And he said, "Let anyone with ears to hear listen!"

a. Transplant some of them by simply pulling them up by the roots and carelessly putting them in another location.

b. Carefully dig up several others and transplant them in a location that has been prepared to receive them.

Continue to monitor and record the growth of all the plants for the remainder of the growing season and note the results.

2. Gardening with Immediate Results (for those who just can't wait)

Buy seedlings or bedding plants that are already growing so you don't have to wait for germination. The growth process can be seen and charted immediately. You could also plant seeds at the same time and see how long it takes the plants growing from seed to catch up with the seedlings.

Long-range follow-up activity and discussion:

Sometime later in the summer, after the seeds have grown and you can see some difference in their growth, the family could either have a follow-up family night or simply discuss the differences in growth, making connections between the plants, people, and other elements in our environment. For example, look around your own city or town, state, and other parts of the world. Note the similarities to the sets of plants. People who are not properly cared for or nurtured from conception through their growing years suffer fates similar to the plants that were not nurtured and cared for. They survive but almost never grow and develop into the healthy, productive people they could be.

Similarly, people who start out with the proper care and nurturing, but are uprooted recklessly without regard for their health and well-being, also have a harder time becoming healthy, productive citizens. However, those who are uprooted and *carefully transplanted* and *properly nurtured* may lag in development, but they are still able to overcome the trauma they suffered.

 **TREAT**

Try to find something homegrown that you'd like as a treat. Since this experiment will take place early in the growing season in most parts of the country, there will be little fresh produce available. Perhaps you have berries frozen from last summer. If you don't have fresh produce, enjoy any favorite dessert.

—Mike Magrath

MODELS OF STRENGTH AND DIGNITY

Mother's Day (or International Women's Day—March 8)

FAMILY NIGHT 23

 OPENING

Light a candle and sing a song about women or motherhood. You could sing "We put all women in God's hands . . . " to the tune of "He's Got the Whole World in His Hands."

For Mother's Day add verses such as: "We put all mothers [name your own mothers, pregnant women, grandmothers, suffering mothers] in God's hands."

For International Women's Day add verses such as: "We put African [Chinese, American, etc.] women in God's hands."

Reading:
Proverbs 31:10-22, 24-31 *or*
Baha'i reading

 PRESENTATION OF THEME

We are honoring and celebrating the contributions that women in the world have made throughout time. Let's take a few moments of quiet to thank our Creator for women and then share stories of how women have affected our world. We hope this will make us aware of our ties with women throughout the world and strengthen our resolve to work for justice and wholeness for all women.

Examples of some notable women in history are:

Rigoberta Menchu—In 1993 this young Guatemalan woman received the Nobel Peace Prize for her work on behalf of oppressed indigenous people of her country.

Mary McLeod Bethune—As a child in Mayesville, South Carolina, she deplored the lack of schools for blacks in the South. After completing her education, she became a teacher in 1904 and from then on worked to establish schools, hospitals, job training, and dignity for all Black people.

Sojourner Truth—Sojourner Truth was born into slavery. When she was freed in 1827, she devoted her life to speaking out against slavery and campaigning for women's rights.

Helen Caldicott—As an Australian physician, she has been a leader in the movement against the development of nuclear weapons for over a decade. She is also the founder of Physicians for Social Responsibility.

YOU WILL NEED...

☐ stories of women, preferably from diverse religious and ethnic backgrounds (or use the sample list). Stories of women from our own families are good too.

☐ the names of well-known women on small pieces of paper, pins or tape

☐ magazines with pictures of women from around the world

 READING

Proverbs 31:10-22, 24-31

A capable wife who can find?
    She is far more precious
    than jewels.
The heart of her husband
    trusts in her, and he will
    have no lack of gain.
She does him good, and not
    harm, all the days of her
    life.
She seeks wool and flax, and
    works with willing hands.
She is like the ships of the
    merchant, she brings her
    food from far away.
She rises while it is still night
    and provides food for her

(cont.)

household and tasks for
her servant girls.
She considers a field and
buys it; with the fruit of
her hands she plants a
vineyard.
She girds herself with
strength, and makes her
arms strong.
She perceives that her
merchandise is
profitable. Her lamp does
not go out at night.
She puts her hands to the
distaff, and her hands
hold the spindle.
She opens her hand to the
poor, and reaches out her
hands to the needy.
She is not afraid for her
household when it
snows, for all her
household are clothed in
crimson.
She makes herself coverings;
her clothing is fine linen
and purple. . . .
She makes linen garments
and sells them; she
supplies the merchant
with sashes.
Strength and dignity are her
clothing, and she laughs
at the time to come.
She opens her mouth with
wisdom, and the
teaching of kindness is on
her tongue.
She looks well to the ways
of her household, and

(cont.)

Amelia Earhart—Having passionate belief in the equality of the sexes, she was the first woman to pilot a plane across the Atlantic Ocean.

Dorothy Day—Best known as founder of the Catholic Worker Movement, which opened houses of hospitality for homeless people, she was also a journalist and activist who spoke out against war and worked on behalf of oppressed people.

Helen Keller—Keller was an author, lecturer, and humanitarian who, through her unusual life as a person without sight or hearing, had an influence on the lives of people with handicaps throughout the world.

Susan B. Anthony—As the leader of the women's suffrage movement, she made women's right to vote a powerful and successful movement in both America and Europe.

FAMILY RESPONSE

Read several stories about women's lives (or read the stories beforehand and paraphrase them on family night for the children). Older children can be invited to share the story of a woman they particularly admire.

Do one or more of the following, depending on your time and the ages of the children:

1. Have each person draw a picture of a well-known woman showing why she is important. Have everyone guess who it is—making a game of it.

2. Play this fun and simple game: Write the names of well-known women on small pieces of paper (one name on each sheet) and pin or tape one on each person's back so they do not know who it is. Each person must try to guess whose name is on his or her back by asking questions of the others that can be answered yes or no, such as: Is she alive? Is her hair black? Is she a singer?

3. Using pictures from magazines such as *National Geographic* and news or missionary magazines, create a collage depicting women around the world. Display the collage in a prominent place in your home.

4. Have a discussion about sexism.

◆ Are there some jobs around the house that males are physically able to do better than females? or vice versa?

◆ Are there some jobs in our home that only women do? Why?

- ◆ Are there any jobs in our society that women are not able to do? Why?

- ◆ Are there any jobs for which a man would get paid more than a woman? or vice versa?

 TREAT

Let the female(s) in the family choose any favorite treat (within reason) and have the male(s) prepare it.

AGE ADAPTATION

Older children or teens could search current news articles for positive and negative views of women and discuss how sexism has affected their own lives. Other topics for discussion might be: Why are 97 percent of nurses women? Why is it that women get paid less money than men for doing the same work?

does not eat the bread of idleness.
Her children rise up and call her happy; her husband too, and he praises her:
"Many women have done excellently, but you surpass them all."
Charm is deceitful, and beauty is vain, but a woman who fears the LORD is to be praised.
Give her a share in the fruit of her hands, and let her works praise her in the city gates.

———

For mothers are the first educators, the first mentors; and truly it is the mothers who determine the happiness, the future greatness, the courteous ways and learning and judgment, the understanding and the faith of their little ones.

—From the writings of Abdu'l-Baha (Baha'i faith)

—Karen Schneider-Chen

There is much discussion these days about what is the most "politically correct" language to use when referring to people who have disabilities. Long ago people might have been called cripple, moron, deaf and dumb, imbecile, or mongoloid. Today people debate whether it's more respectful to say a person is differently abled, visually challenged, or disabled.

Whatever way we refer to a disability, it is important to remember that no disability completely defines who someone is. It isn't always easy to describe a person with a disability in our language without sounding awkward or wordy. That's how the joke developed about short people being "vertically challenged." The main point to remember in the discussion over terminology is *people first*. It is important to focus first on the fact that we are talking to and about individuals who happen to have a noticeable impairment, that is "a person who has a disability," not a disabled person.

The Reverend Harold Wilke, well-known advocate and pastor, born without arms, likes to say: "People have physical or sensory or mental impairments that contribute to one or more disabilities. Society puts handicaps on them such as physical barriers, discriminatory treatment, and so forth." All of us, if we live long enough, will suffer some impairment severe enough to interfere with normal daily functions and our independence. It's the human condition.

Our society likes to applaud heroes and heroines. What makes a person heroic? Is it appearance? talent? character? The following are examples of several people with disabilities who are true heroes and heroines:

◆ a man with Down's Syndrome who died trying to rescue his brother from a burning house

◆ a woman with cerebral palsy, who pulled an angry, biting police dog off a seven-year-old child

◆ a teenager with a mental impairment who calmly cared for his friend who had experienced a seizure in a theater lobby and, through his explanations to bystanders, helped them to relax

◆ a woman with Down's Syndrome who stayed all night at the bedside of a seriously ill, elderly neighbor who lived in the next apartment.

—Robert and Martha Perske, *New Life in the Neighborhood*

WALKING IN ANOTHER'S SHOES

Optional

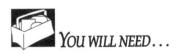 YOU WILL NEED...

☐ a dinner meal, if at all possible

☐ materials to simulate physical impairments

   ☐ blindfold (an old dark sock and large pin work well)

   ☐ ear muffs, ear plugs, or cotton

   ☐ tape for mouth

   ☐ sling for an arm (or a rag that can approximate a sling)

   ☐ crutches (a rag could be used to tie up one leg)

   ☐ mitten to cover a hand (attach the thumb so it can't be used)

☐ slips of paper, each designating a handicap: blindness, deafness, muteness, leg amputee, arm amputee, paralysis, etc.

 OPENING

Carefully arrange the items from the preparation list on the table. Light a candle and have members silently ponder: If I had to choose a disability, what would I choose?

PRESENTATION OF THEME

Of course, people who have physical, mental, or emotional impairments never had the chance to choose their limitation. We can never fully know what it's like to walk in another person's shoes, to experience his or her disability, but tonight we're going to try to get at least a sample of what some people in our society have to live with every day.

Reading:
1 Corinthians 12:14-26 *or*
Excerpt from *New Life in the Neighborhood*

> Donald Shannon, a nine-year-old boy who could not walk, was learning to move his wheelchair up a fifty-foot ramplike hall in a special education program in Topeka, Kansas. He was promised a job as a mail messenger if he made it. On the back of the wheelchair was a sign: DON'T PUSH ME. I GOTTA DO IT MYSELF. The young man accosted that rising hallway five days a week, for more than two months, in unsuccessful attempts to reach the top. During that period, frustration, tears, and anger were daily companions. Then he made it, and nearly thirty people gathered around him and applauded. That day it was obvious that Don Shannon was experiencing the same thrill that you or I might enjoy if we had reached the summit of Mount Everest.

From New Life in the Neighborhood.
Copyright © 1980 by Robert and Martha Perske.
Excerpted by permission of the publisher,
Abingdon Press.

 FAMILY RESPONSE

Put all the slips with disabilities written on them in a basket and have each family member randomly pick one. Each person then uses the items on the table to simulate that disability. The task, of course, is to "stay in role" for a predetermined period of time. The length of time depends upon the ages of the children and the day's schedule. You may want to include a meal to experience what a person with a disability experiences in accomplishing an ordinary task. Very young children may be able to do this for only fifteen to thirty minutes. Families with older children can "stay in the role" over a longer period of time.

When disabilities have been assigned, the family is then free to go about their normal activities until the time is up.

When the time is up, the family gathers to debrief what the experience was like for each of them.

◆ What did it *feel* like?

◆ Did any of the disabilities seem like fun in the beginning? If so, how long did it take for the glamour to wear off?

◆ Did the particular disability you had make a difference? Would you have preferred a different one? Which one? Why?

◆ What if you had a disability that was not physical, such as an emotional or mental disability? Would that be better or worse? Why?

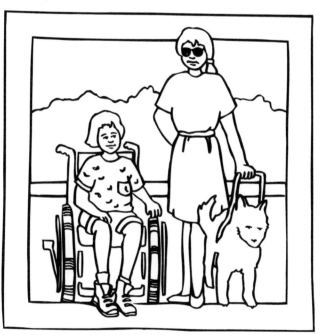

 READING

1 Corinthians 12:14-26

Indeed, the body does not consist of one member but of many. If the foot would say, "Because I am not a hand, I do not belong to the body," that would not make it any less a part of the body. And if the ear would say, "Because I am not an eye, I do not belong to the body," that would not make it any less a part of the body. If the whole body were an eye, where would the hearing be? If the whole body were hearing, where would the sense of smell be? But as it is, God arranged the members in the body, each one of them, as he chose. If all were a single member, where would the body be? As it is, there are many members, yet one body. The eye cannot say to the hand, "I have no need of you," nor again the head to the feet, "I have no need of you." On the contrary, the members of the body that seem to be weaker are indispensable, and those members of the body that we think less honorable we clothe with greater honor, and our less respectable members are treated with greater respect; whereas our more respectable members do not need this. But God has so

(cont.)

arranged the body, giving the greater honor to the inferior member, that there may be no dissension within the body, but the members may have the same care for one another. If one member suffers, all suffer together with it; if one member is honored, all rejoice together with it.

RELATED READING

Circle of Friends by Robert Perske. Abingdon, 1988.

Don't Feel Sorry for Paul, Bernard Wolf, ed. HarperCollins Children's Books, 1988.

Knots on a Counting Rope by Bill Martin and John Archambault. Holt, Henry, and Company, 1987.

My Friend Leslie: The Story of a Handicapped Child by Maxine B. Rosenberg. Lothrop, Lee and Shepard Books, 1983.

New Life in the Neighborhood by Robert and Martha Perske. Abingdon, 1980.

Nobody is perfect. In one sense all of us have disabilities, but they may not be as noticeable or severe as the kind we've just sampled. What limitation or disability do you really have?

Extending the session:

Use a finger-spelling chart available in some larger dictionaries and encyclopedias to learn to spell your names in sign language.

If the family knows a person with a severe disability, plan to visit him or her. Talk with them about their feelings and their experiences. If you don't know anyone, perhaps a social agency in your community could put you in contact with such a person.

TREAT

Why not try to make (or at least eat) a dessert using your less dominant hand—unless you're ambidextrous of course!

—Susan Vogt

SUGGESTIONS FOR TEACHING PEACE AND NONVIOLENCE TO CHILDREN IN THE HOME

1. Cultivate a good home life.

- ◆ Affirm each other.

- ◆ Share feelings, information, and experiences in order to learn to understand others.

- ◆ Be a community that allows people to work together on problems.

- ◆ Provide practical experience for children on different ways to solve problems.

- ◆ Enjoy life together.

2. **Join a parent support group.** If parents want to provide the proper kind of environment for their children, they themselves should use available resources to work through problems and deal with frustrations.

3. **Provide a good example.** Adults need to be the kind of people they want their children to become.

4. **Help children experience forgiveness.** To become peacemakers, children need to experience forgiveness from their parents when they make mistakes. They must also be helped to forgive others who wrong them.

5. **Don't buy war toys.** Research shows that playing with toy guns prompts aggression and antisocial behavior.

6. **Avoid entertainment that glorifies violence.** The peace-loving family will shun entertainment based on violence or the acceptance of violent solutions.

7. **Curb backyard fighting.** A way to teach peace values to children is to work with them on handling the conflicts that erupt during their play.

8. **De-emphasize possessions.** Much conflict in the world is about who owns what. Toning down the need for possessions will take away much of this source of conflict.

9. **Stress cooperative play.** In our Western world, we have overstressed competitive activities vocationally and in many other ways. Cooperative players in an orchestra make better music than competitive players.

10. **Tell stories.** To become peacemakers, children need to have a sense of belonging to a history of peacemakers. Parents can give them this sense by telling them stories. Stories can help children see that peacemaking is as heroic as making war.

11. **Encourage autonomy.** The willingness of parents to stand back and let their children experiment on their own and think for themselves appears to

be equally as important as warmth in the development of creative peacemakers.

12. **Learn to recognize situations that might provoke conflict.**

13. **Provide international experiences.** Invite visitors from other nations into your home to interact with the family. As children learn to know and like people from other cultures, violence becomes less of an alternative for settling problems with people who are different.

Adapted from *How to Teach Peace to Children*
by J. Lorne Peachey. Copyright
© 1981 Herald Press.
Used by permission.

 ## OPENING

Invite the family around the kitchen table or other gathering place. Light a candle in the center of the table. Sing a song about peace.

 ## PRESENTATION OF THEME

The line "Let peace begin with me," from the song "Let There Be Peace on Earth," is a great starting point for examining how we teach peace and nonviolence at home. Often we find other families or people in our community who encourage and inspire us in their efforts to work for justice and peace.

Reading:
Romans 12:14-19 *or*
a reading from *The Big Book for Peace*   *or*
a Native American reading

 ## FAMILY RESPONSE

Discuss the characteristics of a peaceful family. (See background.) Discuss what you do as a family to nurture a peaceful household. What *more* can you do as a family to be at peace with one another?

Choose to do one or more of the following activities:

1. Peacemakers We Know

Renowned peacemakers such as Gandhi, Martin Luther King, and Oscar Romero aren't the only people who made peace. Name the ordinary people among your extended family and friends who work for peace and justice. Think of people with great perseverance who work to promote peace and justice in your neighborhood or community, no matter how small the task.

2. Pantomime

Take turns pantomiming acts of peacemaking performed by the people above. Let other family members try to guess who it is.

3. Peacemaker Award

Design a family "Affirm a Peacemaker" award.

 ## YOU WILL NEED...

Option 3: Peacemaker Award

☐ supplies to create a peacemaker award: paper, markers or crayons, stickers or ribbons

Option 4: Affirming a Peacemaker

☐ stationery

☐ pens or pencils

Option 5: Famous Peacemakers

☐ scrap paper and pens or pencils

☐ *The Big Book for Peace*, Ann Durrell and Marilyn Sacho, eds., Dutton Children's Books, 1990, optional

 ## READING

Romans 12:14-19

Bless those who persecute you; bless and do not curse them. Rejoice with those who rejoice, weep with those who weep. Live in harmony with one another; do not be haughty, but associate with the lowly; do not claim to be

(cont.)

wiser than you are. Do not repay anyone evil for evil, but take thought for what is noble in the sight of all. If it is possible, so far as it depends on you, live peaceably with all. Beloved, never avenge yourselves, but leave room for the wrath of God; for it is written, "Vengeance is mine, I will repay, says the Lord."

———

The truest and greatest power is the strength of Peace because Peace is the will of the Great Spirit.

—Native American, Hopi Tribe.

RELATED READING

The Animals' Peace Day by Jan Wahl.

God on Our Side, Michael Moynihan, ed.

How to Teach Peace to Children by J. Lorne Peachey. Herald Press, 1981.

One Silver Second by Daphne Hogstrom.

Peace Be with You by Cornelia Lehn. Faith and Life Press, 1980.

Peace Begins with You by Katherine Scholes. Sierra Club Books, 1990.

—Ann Marie Witchger Hansen

4. Affirming a Peacemaker

Each family member writes a letter to his or her chosen peacemaker, affirming that person's life and work. Send along to each one a personalized copy of your homemade "Affirm a Peacemaker" award.

5. Famous Peacemakers

In an encyclopedia, read about the lives of famous peacemakers such as Andre Trocme, Gandhi, King, Oscar Romero, Dorothy Day or Tich Nat Hahn. Write the names of these people on slips of paper. Form teams and take turns choosing a name and pantomiming or role playing an event in that person's life for the other team to identify.

TREAT

Serve Dove ice cream bars.

AGE ADAPTATION

Help younger children compose an affirming letter to a peacemaker.

A LITTLE R&R

OPENING

Light a campfire (or grill, if your community does not permit campfires). Ask everyone to sit comfortably. Close your eyes and breathe in the fresh evening air. Exhale concerns and distractions. Repeat several times until everyone appears relaxed. Slowly open your eyes and refocus. Sing in rounds "O How Lovely Is the Evening" (Appendix A, Music).

PRESENTATION OF THEME

Summer is a time when many families plan recreational activities for the children and outings or a vacation for the entire family. As you plan family activities for the coming summer, reflect on past summers and the activities everyone liked and didn't like, to see which activities to repeat and which to avoid.

Tonight everyone will have a chance to talk about their needs and wishes for the summer. With all expectations presented, the family will be able to make summer vacation plans cooperatively.

Reading:

Psalm 8:4-9 *or*
"Prayer for the Season"

FAMILY RESPONSE

Browse through the pictures and mementos of summers past. Take turns telling stories about a favorite summer. Form two teams of two or more people. One team pantomimes a funny incident during a summer vacation and the other team guesses what happened.

Ask family members what they are looking forward to and concerns they have in planning this summer's activities. Write down all the things that are already scheduled—ball practice, swimming lessons, church camp, summer jobs. When you see everything that is already planned, discuss how the family would like to spend the remaining time. Be sure to balance responsibilities with recreation and activities with rest and relaxation.

> **NOTE:** Family Night 29 (Recharging Our Batteries) will give you more practice in balancing the different parts of your lives.

YOU WILL NEED...

- ☐ a meeting place in your backyard

- ☐ blankets and lawn chairs

- ☐ a campfire (if your city/county ordinance permits) or a grill

- ☐ picture albums and/or mementos from summers past

- ☐ an alternate indoor meeting place in case of bad weather or if you don't have a yard

- ☐ houseplants or flowers for alternate site

READING

Psalm 8:4-9

[W]hat are human beings that you are mindful of them, mortals that you care for them?

Yet you have made them a little lower than God, and crowned them with glory and honor. You have given them dominion over the works of your hands; you have put all things under their feet, all sheep and oxen, and also the beasts of the field, the birds of the air, and the fish of the sea, whatever passes along the paths of the seas.

(cont.)

O LORD, our Sovereign, how majestic is your name in all the earth!

———

Prayer for the Season

God of all creation,
Grant us this summer day
    some meeting with bird
    or moon,
sheep or star, insect or the
    sun itself
that we might marvel and
    know our place
and praise you again and for
    ever and ever. Amen.

—Source unknown

 RELATED READING

Amy Loves the Sun by Julia Hoban. HarperCollins Children's Books, 1988.

Sanity in the Summer by Linda Dillow.

School's Out—Now What? by Joan M. Bergstrom. Ten Speed Press, 1990.

Under the Snowball Tree by Ellie Kirby. Fox Creek Press, 1986.

 TREAT

Make S'mores over the campfire. (See Appendix B, Recipes.)

 AGE ADAPTATION

Tell stories about past summer activities and vacations to the little ones if they are too young to remember their past summers.

—Ann Marie Witchger Hansen

LOVE TO GIVE, GIVE TO LOVE

Optional

NOTE: For several weeks before you do this family night, save all of the charitable solicitation letters that you receive in the mail. If you have a Shalom Box, this would be a good place to collect the mail. If not, directions are included here for making one.

OPENING

Light a candle and sing "Simple Gifts" (Appendix A, Music).

PRESENTATION OF THEME

Explain that the family has received a lot of mail lately that needs to be opened:

> Usually mail is fun to open, but I saved these particular letters because I could tell by the envelope that probably all of them are from people who want our help. These are from people and organizations who are asking us to give them money. These are different from bills, though. We don't *owe* these people money. They hope that when we learn of their needs, we will want to give them some of our money to help them out. In a way, we do owe our poorer world neighbors some help. When we have more than they, we want to share to make things more even.

Reading:
Matthew 19:16-22 *or*
Giving Tree

FAMILY RESPONSE

Let everyone in the family help open the mail and take turns summarizing the requests.

Decide to donate time, money, or goods to one or two causes. Determine how each person in the family can contribute something.

To remind each other of the cause(s) you've taken on, draw or make a symbol of your charity and put it in a visible place in

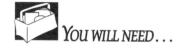

YOU WILL NEED...

☐ solicitation letters from charitable organizations collected over several weeks

☐ a Shalom Box for collecting mail, optional

☐ names of causes your family supports financially

☐ *Giving Tree*, Shel Silverstein, HarperCollins Children's Books, 1964, optional

READING

Matthew 19:16-22

Then someone came to him and said, "Teacher, what good deed must I do to have eternal life?" And he said to him, "Why do you ask me about what is good? There is only one who is good. If you wish to enter into life, keep the commandments." He said to him, "Which ones?" And Jesus said, "You shall not murder; You shall not commit adultery; You shall not steal; You shall not bear false witness; Honor your father and mother; also, You shall love your neighbor as yourself." The young man said to him, "I have kept all these; what do I still lack?" Jesus said

(cont.)

to him, "If you wish to be perfect, go, sell your possessions, and give the money to the poor, and you will have treasure in heaven; then come, follow me." When the young man heard this word, he went away grieving, for he had many possessions.

RELATED READING

A Birthday for Frances by Russell Hoban. HarperCollins Children's Books, 1976.

Gogo's Pay Day by Anne Rockwell.

The Scarebunny by Dorothy Kunhardt.

—Susan Vogt

your home. Or make a Shalom Box and put the artwork in or around this box. A Shalom Box is a shoe box or similar box decorated with symbols of peace, unity, and caring to remind the family of their values and goals. Use the box to hold symbols of the charitable groups you support financially or to collect appeal letters from charitable organizations. For a fuller description of a Shalom Box, see page 107 in *Helping Families Care*.

If possible, mail your contributions at the close of the gathering. As a family, walk or ride bikes to the nearest mailbox or post office.

Extend the activity:

Stewardship also involves taking care of the earth, not only taking care of our own belongings, but also caring for public land and goods. Pick a park close to your home and go on a clean-up expedition. Take bags for paper, cans, glass, and other trash. An energetic family may even decide to "adopt" this park and pick up trash there on a regular basis.

TREAT

If there's an ice cream shop on the way to the post office, stop for cones. (Once we had enough Dairy Queen coupons to treat the whole family for free.)

AGE ADAPTATION

Talk with teens in more detail about charitable contributions, asking questions such as:

◆ How do we know what percent of our money really goes to the charity? The Annual Charity Index can be obtained from:

Council of Better Business Bureaus
c/o Philanthropic Advisory Service
4200 Wilson Blvd., Suite 800
Arlington, VA 22203

◆ Should we give to sidewalk beggars?

◆ How much of our money should we give away?

◆ How can we use time as well as money responsibly?

LAUGHING AND LOVING WITH DAD

Father's Day

 ## OPENING

Light a candle and think of your own father, grandfather, or great-grandfather if you remember them. Think of the qualities these fathers have that you admire. Also, are there "fathers" not related to you who you think do a very good job of parenting? Quietly think about these special men.

 ## PRESENTATION OF THEME

Fathers come in many shapes, sizes, and kinds. Most fathers are good and loving to their children, but like all humans, no father is completely perfect. Tonight we're going to poke some good-hearted fun at fathers, and in the process we might even understand fatherhood a little better.

Reading:

Luke 11:11-13 *or*
Luke 15:11-32 (the story of the Prodigal Son) *or*
"What Fathers Really Want as Gifts"

 ## FAMILY RESPONSE

Choose one or more of the following activities.

1. Imitating Dad

Everyone but Dad dresses up in the "dad type" clothes that have been collected. Dad is the audience and his main job is to laugh heartily, clap loudly, and enjoy everything. The rest pretend they are "Dad" and exaggerate his mannerisms and expressions. The only rule is that the acting must not be hurtful or bothersome to Dad. When the frivolity dies down, close with each person completing the sentence, "If I were really a father, the most important thing I would do (or be) is _____."

2. Dad: Leading Man

Everyone in the family but Dad thinks of a significant event in the family's life in which Dad had a major role. It could be something serious in which Dad was a protector or hero, or it could be

 ## YOU WILL NEED...

**Option 1:
Imitating Dad**

☐ Dad's or Grandpa's old clothes, hats, shoes, ties, coats/jackets

**Option 2:
Dad: Leading Man**

☐ several puppets (If you feel like making your own, use socks and sew on buttons for eyes and nose, use markers for mouth and yarn for hair.)

**Option 3:
Where's Dad?**

☐ family picture albums, recent and past

 ## READING

Luke 11:11-13

Is there anyone among you who, if your child asks for a fish, will give a snake instead of a fish? Or if the child asks for an egg, will give a

(cont.)

scorpion? If you then, who are evil, know how to give good gifts to your children, how much more will the heavenly Father give the Holy Spirit to those who ask him!

———

Luke 15:11-32 (the story of the Prodigal Son)

———

What Fathers Really Want as Gifts

Fathers prefer experiences, help with chores, and appreciation from time to time. They like to be told they're good fathers and that they are loved, because they aren't really sure they are.

   Maybe the best gift we can offer is the risk of sharing what he means to us in our own words. We can say it to him in person or on the phone. If it's tough to say, we can begin with, "I don't want to embarrass you, Dad, but I have never told you I loved you or thanked you for being my dad."

—Dolores Curran, *Messenger* (June 11, 1993). Copyright © 1993 Alt Publishing Co.

something funny such as a silly thing he did. Once everyone has his or her event in mind, use puppets to act out the situation for Dad.

3. Where's Dad?

Pull out the family's picture albums. Everybody makes a guess as to how many times "Dad" is in an album. Then play "Where's Dad?" by finding and counting how many times Dad appears. Encourage lingering over pages that remind you of stories about Dad.

Discussion:

After spoofing Dad awhile, discuss some of the following questions:

- ◆ Are the qualities typical of fathers different from the qualities of mothers? If so, how?

- ◆ Unfortunately, not everyone has a loving father. Either their father is dead, no longer present, or perhaps he just doesn't know how to be a good father. How can people in these situations learn to be good fathers themselves?

- ◆ How are fathers portrayed in the media? Realistically? Stereotypically?

- ◆ Not all fathers are the same. What would a father's life be like if he were a single parent? a stepfather? a father with a disability? a father from a foreign country or culture?

Discussing grandfathers and great-grandfathers gives an opportunity to look at genealogy and share oral history. Talk about best memories, funniest stories, and family legends.

Who are the people we know who act like loving fathers to us (uncles, grandfathers, or friends)?

TREAT

Serve up Dad's favorite dessert.

AGE ADAPTATION

In addition to focusing on the discussion questions above, teens might want to talk about how men can be nurturing, caring, strong, fair, openminded, and effective problem-solvers. Some fathers are secure enough in their manhood that they feel comfortable taking on nontraditional roles such as child care, cooking, laundry, and grocery shopping. Why are men often stereotyped as harsh disciplinarians? Can men discipline children effectively without violence? Would it be any easier for a woman? What are some other negative stereotypes of fathers?

—Mike Magrath

RECHARGING OUR BATTERIES

YOU WILL NEED...

☐ a simple picnic meal (i.e., bread, vegetables, cheese, fruit, and cookies)

☐ sports equipment for games the entire family will enjoy

☐ star finder or map of the constellations, optional

READING

Mark 1:32-35

That evening, at sundown, they brought to him all who were sick or possessed with demons. And the whole city was gathered around the door. And he cured many who were sick with various diseases, and cast out many demons; and he would not permit the demons to speak, because they knew him.

In the morning, while it was still very dark, he got up and went out to a deserted place, and there he prayed.

——

Psalm 46:10a

Be still, and know that I am God!

OPENING

Find a quiet picnic spot under a tree or near a stream at your favorite local park. Everyone sit comfortably on the blanket with legs crossed.

Have family members close their eyes and breathe in the fresh evening air. Exhale concerns and distractions. Repeat several times until everyone appears relaxed. Slowly open your eyes and refocus. Sing in rounds "O How Lovely Is the Evening" (Appendix A, Music), "White Coralbells," "The Ash Grove," or another song about nature. When everyone is relaxed and in tune with nature, play a game of follow-the-leader. Take turns being the leader who leads others with their eyes closed: lead everyone to things in nature—grass, leaves, trees, rocks—and try to identify them by feel.

PRESENTATION OF THEME

Summertime can be just as hectic as the busy school year. Families often plan many outings and recreational activities for the kids just "to keep them busy."

Summertime, however, can also be a time to renew both our "inner" selves as well as our "outer" selves. Taking time out of our busy schedules each day to sit quietly, listen to the sounds around us, or simply to close our eyes may give us new insights and replenish our spiritual and emotional energy.

Reading:
Mark 1:32-35 *or*
Psalm 46:10a *or*
"Becoming Friends with the Earth"

FAMILY RESPONSE

While eating your picnic supper, ask each person to recall a time when he or she felt worried or scared and another time he or she felt at peace (e.g., walking along the shore, hiking in the woods, lying on the bed, petting a kitten). Reflect on the opening exercise of getting in touch with your surroundings.

After supper, play a sports game together in the park just for the fun of it. Adapt it as a cooperative game so no one loses.

Chase lightning bugs if there are any around. When it gets dark, tell stories and sing.

Extending the activity:

For assorted nature activities, refer to *Educating for Peace and Justice* (Appendix D, Resources).

 TREAT

After the game, have some juice and then sit down together on the blanket and gaze at the stars. Perhaps use a star finder to identify constellations.

Becoming Friends with the Earth

The first peace, which is the most important, is that which comes within the souls of people when they realize their relationship, their oneness, with the universe and all its powers. And when they realize that at the center of the universe, dwells the Great Spirit, and that this center is really everywhere, it is within each of us.

—From *The Sacred Pipe: Black Elk's Account of the Seven Rites of the Oglala Sioux.* Copyright © 1953 University of Oklahoma Press.

 RELATED READING

Weekend at Muskrat Lake by Nicki Weiss.

—Ann Marie Witchger Hansen

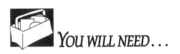 YOU WILL NEED...

☐ clothes reminiscent of parents' youth for everyone to wear

☐ old yearbooks, scrapbooks, photo albums, memorabilia

☐ a dance floor (reminiscent of parents' era) re-created with crepe paper, balloons, and signs

☐ old records and tapes from the Fifties, Sixties, or Seventies (Borrow from friends or the library, or play an "oldies" station on the radio.)

 READING

Luke 2:41-50

Now every year his parents went to Jerusalem for the festival of the Passover. And when he was twelve years old, they went up as usual for the festival. When the festival was ended and they started to return, the boy Jesus stayed behind in Jerusalem, but his parents did not know it. Assuming that he was in the group of travelers, they went a day's journey. Then they started to look for him among

(cont.)

 OPENING

Explain to your children that part 2 of tonight's activity is a surprise. Ask them to follow your example and dress in the appropriate attire you have found for them. If possible, do not let them see the "dance floor." Gather around the kitchen table or other meeting place. Light a candle. Sing a song reminiscent of the parents' teen years.

 PRESENTATION OF THEME

Sometimes children forget that parents were kids once, too! By reminiscing with our children, we will remember what it's like to be children and also help the children understand "why we are as we are."

Reading:

Luke 2:41-50 *and/or*

Parents tell stories of how "We were kids once, too!" Bring out your high school yearbooks, photo albums, scrapbooks, and memorabilia, and tell a few stories about your school days.

FAMILY RESPONSE

Ask the children what is most important to them today—sports, school friends, family, or hobbies, for example. Then, as parents, talk about what was most important to you when you were young. Ask children how they solve problems today, who they talk to when feeling low, and what they do when peer pressure becomes too intense. Then share your experiences, too. Remind kids that you had fun, too!

With the lights down low and the music ready, have the kids follow you to the "school dance" with their eyes closed. Turn on the music before they open their eyes. Teach them the twist, chicken, swim, fox-trot or other favorite "old time" dance steps. Ham it up and rock out!

their relatives and friends. When they did not find him, they returned to Jerusalem to search for him. After three days they found him in the temple, sitting among the teachers, listening to them and asking them questions. And all who heard him were amazed at his understanding and his answers. When his parents saw him they were astonished; and his mother said to him, "Child, why have you treated us like this? Look, your father and I have been searching for you in great anxiety." He said to them, "Why were you searching for me? Did you not know that I must be in my Father's house?" But they did not understand what he said to them.

 ## Treat

Set up popcorn, ice cream sodas, or old-fashioned root beer floats.

 ## Age Adaptation

With older children, dance to some of the current favorite hits when *your* music "gets old"!

—Ann Marie Witchger Hansen

31

FAMILY NIGHT

THE LIFE OF A CHOCOLATE BAR

United States Independence Day—July 4
Canadian Dominion Day—July 1

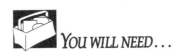 **YOU WILL NEED . . .**

❑ a world map or globe

❑ audiocassette or CD of "We Are the World" or "It's a Small World," optional

❑ *Turkey's Gift to the People*, Ani Rucki, Northland Publishing, 1992, optional

Option 1:
Daily Dependence

❑ piece of plain paper and a pencil for each person

❑ 6-inch circles with a smiling face on each for everyone in your family

Option 2:
Product Development

❑ a polyester blouse or skirt on a hanger, optional

❑ eight script cards with one of the following written on each one: El Salvador, South Carolina, Venezuela, Trinidad, New Jersey, North Carolina, Haiti, New York

 **OPENING**

With a globe in the middle of the table or world map hanging on the wall, join hands and sing or listen to either "We Are the World" or "It's a Small World."

PRESENTATION OF THEME

So often at this time of the year we hear how great it is for our country to have gained its independence. And yet we are a global family. When we celebrate our freedom from tyranny and foreign rule, we also recognize our dependence on others for food, shelter, clothing, and friendships. Today we are going to declare our *interdependence*.

Reading:
1 Corinthians 12:4-11 *or*
Turkey's Gift to the People

FAMILY RESPONSE

Discuss Paul's message in 1 Corinthians 12:4-11 and choose one of the following options.

1. Daily Dependence

Ask each family member to list five to ten daily activities such as hearing the alarm clock ring, dressing, brushing hair, and eating a banana, talking to your mom, calling a friend, listening to your teacher. Next to each activity write the items and people you depend upon to carry out these daily activities (for example, pillow, clock radio, clothing, banana, mom, teacher).

Distribute the smiling faces to family members and have them write the names of two people upon whom they depend. Also have them bring to the table two of the objects on which they depend and take turns explaining their dependence. Then locate on the map where each originated, for example: alarm clock (Japan), sweatshirt (Malaysia), banana (Brazil).

2. Product Development

Select one item that is commonly available around the home, and trace the countries, provinces, and states that contribute to its

development. For example, the ingredients and sources of a chocolate candy bar include:

- chocolate/cocoa from Ghana

- almonds from Brazil

- sugar from the Dominican Republic

- milk from Pennsylvania dairy farms

- corn syrup from Iowa corn fields

- paper wrappers from Canadian lumber mills

- stores selling candy bars in many cities, states, countries

A more elaborate way to trace the development of an item is to act out the "Journey of the Polyester Blouse."

Distribute a script card to everyone in the family. Some members may have more than one. In order, from one to eight, each person reads the script for his or her country. (Readers may read for nonreaders in the family.) Pass the polyester clothing item to each family member to hold as they read. Also have them find their location on the map or globe.

Polyester blouse script:

El Salvador

> Workers in a poor province of El Salvador plant and harvest for our blouse. Children and adults pick the cotton on long hot days. Adults earn the equivalent of about $2 a day, which is less than one percent of the final value of our blouse.

South Carolina

> The ginned cotton is shipped to South Carolina by a company called Cargill. This company can bargain with the Salvadoran landowner for a very low price. In South Carolina, the cotton is sold to Burlington for spinning into thread. Burlington is the largest textile mill in the United States.

Venezuela

> Next we need oil from Venezuela, because polyester is made from petroleum. In South America, Venezuelan workers have a dangerous job drilling and processing oil. They work under hot skies for the equivalent of $6 a day. After they pump and refine the oil for the state company, the oil is sold to Exxon, a giant multinational corporation. Exxon controls the most profitable part of the oil business: the processing, marketing, and final distribution of the oil.

READING

1 Corinthians 12:4-11

Now there are varieties of gifts, but the same Spirit; and there are varieties of services, but the same Lord; and there are varieties of activities, but it is the same God who activates all of them in everyone. To each is given the manifestation of the Spirit for the common good. To one is given through the Spirit the utterance of wisdom, and to another the utterance of knowledge according to the same Spirit, to another faith by the same Spirit, to another gifts of healing by the one Spirit, to another the working of miracles, to another prophecy, to another the discernment of spirits, to another various kinds of tongues, to another the interpretation of tongues. All these are activated by one and the same Spirit, who allots to each one individually just as the Spirit chooses.

Trinidad

Exxon carries the oil by ship to the islands of Trinidad and Tobago. Here the oil is processed again into many petrochemicals. The work is difficult, dangerous, and unhealthy because many of the chemicals are poisonous.

New Jersey

The chemicals are put on another ship and sent to New Jersey. They go to a big DuPont factory where they speed through huge machines and come out as miles and miles of continuous string called filament. This is the polyester part of the thread.

North Carolina

The polyester thread is taken to another Burlington textile mill. The workers' salaries are very low. Here high-powered looms combine the cotton thread from South Carolina with the polyester chemical thread. Then the combined threads are woven into long sheets of fabrics ready to be cut into our blouse pattern.

A big retail company, like Sears, comes to buy the woven cloth. Eventually the retail company will sell the blouse.

Haiti

The polyester and cotton cloth is put onto another ship. It's carried to Haiti. Small Haitian-owned-and-run businesses pay women workers the equivalent of $3 a day to make the blouse. The Haitian women bend over the sewing machines for long hours stitching seams. They have no labor union. They will be fired or punished if they talk about changing their working conditions.

New York

The finished blouses leave the Third World for the last time. They are put on another ship and sent back to New York. In New York, the blouses are packaged and sealed in plastic and finally sent to mail-order buyers around the United States.

We find the blouses on display at our local department store, and we buy one.

Adapted with permission from a poster available from *Seeds Magazine*, June 1987, $3.00 (P.O. Box 6170, Waco, TX 76706, 817-755-7745).

Closing:

To acknowledge our interdependence with workers both here and abroad and the people who touch our lives each day, stand in a circle. Each family member extends both hands to different people in the circle and have one giant handshake.

Even though we recognize our **inter**dependence with all nations on our planet, we want to remember the values on which our country was built, especially freedom. Close by singing "O Freedom" (Appendix A, Music) or other patriotic songs your family enjoys.

 *TREAT*

Make "interdependent" pizza. Someone prepare the crust, another grate the cheese, someone else make the sauce, and so forth.

AGE ADAPTATION

Go with younger children to their bedrooms and/or kitchen. Have them choose one item they use each day. Explain to them where each was made. Also ask them to name people in their lives upon whom they depend. Explain interdependence at their level.

For older children and teens, you may want to explore the complexities of international trade and moral questions that come up. For example:

◆ When we get sugar from the Dominican Republic, we are buying the product raised on land that could be producing food for the people there. We are also paying rich landowners for the sugar, not the people who sweat to make it grow.

◆ A sweatshirt from Malaysia may be less expensive than one made in a developed country because wages are lower. Wages may be lower because the country doesn't have laws to protect their workers from "sweatshop" conditions.

◆ Is it really interdependence when a developed country gets raw materials or labor from an underdeveloped country but gives little of value back, in fact, perpetuating the poverty of the local workers? How could this be changed?

Since older children and teens enjoy a trip to the mall, send everybody out in pairs with paper and pen to find as many countries on clothing labels or packing boxes as you can find. Come back together after an hour to combine lists and see how much of the world you covered.

—Ann Marie Witchger Hansen

B.C.—BEFORE COMPUTERS

 **YOU WILL NEED...**

☐ decks of cards and directions for card games from your childhood

☐ a traditional board game or other game

☐ a paragraph or two from *Little House on the Prairie* (Wilder), *The Education of Little Tree* (Carter), *The Chosen* (Potok), or a similar book you have read describing family time at home, optional

☐ a short written description of your own tradition of family time as a child, optional

☐ invitation to grandparents or older neighbors to join you this night, optional

 **OPENING**

Gather the family in a cozy spot in your home and sit on the floor. If you have a fireplace, gather around it. Light a candle and sing a familiar and loved folk song such as "Let Me Call You Sweetheart" or "I've Been Working on The Railroad"(see Appendix A, Music).

PRESENTATION OF THEME

In the "good old days" before computers, VCRs, microwaves, and color television sets, families often spent more time at home together playing cards or board games and listening to each other tell stories about their week. Tonight we're going to have fun the old fashioned way.

Reading:
Read the passage you chose from a book describing family time
    or a description of family time in your childhood *or*
Psalm 133

FAMILY RESPONSE

Talk about the things we have or do for fun today that we did not have "back then." Try to imagine what life would be like without them. To the sound of a crackling fire or a classical radio station, teach your children a favorite card game or board game: Fish, Poker, Crazy Eights, checkers, Parcheesi, Monopoly.

If necessary, work in two small groups rather than all together all the time. Switch partners occasionally.

Give the kids a chance to teach you a card game or two, also.

In between games or when appropriate, ask kids to describe their favorite "stay-at-home" evening activity with the family (excluding watching television or a video or playing games on the computer).

 ## TREAT

Serve hot apple cider and cookies or popcorn.

 ## READING

Psalm 133

How very good and pleasant it is when kindred live together in unity! It is like the precious oil on the head, running down upon the beard, on the beard of Aaron, running down over the collar of his robes. It is like the dew of Hermon, which falls on the mountains of Zion. For there the LORD ordained his blessing, life forevermore.

 ## RELATED READING

The Chosen by Chaim Potok. Fawcett, 1987.

The Education of Little Tree by Forrest Carter. University of New Mexico Press, 1986.

Little House on the Prairie by Laura I. Wilder. HarperCollins, 1975.

—Ann Marie Witchger Hansen

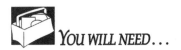

YOU WILL NEED...

☐ a moonlit evening (perhaps combine with a time the family is out late anyway)

☐ a safe and comfortable place to sit outside

☐ one or more flashlights

☐ readings selected ahead of time from the Bible and/or storybooks:

    ☐ *Goodnight Moon*, Margaret Wise Brown, HarperCollins Children's Books, 1977

    ☐ *Papagayo: The Mischief Maker*, Gerald McDermott, Harcourt Brace, 1992

READING

Selections from Psalms:

Psalm 8:1-4

Psalm 19:1-2

Psalm 57:9-11

Psalm 89:5, 11

Psalm 108:3-5

Psalm 139:7-12

Psalm 148:1-6

Psalm 150:1-2

There is something very special about a moonlit evening. Being outside together under the stars can be very intimate and inspirational. Being shrouded in darkness can give us a sense of being hidden, which helps us feel secure enough to talk more freely than usual with each other and with God. This family night, therefore, uses this opportunity to foster prayer and spirituality.

> **NOTE:** Before going outside, allow each family member to choose a story or some verses from the Psalms that express awe and wonder over the heavens that God created. For children who cannot yet read, choose a simple phrase that they can repeat after you. Place a bookmark in the pages so that you can locate the readings easily and read them by flashlight.

OPENING

Gather outside under the stars. Take a few minutes to get used to the darkness and to appreciate the beauty and wonder of the night sky. Then, light one or more candles. Enjoy the soft glow. Observe the way the light dances in the darkness of the night.

PRESENTATION OF THEME

The Psalms are full of verses about the heavens praising God. Perhaps some of them were written by David as he cared for his father's sheep out under the night sky. When everyone seems ready, share the readings that you have chosen. When finished, add any words of appreciation, awe, wonder, or thankfulness that members of the family may be feeling.

Reading:
Story selections or Bible passages

FAMILY RESPONSE

Continue your time together by sharing stories or songs about the night or the night sky. "Twinkle, Twinkle Little Star" is one

well-known example. If you have young children, include actions
with the songs. Reminisce by telling stories of times you spent
outside under the moon and stars, recalling playing hide-and-seek
on those lazy warm nights of
childhood.

Then recall wishing on a star and
tell young children about this
tradition. Teach the words,

> Star light, star bright,
> first star I see tonight.
> I wish I may, I wish I might,
> have the wish I wish tonight.

Talk about what each person
would wish. Then use this poem as
a format for prayer. Challenge each
person to come up with a fourth
line, for example:

> Star light, star bright,
> first star I see tonight.
> I wish I may, I wish I might,
> know how God will use my light.

Other examples of fourth lines are:

> ...pray that everyone is safe
> tonight.
> ...learn to love and not to fight.
> ...care about all who share this sky tonight.

Remind children that they are not praying to the stars, but
rather using this poem as a way of directing their prayers to
God. If this prayer format is too confining, express your prayers
in whatever way is comfortable or familiar to you. Also allow for
family members to offer spontaneous prayers.

End this time by giving a blessing or wish for each person.
Saying special words to each other will help each person
remember this experience for a long time to come. You may want
to bring closure to the "official" part of the family night by
singing a song like "God Bless the Moon" (Appendix A, Music).
As you sing this blessing, stand together in a circle and do a
simple dance as well. Hold hands and take two steps right, then
two steps left; two steps in, then two steps out. Repeat the
pattern twice for each verse.

As you share your treat together, continue to enjoy the evening
and the beautiful heavens God has made.

TREAT

Select a treat that goes along with the theme of moon and stars, for example: Heavenly Hash ice cream, moon pies, sugar cookies made in the shape of the moon or stars, star fruit, a half-moon of cheese (after all, the moon is made of it!), round crackers, or Starburst candies. A round scoop of ice cream with sprinkles on it would make a great moon and stars!

AGE ADAPTATION

This activity may take place later than preschoolers and young children are used to staying up. It may also take on a magical feel for them. Maximize this special feeling. Also be aware that they may not be used to the darkness. Be sure to help them feel comfortable and safe in their new surroundings.

Encourage older children or teens to share some of their memories of how they felt about the darkness when they were young, or have them tell about one of the first times they remember being out in the darkness. Older children may also enjoy looking for constellations and remembering that their ancestors saw the very same pictures in the stars.

—Colleen Aalsburg Wiessner

 ## OPENING

Prominently display the four pictures of people of different races on the table. Light a candle and ask the family to ponder the four pictures for one minute in silence.

 ## PRESENTATION OF THEME

The objective of this session is to heighten the family's awareness of and sensitivity for the feelings of those of another race.

Lift up Martin Luther King, Jr., as an example of one who believed in racial equality. He lived and worked peacefully and died for his beliefs. Share his dream of justice for all races by emphasizing the following points:

- ◆ It is unfair to judge people by the color of their skin.

- ◆ Jobs should be equally available to everyone whether their skin color is red, yellow, black, brown, or white.

- ◆ All people should live together in peace and love.

 ## FAMILY RESPONSE

Have everyone cut out armbands from construction paper. Cut the strips four inches wide and eighteen inches long. Make one orange strip and the rest blue. Fold the strips so that the ends overlap, and staple or paste them together.

Select one person to wear the orange armband. (Each person will be given this opportunity.) The others put on the blue armbands. Have the family members walk into the living room and sit down. Those in blue armbands try to show rejection to the person wearing the orange armband by forcing him or her to sit in the corner. Whisper to each other, saying negative things about that person. Be serious and don't smile. Create this scene several times as everyone takes a turn wearing the orange armband.

> **NOTE:** To vary this activity, have the "orange person" sit in a comfortable seat of honor. All others in blue armbands sit on the floor. The "orange person" is allowed to snack on treats and speak whenever he or she wants. Everyone else must raise a hand to be recognized by the "orange person." The

 ## YOU WILL NEED...

- ☐ four pictures of people (one Caucasian, one African-American, one Native American, one Asian)

- ☐ orange construction paper

- ☐ blue construction paper

- ☐ glue or stapler

 **READING**

Luke 10:27

He answered, "You shall love the Lord your God with all your heart, and with all your soul, and with all your strength, and with all your mind; and your neighbor as yourself."

———

We will match your capacity to inflict suffering with our capacity to endure suffering. We will meet your physical force with soul force. We will not hate you, but we cannot in all good conscience obey your unjust laws. . . . But we will soon wear you down by our capacity to suffer. And, in winning our freedom, we will so appeal to your heart and conscience that we will win you in the process.

—Martin Luther King, Jr.

"blue people" may not eat. The "orange person" is always right and must be pampered.

Reading:

Luke 10:27 *or*
Martin Luther King, Jr., quotation

When the activity is over, the family should gather to discuss their experiences. The leader is responsible for cultivating an atmosphere of openness so that each person feels free to share his or her feelings.

Explore these questions:

- ◆ How did it feel to be the only one wearing the orange armband?
- ◆ How did you feel when you were forced to sit in the corner or on the floor?
- ◆ How did the comments made about you affect you?
- ◆ How did you feel about the rest of the family?
- ◆ What could have been done to create a better relationship between those wearing the blue arm bands and the one wearing the orange arm band?

Relate this activity to real life situations and stress how our words can lift up or put down other people. Discuss the African proverb that states: "Quarrels end, but words once spoken never die."

Close with the traditional civil rights song "We Shall Overcome."

 **TREAT**

Serve anything colorful, like candy or sugar cookies.

AGE ADAPTATION

For younger children, use simple language but don't avoid discussion. Children of all ages can express their feelings.

Ask teens more involved questions:

◆ Is it possible to be prejudiced toward others even though you have been the victim of racism and know how much it hurts?

◆ Are victims of racism justified in treating the oppressor as they have been treated?

◆ Is anger justified?

◆ What can we do with strong negative feelings or guilt?

RELATED READING

Iggie's House by Judy Blume. Dell, 1976.

Maniac Magee by Jerry Spinelli. HarperCollins Children's Books, 1992.

Sneetches and Other Stories by Dr. Seuss. Random House Books for Young Readers, 1961.

—Evelyn P. Wilson

35 FAMILY NIGHT

WATER FROLIC

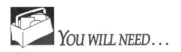 YOU WILL NEED...

☐ water in a small glass bowl

☐ a hand towel

☐ glass of ice water

☐ 4 containers: two-quart bowl, one-gallon bucket, two-gallon bucket, five-gallon bucket

 READING

John 4:7-15

A Samaritan woman came to draw water, and Jesus said to her, "Give me a drink." (His disciples had gone to the city to buy food.) The Samaritan woman said to him, "How is it that you, a Jew, ask a drink of me, a woman of Samaria?" (Jews do not share things in common with Samaritans.) Jesus answered her, "If you knew the gift of God, and who it is that is saying to you, 'Give me a drink,' you would have asked him, and he would have given you living water." The woman said to him, "Sir, you have no bucket, and the well is deep. Where do you get that living water? Are you greater than our ancestor Jacob, who gave us the well, and with his sons and his flocks drank from

(cont.)

OPENING

Light a candle and sing "Simple Gifts," or sing "Itsy Bitsy Spider" for very young children. (See Appendix A, Music.)

PRESENTATION OF THEME

Water is the source of our human and spiritual life. It is very precious to us.

Reading:
John 4:7-15 *or*
Excerpt from *Many Winters*

> This time the white man wants our water which flows out of our sacred Blue Lake. It flows through our land and down into the pueblo where we use it for drinking and cooking and washing. It nourishes our crops as well. It is all we have. The white man does not need it. It is so small anyway, just enough for us and for our children. We have been careful with the water which flows from Blue Lake and it will last forever.
>
> When the white man gave Blue Lake back to us, some of us said, it will not end here. The white man is angry because he has had to give up this land which was ours to begin with, ever since we were put here as a people by the Great Father. We said, the white man will think of some new way to get what he wants. And now that has happened.
>
> If the white man takes our water, what do we have left? The land is no good without it. And we will shrivel up and die.
>
> What we have to do now is walk quietly among them. They have every weapon there is. We have only what we believe. Perhaps they will listen to us. Perhaps they will not. But we are a people of strong beliefs. Our hearts are where they should be. Everything is in place here. We are going on together. They cannot kill us.

—From *Many Winters* by Nancy Wood.
Copyright © 1974 Doubleday. Used by permission.

 FAMILY RESPONSE

Brainstorm what our lives would be like without water. Water is important to life because, among other things, it quenches our thirst and it cleans. Pass around a bowl of water. Each person dips a hand in the water, naming a habit he or she wants to be cleansed of, for example: teasing, putting down other people. Pass around a glass of ice water. Before drinking from it, each person mentions something she or he has been thirsting to do, become, or find, for example: putting files in order, becoming better at basketball, or finding time for regular family nights.

In many places around the world, water is very precious because it is very difficult to get. We can turn on the tap and have clean water any time we wish, but many people have to walk long distances for water and carry it home in buckets and jugs. See what it's like to carry water. Outside, fill a two-quart bowl, a one-gallon bucket, a two-gallon bucket, and a five-gallon bucket. Then put on your bathing suits and practice carrying the bowl of water on your heads as people would do in countries where water is scarce. Make a relay out of this activity or see who can carry the water the farthest.

Close by saying water rhymes or singing water songs such as "Row, Row, Row Your Boat," "Michael Row Your Boat Ashore," "Come to the Water," and "Roll On Columbia." Have fun with a water activity such as running through a sprinkler, tossing water balloons, or bobbing for apples.

it?" Jesus said to her, "Everyone who drinks of this water will be thirsty again, but those who drink of the water that I will give them will never be thirsty. The water that I will give will become in them a spring of water gushing up to eternal life." The woman said to him, "Sir, give me this water, so that I may never be thirsty or have to keep coming here to draw water."

RELATED READING

Many Winters (a collection of Pueblo poetry) by Nancy Wood. Doubleday, 1974.

—Mary Joan Park

 TREAT

Eat watermelon outside.

AGE ADAPTATION

Teens can discuss the dangers of floods and storms. Reflect on how even good things like water can be harmful when overdone or not controlled. For example, washing with water is good, but floods are bad. Eating is good, but overeating or undereating is harmful to our health. Likewise, our sexuality and ability to form caring, affectionate relationships are gifts from God. But using sexual power promiscuously and without commitment is destructive.

 BOMBS "AWAY"

Bombing of Hiroshima—August 6
Bombing of Nagasaki—August 9

 YOU WILL NEED...

Option 1:
Floating Japanese Lanterns

☐ several plastic gallon milk cartons

☐ the same number of small votive or tea candles

☐ matches

☐ a body of water (a lake, river, pond, or if all else fails, a child's swimming pool)

Option 2:
Paper Cranes

☐ *Sadako and the Thousand Paper Cranes*, Eleanor Coerr, Dell, 1979

☐ someone to demonstrate making paper cranes

☐ origami paper (writing paper or wrapping paper cut in 9-inch squares is a fine substitute)

Option 3:
Peace Poetry

☐ pens or pencils and paper

READING

Isaiah 2:4

He shall judge between the nations, and shall arbitrate for

(cont.)

 OPENING

Wait until dusk or dark to start. Light a candle and ask the family to pause for a moment to think about the power of fire for good and beauty, as well as evil and destruction.

PRESENTATION OF THEME

On August 6, 1945, the U.S. dropped the first atomic bomb on the people of Japan in the city of Hiroshima. On August 9, a second bomb was dropped on the city of Nagasaki. Japan was our enemy at the time, and the U.S. government believed that dropping this new and powerful bomb would show such overwhelming might that the U.S. would win the war very quickly and decisively and probably save many American lives. But no one knew the full horror of this new kind of bomb—a nuclear bomb. It not only killed people who were directly hit by it, but it also caused invisible harm to many people who got sick and died.

Although the world now realizes the full inhumanity of nuclear bombs like the ones dropped on Nagasaki and Hiroshima, many countries continue to develop more and even bigger bombs. Nobody wants to use these especially dangerous bombs, but many government leaders fear that if the leaders of another country really become angry enough—or crazy enough—they might use their nuclear weapons, even though such bombs could destroy the whole planet, including themselves.

In memory of the many Japanese people who died horrible deaths in the first atomic bombing, the Japanese hold a special ceremony each year on the anniversary. In the evening, as a sign of hope and commitment that nuclear weapons may never be used again, the people float lanterns on the rivers to honor the spirits of those who died. We join in solidarity with them by our own commemorative ceremony.

Reading:

Isaiah 2:4 (Perhaps sing the reading. For example, see the song "Vine and Fig Tree" in Appendix A, Music.) *or*
Santayana quotation *or*
"The Story of a Japanese Farm Woman"

FAMILY RESPONSE

Choose one or more of the following activities.

1. Floating Japanese Lanterns

Cut the top off of empty plastic gallon milk containers (cut about one-fourth from the top). Place a small votive or tea candle in the bottom (dripping some wax onto the bottom of the jug will help hold the candle in place). If you will be floating your lanterns on a large or swift body of water, tie string to the handles so they won't get away from you. Light the candles (long fireplace matches are helpful). One by one reverently place each lantern in the water and let them float around.

Silently ponder the beauty and meaning of the sight.

2. Paper Cranes

Familiarize your family with the story of *Sadako and the Thousand Paper Cranes* by reading an excerpt or using the following summary:

> Sadako Sasaki was a two-year-old Japanese child when Hiroshima was bombed. Ten years later she died of leukemia because of the radiation from the bomb. Before she died, she tried to fold a thousand origami paper cranes as a prayer for recovery and peace. She made only 644 but her Japanese classmates finished the thousand, and children all over the world continue to make paper cranes as a reminder to work for peace.

Make paper cranes and give them to friends or neighbors.

> **NOTE:** Although paper-folding is usually enticing to young children, it's much more difficult than it looks, even with the best of instructions. Usually children need to be at least eight to ten years old to do it successfully. If you know someone who can demonstrate this activity for you, it will be much easier. Practice ahead. As an alternative, you may wish to make cutouts of cranes or doves, or make the familiar paper airplanes and then trim them to look like cranes and decorate them.

many peoples; they shall beat their swords into plowshares, and their spears into pruning hooks; nation shall not lift up sword against nation, neither shall they learn war any more.

———

Those who do not remember the past are condemned to repeat it.

—Santayana

———

The Story of a Japanese Farm Woman (a translation)

(To be read by the oldest female in the family)

Hello, everyone. My name is Michiko Fukai. I am Japanese.

I am from the city of Hiroshima, Japan.

I want to tell you what happened to me on August 6th, 1945.

It was a fine summer day. The crickets were singing. I was a young school girl.

I loved animals. Our next door neighbor had a pretty kitten. I gave it fresh milk.

At 8:15 on August 6th, I went out to feed the kitten.

Suddenly . . . something *terrible* happened!

Out of the blue sky came a bomb. It was the first atomic bomb ever used.

(cont.)

It made a bright flash. The pretty kitten was blinded. I was badly burned.

More than a hundred thousand people were killed in an instant.

People died of burns even six miles away. Everything began to catch on fire.

After three hours, the whole city was burning. Many people died.

My mother . . . my father . . . and my three sisters were killed.

Every year after that, even today, people in Hiroshima die from the effects of radiation.

Did you know that the nuclear bombs today can multiply the destructive power of that atomic bomb a million times?

We want peace in Japan. We want peace in the world.

Please work together with me for peace.

—From *Helping Kids Care* by Camy Condon and James McGinnis.

RELATED READING

The Butter Battle Book by Dr. Seuss. Random House Books for Young Readers, 1984.

Hiroshima No Pika by Toshi Maruki. Lothrop, 1982.

Sadako and the Thousand Paper Cranes by Eleanor Coerr. Dell, 1979.

—Susan Vogt

3. Peace Poetry

If your family enjoys writing, try composing a haiku about peace. This Japanese poetry form consists of three lines. The first line has five syllables, the second line seven syllables, and the third line five syllables. For example:

Peace is our desire, (5)
But sometimes it takes so long, (7)
We must persevere. (5)

Peace is like a dove, (5)
She is often hard to grasp, (7)
But worth the effort. (5)

TREAT

If it is convenient, have food that is characteristic of Japan. Or try rice cakes with jam and peanut butter.

AGE ADAPTATION

Teens may find it intriguing to read the excerpt from Kurt Vonnegut's novel *Slaughterhouse Five*, in which Billy Pilgrim watches an old World War II movie about American bombers making raids over Germany. In a dream sequence, he sees the movie running backward as the bombs leave their targets, return to the airplanes, and eventually return to the earth from which the metal was mined.

Everybody Wins!

 ## Opening

Display the symbols of play activities on the table. Light a candle. Ask family members to think silently about how they feel when they win a game or lose a game. Play the theme from *Chariots of Fire* softly in the background as people think. Explain to the family that this movie is an inspiring story about two runners whose moral principles overrode their competitive spirit when they competed for England in the 1924 Olympic Games.

Reading:

1 Corinthians: 10:24 *or*
2 Timothy 2:5 *or*
"Hug O'War" from *Where the Sidewalk Ends or*
"No One's a Loser"

No One's a Loser

> To win is something everyone chooses,
> But when someone wins, at least one loses.
> Wouldn't it be nice if life were a game
> Where everyone shared the winning and fame.
>
> —Susan Vogt

 ## Presentation of Theme

Tonight we're going to play. Most people think of fun when they think of play. We're especially happy if we *win* a game or a contest. Training and practicing to win help us to become better at whatever we're trying to do. Competing against our peers also helps motivate us to do our best and that's good. But sometimes play makes us sad or even angry. Often that happens when the game is unfair or we lose. Every time we play a game in which someone wins, at least *one* person loses. It's important, of course, to be a good sport at both winning

 ## You Will Need...

☐ books of cooperative games (see list of related resources on page 110) or ask each member of the family ahead of time to think of or create a game in which nobody loses

☐ theme music from the movie *Chariots of Fire*

☐ several simple symbols of play activities (a ball, a deck of cards, a cooperative board game)

☐ *Where the Sidewalk Ends*, Shel Silverstein, HarperCollins Children's Books, 1974

 ## Reading

1 Corinthians 10:24

Do not seek your own advantage, but that of the other.

———

2 Timothy 2:5

And in the case of an athlete, no one is crowned without competing according to the rules.

RELATED RESOURCES

Books:

The Cooperative Sports and Games Book by Terry Orlick. Pantheon Books, 1978.

New Games Book, Andrew Fluegelman, ed. Doubleday and Co., 1976.

Playfair by Matt Weinstein and Joel Goodman. Impact Publishers (Calif.), 1980.

Games:

Animal Town Game Co., P. O. Box 2002, Santa Barbara, CA 93120.

Board games that emphasize cooperation, conservation, self-sufficiency, simple and peaceful living for the whole family.

Family Pastimes, R. R. #3, Perth, Ontario, Canada K7H 3C6.

Some titles of their board games are Community, Earth Game, Harvest Time, New American, Our Town, Space Feature, Yin Yang.

The Ungame Co., P. O. Box 6382, Anaheim, CA 92806.

These board games include Ungame, Reunion, and Social Security. Our favorite for families is Reunion.

and losing. Most games are set up to teach us that. Tonight we're going to learn more games in which *everyone wins*—cooperative games.

FAMILY RESPONSE

Invite family members to tell about when they won a game and a time they lost. How did they feel? Next, each member takes a turn teaching the family a game in which nobody loses. If you are unfamiliar with cooperative games or don't have easy access to one of the books listed below, here are two possibilities.

Cooperative Pin the Tail on the Donkey

If you don't have this game, use a large picture of an animal from a poster or magazine and make some "tails." One player is blindfolded as usual, but then it is the job of the onlookers to call out directions to help the player put the tail as close as possible to the right spot, for example: "Up a little, to the left...." Then everyone cheers the "team's" success.

Frisbee

Toss the Frisbee (or ball) around the circle of family members, seeing how many tosses the family can make before a drop. The family keeps trying to top its own record. You can make this game more difficult by moving back a step each time. You can make almost any board game into a cooperative game by not keeping score. Drawing games, quiz games, and word games lend themselves well to noncompetitive fun.

TREAT

Cooperatively make Orange Julius drinks or Smoothies (Appendix B, Recipes) or any snack that has several parts to put together like sundaes or milkshakes. Discuss how you liked the new games.

—Mary Joan Park and Susan Vogt

OPENING

Invite the family around the kitchen table or other gathering place. Light a candle and ask everyone to close their eyes and imagine a grand, festive, neighborhood or block party with all your neighbors singing, dancing, and enjoying each other's company. Open your eyes.

PRESENTATION OF THEME

Whether we live in cities or towns, rural or suburban areas, we all have neighbors next door or down the road. Discuss these questions:

- ◆ Do we take time to get to know these people?

- ◆ What does it mean to be a good neighbor?

- ◆ To whom do we reach out in our neighborhood?

- ◆ Who are our neighbors who care about us and our family? How do they show it?

Reading:
Luke 10:29-37 (The Good Samaritan) *or*
"Who Is My Neighbor?"

FAMILY RESPONSE

Our "Immediate Neighbors"

Divide into two teams for charades. Act out the helpful deeds or positive qualities of your neighbors, and let the other team try to guess whom your team is imitating.

After the game, talk about the neighbors you do not know or would like to get to know better. Plan to invite a new family and a family you know well to your next family night of games and fun.

Set a date for the party. Use the paper and markers to create personal invitations for each person or family. If you want to have a talent show, ask them to bring a musical instrument, piece of art, favorite story, poem, or song to the party. Plan several get-acquainted games to break the ice and decide what kind of food to have. Compose together a tribute to neighbors in prose or poetry, which you can read to your guests at the party.

YOU WILL NEED...

☐ colored paper

☐ pens, markers, crayons

READING

Luke 10:29-37

But wanting to justify himself, he asked Jesus, "And who is my neighbor?" Jesus replied, "A man was going down from Jerusalem to Jericho, and fell into the hands of robbers, who stripped him, beat him, and went away, leaving him half dead. Now by chance a priest was going down that road; and when he saw him, he passed by on the other side. So likewise a Levite, when he came to the place and saw him, passed by on the other side. But a Samaritan while traveling came near him; and when he saw him, he was moved with pity. He went to him and bandaged his wounds, having poured oil and wine on them. Then he put him on his own animal, brought him to an inn, and took care of him. The next day he took out two denarii, gave them to the innkeeper, and said, 'Take care of him; and when I come back, I will repay you whatever

(cont.)

more you spend.' Which of these three, do you think, was a neighbor to the man who fell into the hands of the robbers?" He said, "The one who showed him mercy." Jesus said to him, "Go and do likewise."

———

Who Is My Neighbor?

The diversity in the human family should be the cause of love and harmony, as it is in music where many different notes blend together in the making of a perfect chord. If you meet those of a different race or color from yourself, do not mistrust them and withdraw yourself into your shell of conventionality, but rather be glad and show them kindness. Think of them as different colored roses growing in the beautiful garden of humanity, and rejoice to be among them.

—Paris Talks of Abdu'l-Baha
  (Baha'i faith)

RELATED READING

Who Is My Neighbor? (for young children) by Virginia Mueller. The Standard Publishing Co., 1980.

—Ann Marie Witchger Hansen

Our "Other Neighbors"

It's usually easy to like those people who are nice to you or with whom you have a lot in common. As a family, talk about whether there are any people in your neighborhood whom you don't like? Why? Can you think of a way to offer them kindness or friendship? Who would be an outcast (like the Samaritan) in your community or in the world (perhaps a foreigner, a poor person, someone with different religious or political beliefs)? If you have trouble thinking of someone, find your home on a globe and locate the most distant country from you on the other side of the globe. Who lives there?

Draw a picture or make a collage showing your family living next door to people from this nation or region. We don't have to *like* everyone on this earth, but how can we *understand* this person or group better?

TREAT

Try two tasty but very different treats: fresh vegetables and dip with milk shakes.

WHO IS MY NEIGHBOR?—PART 2

 OPENING

Welcome your neighbors into your home and invite them to sit down. If the group enjoys singing, sing songs together such as "The More We Get Together" or "Make New Friends."

 PRESENTATION OF THEME

Neighbors are a special group of people we often take for granted. This is an attempt to become better acquainted with our neighbors and show our gratefulness for who they are and what they do.

Reading:

"A Tribute to Our Neighbors" (composed as a family at your last family night)

FAMILY RESPONSE

Play a mime game, drawing game, or quiz game as an ice breaker. If you have *The Book of Questions*, show it to your guests and then discuss a few of the questions. Try to learn more about each other's lives.

   If you think your guests would enjoy a "mini" talent show, invite them ahead of time to be prepared to share their talents with your family and vice versa.

   If your new neighbors are housebound, take tea, cookies or other homemade treats to them. If they welcome you in, take time to share stories about your lives and the neighborhood. Bring along a story, poem, song, or musical instrument to provide entertainment.

 TREAT

Treat your neighbors to your family's favorite snack, or create your own pizza with English muffins, sauce, and several simple toppings.

 YOU WILL NEED . . .

☐ games

☐ name tags

☐ food for the party

☐ instruments, art, music, stories, or poetry

 RELATED READING

The Book of Questions by Gregory Stock. Workman Publishing Company, 1987.

—Ann Marie Witchger Hansen

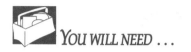

YOU WILL NEED ...

- [ ] items that remind each person of the past summer (i.e., bathing suit, baseball, vacation souvenir)

- [ ] new school supplies

- [ ] a bag, box, or basket to conceal the new supplies

READING

Luke 2:41-47

Now every year his parents went to Jerusalem for the festival of the Passover. And when he was twelve years old, they went up as usual for the festival. When the festival was ended and they started to return, the boy Jesus stayed behind in Jerusalem, but his parents did not know it. Assuming that he was in the group of travelers, they went a day's journey. Then they started to look for him among their relatives and friends. When they did not find him, they returned to Jerusalem

(cont.)

OPENING

We have gathered here to say goodbye to the summer and to welcome the new school year. Let us pray together: Dear God, you are the Lord of beginnings and endings. We ask you to bless us as we leave the summer behind and prepare for a new school year.

PRESENTATION OF THEME

Starting or returning to school usually brings a bag full of mixed feelings:

- ◆ Sorrow that carefree days of summer are over and work will begin

- ◆ Excitement about starting something new

- ◆ Fear about leaving home

- ◆ Parental anxiety about a first or youngest child leaving home for the first time, letting go

- ◆ Hope for new adventures

- ◆ Anticipation of reuniting with friends

The start of a new school year is a time of transition for everyone in the family, not only the students. When one or more members leaves for school, the daily routine of parents and younger children who are still at home is also affected. A family is a system and any change in the routine is a change in the family system.

There is more to education than just "going to school." What might the parents be learning new this year? What lessons (music, sports, cultural) might each of us be starting or resuming? Before we say hello to the new, however, we need to say goodbye to the past.

Reading:

Luke 2:41-47 (If you are having trouble letting go of a child, you may want to meditate on the verses that follow this passage—Luke 2:48-50.) *or*

Excerpt from *All I Ever Really Needed to Know I Learned in Kindergarten*

 **FAMILY RESPONSE**

Ask each person to share their symbol of a favorite summer activity or memory. When everyone is finished, the leader prays:

Dear God, We ask you to bless these symbols of our summer and to allow us to keep their memories alive in our hearts.

Then uncover the new school supplies and display them on the table. Ask each person to express his or her hopes and fears for the new school year. Have everyone extend their hands over the supplies as the leader prays:

Dear God, we thank you for our school and the teachers who will teach our children. We thank you for giving us the ability to learn new things. Please bless our children and the instruments of learning that we place before you. Help the children to use them to become more knowledgeable of the marvelous world you have created for us.

If the children are receptive, parents may want to share stories of what they remember about their first day of school.

 **TREAT**

Prepare and serve anything with apples: apple pie, apple dumplings, apple slices coated with peanut butter and raisins.

AGE ADAPTATION

If any of your children are preschoolers, focus on the new skills they will learn this year: potty training, getting dressed, learning to count. Find symbols for these activities. Also, don't forget to recognize parents who are returning to school or attending a seminar.

to search for him. After three days they found him in the temple, sitting among the teachers, listening to them and asking them questions. And all who heard him were amazed at his understanding and his answers.

———

Share everything.
Play fair.
Don't hit people.
Put things back where you found them.
Clean up your own mess.
Don't take things that aren't yours.
Say you're sorry when you hurt somebody.
Wash your hands before you eat.
Flush.
Warm cookies and cold milk are good for you.
Live a balanced life—learn some and think some and draw and paint and sing and dance and play and work every day some.
Take a nap every afternoon.
When you go out into the world, watch out for traffic, hold hands and stick together.
Be aware of wonder.

—Excerpted from *All I Ever Really Needed to Know I Learned In Kindergarten* by Robert Fulghum. Copyright © 1988 Random House.

—Peggy Haupt

A LABOR OF LOVE

Labor Day in the U.S.

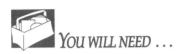 YOU WILL NEED . . .

☐ pictures of people at work in their community

☐ *The Man Who Made Fine Tops*, Marie Winn, Simon and Schuster, 1970, optional

 READING

Matthew 20:1-8

For the kingdom of heaven is like a landowner who went out early in the morning to hire laborers for his vineyard. After agreeing with the laborers for the usual daily wage, he sent them into his vineyard. When he went out about nine o'clock, he saw others standing idle in the marketplace; and he said to them, "You also go into the vineyard, and I will pay you whatever is right." So they went. When he went out again about noon and about three o'clock, he did the same. And about five o'clock he went out and found others standing around; and he said to them, "Why are you standing here idle all day?" They said to him, "Because no one has hired us." He said to them, "You also go

(cont.)

 OPENING

Light a candle and hold hands in silence for a few minutes. Then say the following prayer:

> Lord, we thank you for the gift of the summer and for all the fun and relaxation it has brought us. Help us face the new fall with energy and love so that we may be faithful stewards of your creation. Help us appreciate the opportunities we have to do good work, whether at school, in the community, or at home. Amen.

Sing "Our Life Is More Than Our Work" (Appendix A, Music) or a favorite family song, preferably one about work.

PRESENTATION OF THEME

For many, Labor Day is eclipsed by the beginning of the new school year, an important event. But we also celebrate the value of work on Labor Day. For many children, work is what one does to get money. Since they are not responsible for a livelihood, children usually pay little attention to the importance of work. During this evening we will reflect on the work each of us does and why it is important beyond its monetary value.

Ask the family about the work around your home that makes your lives better. They might suggest meal preparation, doing the yard work, washing clothes, making curtains and bedspreads, or painting rooms. Be sure, as these tasks are being named, that the work of even the smallest child is mentioned. Emphasize that each one is important to the operation of the family and should be acknowledged for it.

Going to school is also work for some of us. It is how we prepare to be contributing members of our community. Ask the children what they would like to be when they grow up. As each one tells of his or her dream, say a little about the value of that occupation to the community.

Reading:
Matthew 20:1-8 *or*
The Man Who Made Fine Tops

 **FAMILY RESPONSE**

Choose one or more of the following activities.

1. Community Workers

Look at the pictures of people at work in their community. Talk about workers in the community who are important to the well-being of the community, just as each family member is important to the well-being of the family (mail carriers, firefighters, teachers, people who repair our roads, and farmers). How can we express our gratitude for the work they do for each of us? Write a letter to someone who has been especially helpful, such as your auto mechanic or mail carrier, or write a letter to the local newspaper expressing gratitude for some of the people in these occupations. Mention specific people who have made your lives better.

2. Mystery Workers

Put each family member's name in a basket. Draw names (if anyone gets their own name, switch with someone else). One at a time each person pretends that he or she is doing the "work" of the person whose name they have drawn. The rest of the family tries to guess the "mystery worker." (Parents might be surprised at what their *important* work really looks like to a child.)

3. Family Jobs

Negotiate family jobs for the coming year. Talk about what needs to be done around the house and who should do it. Make specific decisions if at all possible, and agree to check back at the end of the month to see how things are working out.

 **TREAT**

In a spirit of "laboring," the whole family could make pizza and enjoy it together!

 **AGE ADAPTATION**

If you have teens who are working at paying jobs, talk a little about responsibility and good work habits. What loyalty do they owe to their employer? Do they have an obligation to be aware of unjust things that might happen in the workplace? This is an appropriate time to reflect on these obligations and the importance of the work they do.

into the vineyard." When evening came, the owner of the vineyard said to his manager, "Call the laborers and give them their pay, beginning with the last and then going to the first."

RELATED READING

How to Find Your Mission in Life by Richard N. Bolles. Ten Speed Press, 1991.

What Color Is Your Parachute? by Richard N. Bolles. Ten Speed Press, 1993.

Working by Studs Terkel. Ballantine Books, 1985.

—Wendy Bauers Northup

Change Me, Change the World

Rosh Hashanah is the beginning of the Jewish ritual year, though it is celebrated in the seventh month of the Hebrew calendar, which is our fall. Passover, which comes in our spring, is the beginning of the calendar year, demonstrating how central the theme of liberation is to Jewish identity. The first month is also calculated according to the agricultural new year when crops are planted and the growing season begins. Judaism has several "new years."

In addition to bringing in the new religious year, Rosh Hashanah opens Yom Kippur, a ten-day period of atonement for sins. Rosh Hashanah awakens the people to their sins and failings and prompts them to review their relationship with God.

The Shofar

The new year opens at the sound of the shofar, a ram's horn that is blown like a trumpet. When the people hear the shofar each year, they are awakened to the day of judgment. They are drawn back to God and to themselves, to the people they are called to be. The Hebrew Scriptures also mention that the shofar sounded as Israel went into battle and, more importantly, when God gave Moses the Torah on Mount Sinai.

The Book of Life

As the new year opens, God sits with the Book of Life and gazes into it. Through the ten days of Yom Kippur, the Book of Life is inscribed with God's judgment and sealed on the last day. Hoping that their atonement will restore them to God at Yom Kippur and that God will inscribe them a righteous judgment, Jews commonly wish each other "a good inscribing and a good sealing."

CHANGE ME, CHANGE THE WORLD

Rosh Hashanah—Fall

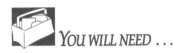 YOU WILL NEED . . .

- ☐ a shofar (ram's horn) or a trumpet or coronet (If not available, try a whistle, recorder, or paper towel core.)
- ☐ two candles
- ☐ a nice notebook

 READING

Leviticus 23:24-25

Speak to the people of Israel, saying: In the seventh month, on the first day of the month, you shall observe a day of complete rest, a holy convocation commemorated with trumpet blasts. You shall not work at your occupations; and you shall present the Lord's offering by fire.

Psalm 81:3-4

Blow the trumpet at the new moon, at the full moon, on our festal day. For it is a statute for Israel, an ordinance of the God of Jacob.

 OPENING

Light two candles and recite the following blessings:

> Blessed are You, Eternal God, Creator of the Universe, who has made us holy with commandments and has commanded us to light the lights of this celebration.

> Blessed are You, Eternal God, Creator of the Universe, who has made us holy with commandments and has commanded us to hear the sound of the shofar.

Sound the shofar (ram's horn) as long as one breath will last.

PRESENTATION OF THEME

The theme of the holidays that begin with Rosh Hashanah is *introspection* (an "inventory of the soul"). To atone and want to do better is a matter of changing our inner lives and the way we feel, then changing our outer lives or the way we behave. The *inner* work of transformation is reflected in the *outer* work of reconciliation and peacemaking. How do we change the world? We change it one person at a time, beginning with the individual.

Reading:
Leviticus 23:24-25 *and*
Psalm 81:3-4

Sound the shofar again. To *hear* the shofar is the central "mitzvah" (literally, commandment) of Rosh Hashanah. Then ask your family members what the sound reminds them of. At Rosh Hashanah, the horn is used to *awaken*. We are sometimes asleep to the hard work of inner change and the outer work of peacemaking. The blowing of the shofar wakes us up to do the work of becoming our best selves.

Illustrate this use of the shofar with the following story.

> What is the significance of the sound of the shofar? Once there was a king, who had an only son whom he loved more

than the world. The king reared the son in the castle, and there came a day when there was nothing more for the son to learn there. The king understood that and with a heavy heart sent his child off into the world. The son was eager to learn the wisdom that only other peoples could teach him, so he traveled outside of the kingdom. He learned the language of the next kingdom, spent time learning its wisdom, and then went on to the next kingdom. There he learned the language and wisdom and then went on to the next kingdom, and so on. One day he recognized that he was so far away from home that unless he turned back, he might never return. Do you know what it feels like to be that far away, so far away that you might never return unless you return immediately? That is what the son did. He traveled back home, from kingdom to kingdom, and finally he arrived at his own. He had been so far away and had learned so many languages that he had forgotten his own tongue. No one recognized him. He went into the courtyard of his castle and, looking up at the chambers of his beloved father, he began to cry out for him. He had forgotten the words, but his father heard the boy's sounds of longing for home and welcomed him home with tears of great joy.

—Adaptation of a traditional Jewish story

The sound of the child's voice is the sound of the shofar. And the return home is its purpose.

FAMILY RESPONSE

Jewish people believe that God keeps an accounting of their good and bad deeds, inscribing them in the Book of Life. Each year they look inward, hoping that God has taken note of their best selves. Refer the family to the special notebook that is to be used for this session. You may print "The Book of Life" on the cover if you like. Devote one page to each family member. Have each person pause and think of one talent that he or she has. Record this on his or her page.

Next ask each person to say something genuine and positive about the person to his or her right, such as "you are kind" or "you are a great athlete." Put these comments on each person's page. As compliments are given, receive them with a simple "thank you."

To connect the inner work of feelings and beliefs with the outer work of justice, ask each person to think of a way to use the talent or strength just named for the good of others. For example, if a sister says to her brother, "You are kind and caring to younger children," her brother might say, "Thanks. I am willing to use that talent this week to play games with our young neighbor who doesn't have many kids to play with."

Record the commitment on the person's page in your "Book of Life."

Close by wishing each other "a good inscribing."

TREAT

Apples, cut up and dipped in honey, are a traditional treat at Rosh Hashanah. So is a challah, egg bread often made with raisins and sweetened with honey. (See Appendix B, Recipes.) Another traditional exchange at Rosh Hashanah is "have a good and a sweet year."

—Jim Goodman

AN UNFINISHED REVOLUTION

NOTE ON LANGUAGE: The Spanish word for the original inhabitants of Mexico is *indígena*, although many Hispanics still use the term *Indian*. In this family night, we use the term *Indian* since it may be simpler for many children. These "Indians," however, are not to be confused with the "cowboys and indians" of the old west. (In Family Nights 45 and 54, the term "Native American" is preferred over "Indian" for the indigenous people of North America.)

On the night of September 15, 1810, Father Miguel Hidalgo let the cry for independence ring out, and the revolution against the Spanish Crown began the next day, September 16. Mexico had belonged to Spain since the conquest by Hernán Cortés in 1521.

In Mexico at that time, only Spaniards born in Spain, living in Mexico, could hold top government posts. Spaniards born in Mexico were relegated to less important positions. Those of mixed Indian and Spanish blood, called Mestizos, and those born to Indians were more repressed. Most of the land belonged to the Crown or to the Spanish and to the Church whose leaders were Spaniards and who supported the monarchy. As the number of Spaniards born in Mexico increased, they became discontented over the restrictions imposed on them by the Crown.

Add the unhappiness of the large Mestizo population to the unrest among the Spaniards and the suffering of the Indians who were treated no better than slaves. Thus, the church preached a suffering Christ to the Mestizo and Indian populations. Today many of these bruised and bloody Christs hanging from the cross can still be seen in the old churches.

The Mexican-born Spaniard wanted a less repressive government. And the Mestizos and Indians wanted land, better living conditions, and a better future for their children. The banner under which they fought was that of the image of Our Lady of Guadalupe, whom the Mestizo and Indian considered their own because of her skin color and because she called them sons and daughters and assured them that they were loved. (See Family Night 57.)

The initial struggle for independence failed, and its leaders' heads were hung on the four corners of the granary in the City of Guanajuato. The struggle continued, however, led by others until Mexico won its freedom from Spain. Sadly, its people had no experience in governing, and Mexico quickly found itself ruled by inept officials or outright dictators.

While Mexico struggled to build a new nation, it also had to face enemies from other countries. In 1864, France put Maximillian on the throne in Mexico, and in 1848, the United States took what is now the southwestern United States from a weak and corrupt Mexican government. Mexicans have also had to struggle and fight against the church, whose hierarchy was rooted in the colonial period and was more interested in preserving its power than in liberating its people.

43

The revolutionary struggle is still widening to embrace not only independence, democracy, and justice, but also equality for women in government, church, and society. The struggle for better working conditions and more educational opportunities continues along with concerns for the environment.

The Mexicans are still working after five hundred years to become a people. It has not been easy. Learning to respect one another and to work together is never easy. The one rallying symbol for the Mexicans still continues to be the image of Our Lady of Guadalupe—"La Morenita"— who calls everyone sons *and daughters*.

Viva Mexico!

Mexican Independence Day—September 15-16

NOTE: If you have Mexican friends, perhaps you would like to invite them to join you.

Opening

The leader puts on the bandanna and collar to become Padre Miguel Hidalgo. He or she rings the bell and loudly calls to all in the family: "Hear ye! Hear ye! You are all invited to a Revolution Party." When the family is gathered, Padre asks for help in getting the treats ready for the party.

Joint preparation of the party food:
   The piñata could already be prepared or the family could assemble it together and hang it from a tree or the ceiling. Also, make the chocolate drink.

Presentation of Theme

The leader briefly summarizes the struggle the Mexicans had for independence, justice, and equality, adapting the background material for young children. Tonight, we are going to use the treats we prepare to celebrate the day Mexicans began to fight for their freedom from Spain. Mexican parties usually involve special food and games, so we will begin with a traditional Mexican game—the breaking of the piñata. There is one big difference, however, from other parties. Once we break the piñata, *no one is to keep or eat any of the treats right away*! We will gather them into a basket for use later tonight.

Family Response

Starting with the youngest, have family members take turns swinging at the piñata.

   NOTE: Children sometimes get overly rambunctious swinging at a piñata. Talk about common-sense safety guidelines before they begin. After the piñata is broken, gather the treats as promised.

 *You Will Need ...*

- a bell
- a bandanna and white collar
- a Mexican hat
- a tilma (simple poncho) for the Indian (or white pants or shirt)
- sandals for the Mestizo
- a piñata suspended from a ceiling light, tree branch, or rafter (If making or buying a piñata is not practical, a basket or paper bag filled with treats could be substituted.)
- a stick or broom handle
- food: whipped chocolate drink (see directions under treat), juice, bread, beans (or other simple protein), water
- a map or flag of Mexico, optional

The leader, Padre Miguel Hidalgo, explains that before we continue our party, we're going to do a little play to help us understand what life was like for the people who lived in Mexico *before* the Revolution in 1810.

Pick one or more family members to play the following roles.

> **NOTE:** Picking roles randomly from a hat might prevent competition over the more desirable roles. Make sure everyone agrees to accept his or her role without complaining.

Indian(s)—wears a tilma or substitute garment

Mestizo(s)—wears a Mexican hat and sandals

Spaniard(s) born in Mexico— wears a Mexican hat and nice clothing

Spaniard(s) born in Spain—wears nicer clothing

> **NOTE:** The roles of the two Spaniards could be combined if necessary.

The Scene: *A dining room table or wherever the family normally eats. Display all the food on a counter or another table (piñata treats, chocolate drink, bread, beans, juice, water). The Spaniards sit comfortably at the family table. The Mestizo and Indian stand waiting at the side. Padre Hidalgo guides the action along as needed. Introduce the play by saying: "Our play is about how these several characters lived together about two hundred years ago."*

ACT I: The Spaniard born in Mexico leaves his or her place to serve the Spaniard born in Spain a generous serving of piñata treats and chocolate drink. The server then returns to his or her place at the table.

ACT II: The Mestizo and Indian together serve similar foods to the Spaniard born in Mexico. They can "ham it up" by exaggerating their servant role if they like. The Spaniards may begin eating.

ACT III: The Mestizo sits at a lowlier place, perhaps at a small separate table. The Indian now serves bread, beans, and juice to the Mestizo. The Mestizo may begin eating.

ACT IV: Finally, the Indian gets his or her food (just bread and water) and sits on the floor to eat it.

Discussion:

As soon as the Indian is ready to eat, stop the play and the eating. Ask: How would each of us feel if our lives were really like this? Did the Spaniard born in Spain do anything to deserve the best food? the Spaniard born in Mexico? the Mestizo? the Indian? What did they do to deserve their positions?

Padre Hidalgo explains that in an ideal world people would voluntarily share their food and all people would have access to similar privileges. There would be no need to revolt against the government. But in the world as it is, people who are treated like slaves and see no chance to improve their situation get so angry that they see no choice but to revolt.

Since fighting, even to combat terrible injustice, hurts many people, brainstorm as many alternative solutions as possible to use if a situation like this occurred today (involving the United Nations, nonviolent resistance, Gandhi-like actions …). What solution would our family try?

When the discussion has run its course, ask everyone to put their food in the center of the table and join the Spaniards at the main table. Then distribute the food fairly. The party continues.

 ## TREAT

For a special conclusion, distribute the piñata treats and serve the chocolate drink made the Mexican way: whip baking chocolate into hot milk until frothy.

AGE ADAPTATION

Very young children may be upset by not getting the role they want or not getting treats initially. If parent(s) anticipate this, give more difficult roles to the adults.

Let teenagers discuss the pros and cons of using violence to right a wrong. At what point does oppression warrant armed revolt? How do you feel about conscientious objection to war? Is it possible to object to some wars but be willing to fight in what is perceived as a "just war" or a defensive war? Do you approve of taking life in other situations, such as euthanasia or capital punishment? Why? *The Mission* would be a good video to rent to promote discussion on this topic.

—Joe Ceja

LEARNING ABOUT PEOPLE
WHO ARE GAY OR LESBIAN

Homosexuality is a sensitive and sometimes controversial theme. Currently there is no consensus in our society or among religious groups about how to talk about and deal with the differences of sexual orientation that exist among us. Regardless of how we might feel about the morality of this issue, we need to respect the human and civil rights of all people. This is the underlying premise of this session.

Sexuality is a very appropriate theme to deal with in a family setting. Since families vary in the ages of the children, beliefs, and comfort level when addressing sexuality directly, we have designed the core of this family night broadly enough that it can be used with very young children. If parents desire, there need not be any direct reference to homosexuality, since respect for people who are different from oneself will, in itself, be a foundation for respecting gays and lesbians.

Adaptations for teens, however, do address homosexuality directly, and it is up to the parents' discretion to decide how much of this material they wish to use with younger children.

Whether we are aware of it or not, gay and lesbian people may be found among members of our family, our friends, schoolmates, and co-workers. What do we know about them? Myths or facts? Is our treatment of them fair or unfair? How fairly or unfairly are they treated by their friends and relatives? by institutions such as schools? by society?

General Facts (to be used as parents find them useful)

1. A heterosexual is a person whose affection and sexual attraction are toward someone of the opposite sex. A homosexual is a person whose affection and sexual attraction are toward someone of the same sex.

2. Homosexuality has been found in almost every culture throughout history.

3. Homophobia is the irrational hatred or fear of homosexuals (referred to as gays, if they are men, or lesbians, if they are women).

4. The Kinsey Institute of Sexual Studies estimates that from five to ten percent of the population is homosexual. Current research indicates that homosexuality is a biological condition, such as left-handedness or allergies, that parents cannot control.

5. Not all homosexuals are the same. Although there is growing evidence that homosexuality is a biological condition, there appears to be a range of intensity, just as there is a range of sexual drive among heterosexuals. Some people are strictly homosexual from birth. Others' sexual orientation may be influenced by their environment or other circumstances. Some people may have a combination of homosexual and heterosexual orientations.

6. A faggot is a piece of kindling used to start fires. Gay people were sometimes burned at the stake in the Middle Ages. Therefore, they came to be called "faggots" or "fags." Derogatory words like these demean the speakers as well as the subject and should not be used.

7. If we assume that five to ten percent of the population is homosexual, one to three students in a class of thirty may eventually discover they are gay. Another two to five people may have gay people in their extended families. When we call someone "fag" or "queer," there is a good chance we may be hurting someone we know and care about.

8. According to research, the percentage of gays and lesbians who molest children is not any higher than the percentage of heterosexual people who molest children.

OPENING

Display the wrapped boxes prominently in the middle of the table. Light a candle and during a minute of silence ask each person to study the boxes and imagine what might be in each of them. If you have the music, play "It's Not Easy Being Green" in the background.

PRESENTATION OF THEME

Some of these boxes are different on the outside and some are the same. (Let the family unwrap the boxes and look at what's inside.) Likewise, on the inside some are different and some are the same.

   People are like this too. People are different colors on the outside (different races) but all have hearts, brains, blood on the inside. Likewise, some people may look a lot alike on the outside, but have different hobbies, talents, and tastes. Tonight we're going to look at how we feel when we are different from others around us and how we feel when someone else is different from us.

FAMILY RESPONSE

Reading:
Galatians 3:26-29
After reading the scripture, read the following:

Southpaw: A Fable
There's something important about me I want to share with you today. You don't know this about me, not because I've lied about it, or even actively hidden it; I just don't talk about it much because it's kind of scary: I'm left-handed.

   I don't talk about it much, or use my hands much, around right-handed people. It's nobody's business. It's private and why do you have to show it? But then I realize right-handed people show their handedness openly all the time. They write in public. They raise their hands in class. They'll walk into a room of strangers and boldly stick out their right hands to shake.

   Why don't I just offer my left hand as glibly? Well, I've seen lefties get "looks" all my life. Once when a friend of my parents offered his left hand to shake, my parents went on and on after he left about why he made such a point of making them

YOU WILL NEED . . .

☐ 4 or 5 small boxes that are of similar size and shape

☐ (Wrap all but two boxes in different colored wrapping paper but enclose a common element, perhaps some wadded up newspaper or fabric. The final two boxes should be wrapped identically on the outside, but have different contents. It doesn't matter what is in these final two boxes as long as they are different from each other.)

☐ "It's Not Easy Being Green" (Kermit the Frog's song from Sesame Street), optional

☐ paper and pencils

44

FAMILY NIGHT

Reading

Galatians 3:26-29

[F]or in Christ Jesus you are all children of God through faith. As many of you as were baptized into Christ have clothed yourselves with Christ. There is no longer Jew or Greek, there is no longer slave or free, there is no longer male and female; for all of you are one in Christ Jesus. And if you belong to Christ, then you are Abraham's offspring, heirs according to the promise.

uncomfortable, of "flaunting his preference." Plus, it's no fun to be different. I noticed very young that all the tools seemed to be made for righties, all the scissors, all the desks. I saw that all the people on TV, in magazine ads, even in my family, used their right hands....except a few who were the butt of jokes. You've all heard those jokes and putdowns about "southpaws." You don't want to be weird like the people they laugh about.

Not My Choice

You know, I didn't choose to be different. It just feels more natural using my left hand. It always has, as far back as I can remember. I tried to change, when I began to realize I was different; I really did. For a while, I did use my right hand the most, but it never felt right. It never felt normal. It felt dishonest.

Even now, I sometimes offer my right hand when people want to shake, just because it's easier, but it feels like a lie. I feel sort of crummy about myself when I do. More often, I pretend not to notice when people offer to shake hands. And in class, I mostly listen and try to remember the important points, rather than take notes publicly with my left hand. In the cafeteria, I get milkshakes with a straw, so I can set them on the table and not use either hand.

For a long time I felt very alone. I didn't think I knew another lefty in the whole world...until I realized the others were just avoiding using their hands in public...the same as I was! When I finally got to talk with other lefties, I found they'd been there all along: ten percent of my family, my friends, my neighbors. It was so exciting to discover they'd felt the same hurts and met the same challenges as I had! And many felt truly at peace with their handedness. Some were living full, happy, productive lives as lefties.

Reasons for Openness

You probably wonder why I'm sharing all this today. I guess there are a number of reasons.

First, I know that some of you thought you'd never met a lefty before today. You have, of course, but you didn't know it at the time. I want you to have a chance to get to know me a little as a person; being left-handed is an important part of me, but it is only a part.

Second, some of you who are right-handed suffer because of hand-prejudice, too. You may be careful not to ever use your left hands in public, even when your right hands are busy, for fear people will think you're really a lefty. You may feel bad when you overhear put-downs and don't know what to say. You end up feeling ashamed for not sticking up for what you believe, and I want to help you learn how to act as proud allies instead.

Third, I feel an obligation to make sure that young left-handed people know there are happy successful lefties out here.

And, most important, I want to protect those young people from the harassment and isolation I grew up with.

But that doesn't mean I would ever try to "convert" or "recruit" a right-handed young person into a lefty. It probably wouldn't work if I did try. And it would hurt. Teachers used to try the opposite: to make left-handed kids learn to write with their right hands…until it was found that this pressure caused some severe reading and learning problems. So it would be wrong to try to change another person. Besides, it's just a myth that left-handed people are into recruiting right-handed people.

Common Myths

There have been a lot of myths and stereotypes about us throughout history. One myth is that everyone *is* either left-handed or right-handed! I have one friend who is ambidextrous: equally at ease using either hand. I have another friend who is mostly a righty, but who bats and catches left-handed. Not everybody is completely one or the other; people are more complex than that. What are some other myths? Some religions used to teach that lefties were possessed by the devil. Now, most religious groups would say that's ridiculous. Psychiatrists once thought that all lefties were mentally ill. Today many would say that's just silly. People used to think all left-handed folks had to dress and act certain ways. Now we know

that's not true. Yes, some lefties act "different," but many live lives very much like righties' lives…so much so that you don't notice us. Many of us, in other words, are invisible. That's not to disparage those who *do* act or dress "different"; they are my

brothers and sisters, too. But you need to understand that only a few of us fit the stereotypes.

No More Prejudice

We can end prejudice against left-handed folks. We can learn to love and respect our brothers and sisters of both handednesses. We can teach our children that hate hurts us all: the haters and the hated. And that there is nothing to fear. Left-handed people don't want to make you into lefties. We won't take over the world.

It just feels more natural to us when we use our left hands. That's all.

—Author unknown

After the reading, invite reactions from the family. Is anyone in the family left-handed? Do we know friends or relatives who are? Since "lefties" generally no longer experience discrimination, is this a silly story? Can we imagine a time when prejudices against other minorities will sound silly?

♦ Each person think of someone you know who is very different from yourself. Write the person's name or draw a picture of the person on a piece of paper. Share how this person is different from you and how you *feel* about this person.

♦ Next, think of a time when you felt like an outsider because you were different. Perhaps you were at a party and everyone else was dressed up but you weren't (or vice versa). Or everyone else knew how to whistle or swim or tie his or her shoes and you didn't. Or you had a cast or bandage or an injury that made you look different from your friends. Share your experience with your family. Did you feel hurt by anyone's words or looks or actions? All of us have had painful experiences when we were ignored or publicly rejected for unfair reasons. Talk about your feelings in this situation.

♦ Finally, think again about the person you chose who is very different from you. For five minutes (use a timer), pretend you are that person. Talk, walk, and dress as you would imagine that person would. The only limitation is that you cannot do anything that would seriously offend another person in your family. As each family member pretends, there may be a lot of silliness, but that's okay and part of the fun.

♦ Discuss how you feel about the other person now. Have you gained any insights? What does it mean to respect a

RELATED READING

For young readers or teens:

How Would You Feel If Your Dad Was Gay? by Ann Heron and Meredith Maran. Alyson Publications, 1991.

Jack by A. M. Homes. Macmillan Children's Book Group, 1990. A story about a 15-year-old boy who discovers that his father is gay.

Two Weeks with the Queen by Morris Gleitzman. Harper-Collins Children's Books, 1993. While visiting London, a 12-year-old learns about Ted who is gay and whose partner is dying of AIDS.

person? How do we act toward people we respect? Can we respect people even though they may be different from us or we may disagree with them? If not, why not?

 ## Treat

If possible pick a treat that no one in the family has ever eaten before—*something different*! If you can't think of something, select a food from another culture.

 ## Age Adaptation

For teens:

1. On a large sheet of newsprint, list in one column all of the negative terms that are used about gay or lesbian people. For example, homosexuals are called fairies, queer, immoral, mentally ill, and sinful. Then list the talents and virtues that are commonly associated with gays or lesbians such as artistic, creative, very kind, loving. Is one list easier to generate than the other? Why? Both of these lists are stereotypes. How do we know the truth about a person?

Do we know anyone who is gay and can be described by either list? If we don't know any homosexuals, despite the fact that five to ten percent of the population is gay, is it likely that someone we know is gay but has not revealed this to us?

If the words on your list are used to describe lesbians or gays, how would their parents feel if they discovered they had a gay or lesbian child? How would *your* family respond? Would a child in your family be able to talk to family members if he or she was gay? What would you do?

2. With role playing, act out what you would do if a good friend told you she or he was gay (or thought he or she might be gay).

3. What specific things can you do or say when you hear slurs or jokes against homosexuals? As an example, you might say, "I know you don't mean any harm, but I have a gay friend who I care a lot about and it hurts me to hear gay jokes." "Bet you don't realize those jokes can hurt people." "I'm not too crazy about gay jokes, or ethnic jokes either."

Why Am I Different? by Norma Simon. Albert Whitman Co., 1976. Differences in physical makeup, personalities, and culture are presented to give children an understanding of others (for ages 4-8).

For adults:

Beyond Acceptance: Parents of Lesbians and Gays Talk About Their Experience by Carolyn Griffin, Arthur G. Wirth, Marian J. Wirth. St. Martin Press, 1990.

Can Homophobia Be Cured? by Bruce Hilton. Abingdon Press, 1992.

The Final Closet by Rip Corley. Editech Press, 1990.

Is the Homosexual My Neighbor? by Letha Scanzoni and Virginia Ramey Mollenkott. Harper San Francisco, 1980.

The Long Road to Love by Darlene Bogle. Revell Co., 1985.

Of Sacred Worth by Paul A. Mickey. Abingdon Press, 1991.

When Someone You Know Is Gay by Susan Cohen and Daniel Cohen. Dell, 1992.

—Arthur and Marian Wirth

Although Native Americans and Native Canadians are often thought of as one group, it is important to remember that we are actually talking about more than 250 different nations (or tribes) that inhabited North America for centuries before the Europeans arrived. Each nation has a distinctive culture, language, and rituals. For the purpose of this family night, however, we will talk about eight groups of nations distinguished by common cultural characteristics. In addition to customs, each of these groups shared geographic location, which affected the type of work they did, their housing, clothing, and food.

> **NOTE:** The term "Native American" is used in this family night in its most popular sense, generally referring to the original people inhabiting southern Canada and the lower forty-eight states. Technically, however, "Native American" could include the Eskimos along with the native people of Alaska, Canada, Central and South America.

1. **Northeast Woodland Cultural Area**—hunters, fishers, some farmers
   Representative nations: Delaware, Iroquois, Huron, Algonquin, Winnebago, Ojibwa (Chippewa)

2. **Southeast Cultural Area**—hunters, fishers, some farmers
   Representative nations: Natchez, Choctaw, Chickasaw, Creek, Cherokee, Seminole, Catawba

3. **Plains and Plateau Cultural Area**—horsemen, buffalo hunters
   Representative nations: Crow, Arapaho, Cheyenne, Comanche, Dakota [Sioux], Pawnee, Shoshoni, Nez Perce, Flathead, Blackfoot, Chinook

4. **Southwest Cultural Area**— "cliff dwellers" (many of these tribes lived in pueblos), farmers, potters, basket weavers
   Representative nations: Taos, Zuni, Hopi, Navajo, Apache, Papago

5. **Northwest Coast Cultural Area**—fishers, woodcarvers, weavers
   Representative nations: Tlingit, Kwakiutl, Nootka

6. **California Cultural Area**—fishers, hunters, gatherers
   Representative nation: Pomo

7. **Basin Cultural Area**—(primarily desert areas) foragers, wanderers, basket weavers
   Representative nations: Ute, Paiute

8. **Subarctic Cultural Area**—fishers, nomadic hunters, fur traders
   Representative nations: Cree, Montagnais-Naskapi, Beaver

Despite the uniqueness of each nation, most Native Americans share some common values, qualities, and characteristics:

- Because they all depended on nature for life, they shared a profound knowledge of and respect for the earth.

- Native Americans commonly emphasize the *extended family* (or clan) and interdependent community.

- Native Americans did not see land as a commodity that could be owned by an individual. Land was seen as communal trust, and in the case of migrating nations, the idea of "owning" land was even more bizarre.

45

FAMILY NIGHT

NATIONS WITHIN A NATION

Native American Day—4th Friday in September

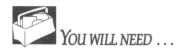

YOU WILL NEED . . .

- ☐ a simple drum (a round oatmeal cylinder would do fine)

- ☐ a mallet (a spoon with a cloth wrapped around it will give a dull, muffled sound)

- ☐ a map of North America

- ☐ paper, crayons or markers

- ☐ modeling clay

NOTE: Although this theme could be used with any age, it is particularly geared for ages eight to thirteen.

OPENING

Have one person in the family start a simple, slow drum beat (a child would probably love to do this). Accent (^) the first of each four beats. The leader begins the chant:

^"My heart speaks to ^your heart [plus two beats]. ^May we listen ^to each other."

Then, one by one (clockwise), each family member joins the chant until the whole family has said it together three times.

PRESENTATION OF THEME

As most of us now realize, Columbus did not actually "discover" America, for many people already lived in the Americas. Columbus, rather, was the first European known to *set foot* in America. Likewise, the people Columbus met were not actually "Indians," which is the name for people from India. To distinguish the two cultures, we now make the effort to use the term Native American when referring to the indigenous people of North America.

For years many of us have held other misconceptions about Native Americans, which have become part of our folklore.

FAMILY RESPONSE

What do you think of the following statements?

1. Native Americans add "um" to the end of many words. ("I lookum for a place to restum.")

2. Native Americans are alcoholics.

3. Native Americans are warlike and savage.

4. Native Americans wear feathers and leather.

5. Native Americans have red skin.

6. Native Americans believe in many gods.

7. Native Americans know more about nature than "white people do."

Except for the first statement, which is completely untrue, there is probably a kernel of truth in each of the above statements. Unfortunately, however, they are also generalizations, exaggerations, and distortions that are unfair and inaccurate.

Responses to the above statements:

1. Untrue

2. Of course some Native Americans are alcoholics just as some people of any group are alcoholics. It is an insult, however, to portray this as a usual trait.

3. Native Americans are no more warlike and savage than European Americans. The warring image is a carryover from the confrontations between European Americans and Native Americans on the western plains. Since the Native Americans of the plains rode horses and hunted bison, they were the nations most able to resist the encroaching Europeans. Thus, they have been portrayed as warlike and savage, an image that is then generalized to include all Native Americans.

4. Some Native Americans wore feathers or leather, but others wore cloth, fur, or other fibers that were available in the region in which they lived.

5. The color tone of a Native American's skin is no more red than a Caucasian's skin is actually white or an African-American's is black. There are many different shades of skin color depending upon the region in which the tribe lives. Variations of a ruddy complexion, however, would be close to many of the commonly known nations. This is how the term *redskin* probably developed.

6. "The Great Spirit" is the term Native Americans use for God, who is considered the Creator.

7. Even this positive notion is not completely true. The Native American's knowledge of nature is not academic. Rather, they have had a very practical understanding of the natural environment and hold a great love and respect for the earth. When Chief Seattle relinquished lands to the U.S. government, he was reported to have talked about the Native American's attitude toward nature. His speech no longer remains, but the reading is one writer's rendition of what Chief Seattle might have said.

Reading:

Speech attributed to Chief Seattle (take turns reading poetically)

READING

We are a part of the earth and it is a part of us. The perfumed flowers are our sisters; the deer, the horse, the great eagle, these are our brothers. The rocky crests, the juices in the meadows, the body heat of the pony, and people—all belong to the same family.

So teach your children what we have taught our children. Whatever happens to the earth happens to the children of the earth. If you spit on the land, you spit on yourselves.

The earth does not belong to us; we belong to the earth. All things are connected, like the blood which unites one family. Mankind did not weave the web of life. We are but one strand within it. Whatever we do to the web, we do to ourselves. All things are bound together.

One thing we know, which the white man may one day discover: our God is the same God and this earth is precious to Him. To harm the earth is to heap contempt on its Creator. Continue to soil your bed, and you will one night suffocate in your own waste.

When the last red man has vanished from this earth, and his memory is only a shadow of a cloud moving across the

(cont.)

prairie, these shores and forests will still hold the spirits of my people, for they love this earth as the newborn loves its mother's heartbeat. So if we sell you our land, love it as we have loved it. Care for it as we have cared for it. And with all your strength, with all your mind, with all your heart, preserve it for your children.

—Attributed to Chief Seattle

RELATED READING

The Girl Who Loved Wild Horses by Paul Goble. Macmillan Children's Books Group, 1993.

One Small Blue Bead, 2nd Ed., by Byrd Baylor. Macmillan Children's Books Group, 1992.

—Susan Vogt
Consultants: Lita Sharone (Blackfoot ancestry) and Golden Eagle (Hopi ancestry)

Tribal awareness:

Using information from the background for this family night, have each family member pick a different cultural area and depict that setting. Depending on the ages and abilities of the family members, they can draw a picture of something as simple as a single tool or product of that culture to something as complex as a picture featuring a Native American performing typical work in his or her geographical environment. You may choose to use modeling clay to form representations of the culture, such as a tent, arrowhead, or pot.

Take turns talking about the artwork and finding the appropriate locations on your map of North America. Display your art for a time in the kitchen or family room.

Be aware that Native Americans today do not live in primitive housing like tepees or wigwams that we have pictured here any more than most "white people" live in log cabins. Their present-day clothes are also "typical modern American." The main differences one *might* notice are physical ones of black hair, a darker complexion, and minor facial differences from the European look.

Closing prayer:

Leader: May the Great Spirit watch over you as long as the grass grows and the waters flow.

All: O Great Spirit, I praise you for Life. I serve you with living.

—Maryknoll Cloister

TREAT

Serve cornbread with honey or jam while you watch an old western movie and critique the portrayal of Native Americans.

THE FRAGILITY OF LIFE

Universal Children's Day—October 1

 **FAMILY NIGHT** 46

 ## OPENING

Cut a bloom from a flowering plant and give one to each person. Ask each person to take a quiet moment to study his or her bloom and become very familiar with its uniqueness.

 ## PRESENTATION OF THEME

Every person is created as a unique child of God. Every person should be nurtured and given the opportunity to grow and mature to his or her fullest potential.

Reading:

Matthew 19:13-14 *or*
Psalm 128 *or*
"On Children" from *The Prophet*

 ## FAMILY RESPONSE

As family members hold their cut flowers, ask them to think and talk about what it means to be severed from the branches and roots that are the source of nourishment and life. While the flower brings pleasure for a brief time, once cut, it is unable to continue to grow and mature, and it will die.

Transplant the house plants into the new pots or move yard plants to small pots.

 ## YOU WILL NEED . . .

☐ a flowering plant

☐ a variety of small house plants that need transplanting or greenery from your yard

☐ empty pots and potting soil

☐ water

☐ *The Prophet*, Kahlil Gibran, Knopf, 1970 or Random House, 1985, optional

 ## READING

Matthew 19:13-14

Then little children were being brought to him in order that he might lay his hands on them and pray. The disciples spoke sternly to those who brought them; but Jesus said, "Let the little children come to me, and do not stop them; for it is to such as these that the kingdom of heaven belongs."

Psalm 128

Happy is everyone who fears the Lord, who walks in his ways.

You shall eat the fruit of the labor of your hands; you shall be happy, and it shall go well with you.

Your wife will be like a fruitful vine within your house; your children will be like olive shoots around your table.

Thus shall the man be blessed who fears the LORD.

The LORD bless you from Zion. May you see the prosperity of Jerusalem all the days of your life.

May you see your children's children. Peace be upon Israel!

RELATED READING

Live and Let Live by P. K. Hallinan. Hazelden, 1990.

◆ Examine and talk about the unique features of each type of plant.

◆ Describe the root system and how the plant is nourished.

◆ List ways the plant must be treated in order to grow and be its best. For example, plants need regular watering, sunshine, an undisturbed place, fertilizer, and pruning.

◆ Ask how people are like plants. For example, suggest that people need food and water, we start life from our parents' seed, our new life is very fragile and needs to be protected and cared for gently and responsibly.

TREAT

Make "dirt" pudding. Line a clean flower pot with clear plastic wrap. Prepare chocolate pudding and pour into pot. Layer crushed chocolate sandwich cookies on the top. Insert Gummi worms if you really want to be authentic.

AGE ADAPTATION

For younger children, read a picture book stressing the uniqueness and value of every child, such as *We Are All Alike, We Are All Different*, by the Cheltenham Elementary School kindergartners, Scholastic Inc., 1991.

With older children, discuss what respect for life means in our society where there is abortion, hunger, lack of education, lack of health care, child abuse, and war.

—Karen Zerhusen

TRUTH FORCE (SATYAGRAHA)

Gandhi's Birthdate—October 2

 **OPENING**

In the middle of the table, display a toy gun (or a picture if you don't have this kind of toy in the house) and a flower. Light a candle, hold hands quietly for a moment, and ponder the gun and flower on the table.

 **PRESENTATION OF THEME**

Guns seem very powerful and people are usually frightened by a gun. Flowers seem very fragile. Some years ago, young people working for peace stuck flowers in the barrels of guns to show the power of love.

Gandhi was a Hindu, a man from India who gave his whole life to teaching nonviolence and living it in his life. He said, "In nonviolence people have a weapon which enables a child, a woman, or even a decrepit old man to resist the mightiest government successfully." He truly believed this and used methods of nonviolence to lead millions of Indian people to bring about a change in their government—using no violence. He also said that "nonviolence is not a garment to be put on and off ...it's seat is in the heart, and it must be an inseparable part of our very being."

A lot of people talk a lot about nonviolence, but most people don't seem to believe it can really happen or can really work. Our goal this evening is to think about the simple power of love and nonviolence—to try to present dramatically the power (and sometimes the surprise or shock effect) of meeting violence with nonviolence. We are going to try to think in a new way!

 **FAMILY RESPONSE**

Pick up the gun and the flower and ask which is stronger, more powerful. Why? Feel them. (Adults can help by talking about seeds, roots, some flowers coming back year after year, after winter, whereas guns rust and break and have no life to come back.) Sometimes something that looks weak may be strong.

Ask family members to think of times when they used (or wanted to use) violence or force. Some examples might be: a playmate is using a toy I want so I pull it away; someone takes a toy I'm playing with away from me, so I hit or kick him or her; a

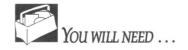 **YOU WILL NEED ...**

☐ a picture of Gandhi, optional

☐ a toy gun (or picture)

☐ a flower

☐ at least two puppets

kid teases me at school (pulls my hair), so I do the same; a bully is bothering my younger brother, so I punch him; a stranger cuts me off in traffic, so I scream at the driver; my daughter ate some candy before dinner when I told her not to, so I spanked her.

In turn, each person takes two puppets (one to represent him or herself and one to represent the "enemy") and acts out the violent or forceful response to the situation he or she recalls.

> **NOTE:** It's okay if the puppets get into tussles since that's part of the fun of using puppets. Parents might comment, however, that in real life this would really hurt. There might be blood and broken bones.

Then ask, "What would you do if a runaway armed prisoner came to your door?" After some back and forth discussion, relate what one woman really did—she acted like Gandhi.

Bless You, Mrs. Degrafinreid

It all started early Tuesday morning, February 21, when Louise Degrafinried's husband, Nathan, got up from bed in Mason, Tennessee, to let out the cat. "Cat" as they call him, stood at the edge of the porch, his hair bristled up on his arched back, and he hissed.

"What do you see out there, Cat?" Nathan asked.

A big man stepped from around the corner of the house and pointed a shotgun at Nathan.

"Lord, Honey," Louise heard her husband shout. "Open the door, he's got a gun."

Before she could open the door, the man with the gun had shoved Nathan inside, pushing him and Louise against the wall.

"Don't make me kill you!" he shouted, thrusting the gun in their faces. The couple knew immediately that the intruder was one of the escaped inmates whom they had heard about on the radio.

Louise Degrafinried, a 73-year-old grandmother, stood her ground. "Young man, I am a Christian lady. I don't believe in no violence. Put that gun down and you sit down. I don't allow no violence here."

The man relaxed his grip on the shotgun. He looked at her for a moment. Then he laid his gun on the couch.

"Lady," he said quietly, "I'm so hungry. I haven't had nothing to eat for three days."

"Young man, you just sit down there and I'll fix you breakfast. Nathan, go get this young man some dry socks."

With that, Louise went to work. She fixed him bacon, eggs, white bread toast, milk and coffee. Then she got out her best napkins and set her kitchen table.

[Louise explained what happened next.]

> When we sat down, I took that young man by the hand and said, "Young man, let's give thanks that you came here and that you are safe." I said a prayer and then asked him if he would like to say something to the Lord. He didn't say anything, so I said, "Just say, 'Jesus wept.'" Then we all ate breakfast.

Why did you tell him to say "Jesus wept"? I asked her later.

"Because," she said, "I figured that he didn't have no church background, so I wanted to start him off simple; something short, you know."

[Then she told me how she prevailed on him.]

> After breakfast, we sat there and I began to pray. I held his hand and kept patting him on the leg. He trembled all over. I said, "Young man, I love you and God loves you. God loves us all, every one of us, especially you. Jesus died for you because he loves you so much."
>
> "You sound just like my grandmother," he said, "She's dead."
>
> Nathan said that he saw one tear fall down the boy's cheek. About that time we heard police cars coming down the road. "They gonna kill me when they get here," he said.
>
> "No, young man, they aren't going to hurt you. You done wrong, but God loves you." Then me and Nathan took him by the arms, helped him up, and took him out of the kitchen toward the door. "You let me do all the talking," I told him. The police got out of their cars. They had their guns out. I shouted to them, "Y'all put those guns away. I don't allow no violence here. Put them

OPTIONAL READING:

Matthew 5:43-48

You have heard that it was said, "You shall love your neighbor and hate your enemy." But I say to you, Love your enemies and pray for those who persecute you, so that you may be children of your Father in heaven; for he makes his sun rise on the evil and on the good, and sends rain on the righteous and on the unrighteous. For if you love those who love you, what reward do you have? Do not even the tax collectors do the same? And if you greet only your brothers and sisters, what more are you doing than others? Do not even the Gentiles do the same? Be perfect, therefore, as your heavenly Father is perfect.

away. This young man wants to go back. Nathan, you bring the young man on out to the car." Then they put the handcuffs on him and took him back to the prison.

That afternoon, two other prisoners who had been separated from [this intruder] earlier entered a suburban backyard where a couple was barbecuing. The husband went into his house and came out with a gun. The escapees shot and killed him and took his wife hostage. They released her the next day.

Was Mrs. Degrafinried frightened? "No, Nathan said he was scared, but not me. I knew God was with me, that God had sent that young man to me for a reason. I knew God would lead me in the right direction."

From the March 14, 1984, issue of
The Christian Century. Copyright © 1984
Christian Century Foundation.
Reprinted by permission.

RELATED READING

Dana Doesn't Like Guns Anymore by Carole Moore-Slater. Friendship Press, 1991.

Gandhi: His Life and Message for the World by Louis Fischer. NAL/Dutton, 1982.

Potatoes, Potatoes by Anita Lobel. HarperCollins Children's Books, 1984.

Tall Man by Dorothy Brandt Davis. Brethren Press, 1963.

Way of Peace—A Guide to Nonviolence by Ed Vanderhaar and Mary Lou Kownacki. Pax Christi, 1985.

If you had been confronted by an armed, escaped convict, which way would you have responded—like Louise or like the suburban husband? Explain. What would you do if someone at school brought a gun?

Optional reading:

Matthew 5:43-48

Have family members again use their puppets to replay their situations but with *nonviolent* response. (Instead of each person handling both puppets, another family member should use the "enemy" puppet. Parents may need to coach younger children with possible nonviolent replies or actions.

TREAT

A family treat for all seasons is popcorn—inexpensive, simple corn—Gandhi would have enjoyed it!

AGE ADAPTATION

You could help teens explore more complex issues of personal or family violence. Is violence or force acceptable in self-defense? to protect a loved one or someone weaker? in the armed forces?

—Jean Chapman

 ## TREAT

Pop a big bag of popcorn to eat during the TV program. Also serve everyone their favorite drink before the show starts to keep people from jumping up during the program and discussion.

 ## PRESENTATION OF THEME

A few minutes before the show, select places in front of the TV to snuggle. It might be helpful to have little ones sit on your lap so that you can focus their attention.

> **NOTE:** One suggested show for this type of family night is *Star Trek: The Next Generation*. It addresses many of today's issues in a nonthreatening and interesting way. Even teenagers can get interested in it. Furthermore, *Star Trek: The Next Generation* is now in syndication so reruns can be found on almost any night. There are, of course, other shows that also deal with pertinent social issues, but often they can be too direct, boring, and/or offensive to members of the family. You must be the judge of what is appropriate for your family.

If the issue turns out to be something different than you originally expected, you must be prepared to redirect the discussion. It is okay to shift to another issue for discussion as the show continues. The objective of the night is to discuss what the family members are seeing and feeling.

Tell the family that tonight we are going to watch TV like the critics do. We are going to talk about what we see and how it makes us feel. Introduce the program you've selected for the family to watch. Give a brief description of the story. Then identify the issue the family will critique during this show (i.e., violence, racism, sexism, consumerism, etc.).

Reading:
Sirach 6:33

 ## FAMILY RESPONSE

Network television is very considerate to provide breaks (also known as commercials) every so often during a program. This will

 ### YOU WILL NEED . . .

- ☐ a weekly TV schedule

- ☐ to select a program you think the whole family can watch together (*Star Trek: The Next Generation* is a suggested option.)

- ☐ an issue to focus on during the show (violence, racism, sexism, consumerism, communication, etc.)

 ### READING

Sirach 6:33

If you are willing to listen, you will learn; if you watch with care, you will be wise.

give the family the opportunity to discuss things. Mute the sound during commercials or assign someone to turn down the sound to avoid distraction. Turning the volume down also helps screen out inappropriate commercials and previews of other prime time programs.

During the commercial breaks, let each person in the family say how well or how poorly the story and characters are presenting the theme. The following options might help get the discussion going:

1. During the first commercial break, each person selects a character to follow. The child watches to see how his or her character is affected by the main issue in the program. How does my character feel? What are my concerns, fears, and joys? After the show the family might want to make up an alternative ending to the show.

2. Each person imagines that he or she is the writer or director and tries to guess what might happen at the end of the show. It is interesting to compare these predictions with the Hollywood plot as it actually unfolds.

3. Use the worksheet from Media Madness, Family Night 20 (Appendix C, Activities), as your family watches the program. For older children and teens, the worksheet for Family Night 20 could help the family scrutinize the dynamics and characters more comprehensively and deeply.

—Tom Kruer

THE WORLD IS OUR FAMILY

United Nations Day—October 24

OPENING

Invite the family around the kitchen table or other gathering place. Place the globe and a candle prominently on the table in the midst of the letters and articles mentioned in "You will need ...." Light the candle and sing "It's a Small World" as you pass the globe around the table.

PRESENTATION OF THEME

Sometimes we become so wrapped up in what we are doing and in our own problems that we forget we are part of a global family with brothers and sisters of all races, religions, and nationalities. Tonight we're going to remember that we are part of the biggest family ever, the human family, sharing one big home, the earth.

Reading:

1 Corinthians 12:12-13, 26 *or*
Garrison quotation *or*
People

FAMILY RESPONSE

Choose to do one or more of the following activities.

1. Pen Pals

Read together the letters or magazine articles you've collected about life in another country. Discuss the similarities and differences in lifestyle and values between us and our brothers and sisters in that country. Write down questions about daily life in these countries that you can't answer. Then assign each family member to write to a pen pal, missionary, or another person living in that country. In your letters you may ask the true experts the questions that arose in the family night.

2. A Collage

Make a collage with the faces of people from all over the world. Give it a title, such as "We Are One Global Family" or "We Are the World." Hang it in a prominent place at home or in your place of worship.

YOU WILL NEED ...

- ☐ globe or map of the world
- ☐ magazine articles, newsletters, or videos on everyday life in a developing country (*National Geographic* is a good resource.)
- ☐ *People*, Peter Spier, Doubleday, 1988, optional

Option 1: Pen Pals

- ☐ writing paper, pens, envelopes, stamps
- ☐ letters from friends or missionaries living overseas (If none of these are available, contact your local library or an international association for pen pal names, or join a "twinning" project like Project MADRE, 853 Broadway, Room 301, New York, NY 10003, a project that pairs young children in the U.S. with children in Nicaragua.)

Option 2: A Collage

- ☐ poster board or large paper
- ☐ picture magazines that treat global issues (*Maryknoll Magazine*, a weekly news magazine, or *National Geographic*)
- ☐ crayons, markers, scissors, glue

Option 3: Friends from Another Country

- ☐ invitation to friends or acquaintances from another country

 **READING**

1 Corinthians 12:12-13, 26

For just as the body is one and has many members, and all the members of the body, though many, are one body, so it is with Christ. For in the one Spirit we were all baptized into one body—Jews or Greeks, slaves or free—and we were all made to drink of one Spirit. . . . If one member suffers, all suffer together with it; if one member is honored, all rejoice together with it.

———

My country is the world. My countrymen are all humankind.

—William Lloyd Garrison

 **RELATED READING**

A Country Far Away by Nigel Gray. Orchard Books, 1991.

Educating for Peace and Justice, Vol. III (Religious Dimensions) by James McGinnis et al. Institute for Peace and Justice, 1993.

Young Peacemakers Project Book by Kathleen M. Fry-Miller and Judith A. Myers-Walls. Brethren Press, 1988.

———

—Ann Marie Witchger Hansen

3. Friends from Another Country

Invite friends or acquaintances from another country for dinner or an evening snack. Ask them to bring along a map, pictures, artifacts, musical instruments, or books from their country. Also ask them to share a folktale, poem, song, dance, or stories about daily life in their country, particularly about the children, their play, school, and other activities.

Close by singing "Under One Sky" (Appendix A, Music).

 **TREAT**

Mix up and serve Chex cereal party mix or some other variety.

DEATH TO LIFE

October 31 (or when the family experiences a death)

 OPENING

Light a candle and ask each family member to take a moment to silently think about a relative, friend, or pet that has recently died. Think about the good they did and the joy they brought to the family when they were alive.

 PRESENTATION OF THEME

If family night takes place near Halloween, explain that the custom of Halloween is connected with the Christian feast on All Saints' Day. Halloween, or "Holy Eve," was the night before we remember the saints who have died. On November 2, All Souls' Day, the Roman Catholic Church now remembers all people who have died.

If this family night is done upon the death of a relative, friend, or beloved pet, merely comment that we are gathering to remember our love for that person and to share our sadness that she or he has died.

Reading:

John 12:24 *or*
The Fall of Freddie the Leaf

 FAMILY RESPONSE

Blow up the balloon and play with it for awhile. Talk about how much fun it is and what color it is and how much you like it. Then pop the balloon. You are left with the physical shell, but the life, the fun, is gone with the air. The air from the balloon, however, is still in the room. When a person dies, we believe that his or her spirit is still with us. The body is dead and will be buried, but as long as we remember the person, he or she, like the air, is still with us even if we can't *see* the person anymore.

If a small pet has died, hold a simple burial. Dig a hole in a corner of the yard, wrap the pet in tissue, and place it in the hole. Before covering the pet with dirt, invite each person to say how the pet brought joy to our lives and how much we loved the pet. Offer a spontaneous prayer, asking God's blessing on the pet and on the family in its sadness over the loss. Conclude by covering the hole and comforting one another.

 YOU WILL NEED ...

☐ balloons

☐ a straight pin

☐ plant or seedling that can be planted outdoors, optional

☐ *The Fall of Freddie the Leaf*, Leo Buscaglia, Charles B. Slack, Inc., 1982, optional

 READING

John 12:24

Very truly, I tell you, unless a grain of wheat falls into the earth and dies, it remains just a single grain; but if it dies, it bears much fruit.

You may wish to plant a plant at the burial site, for a living plant reminds us that life comes out of death. If this is a commemoration of the death of someone who is buried locally, the family could visit the cemetery and say a prayer and place some flowers at the grave.

TREAT

Depending on the nature of the occasion, the family may not be in the mood for a festive treat. If the death you are commemorating is not a recent one, however, and the family is in the mood, blow up a bunch of balloons and play with them. Serving hollow candy or puff pastry might also be fun.

RELATED READING

If I Should Live, If I Should Die by Joanne Marxhausen. Concordia Publishing House, 1987.

Tuck Everlasting by Natalie Babbitt. Farrar, Straus, and Giroux, 1985.

—Janet Fraser and Susan Vogt

OPENING

Invite the family to gather around the kitchen table or other comfortable place. Light a candle and sing "When the Saints Go Marching In" (Appendix A, Music).

PRESENTATION OF THEME

The Feast of All Saints is traditionally celebrated in Christian churches to honor men and women who lived exemplary lives of faith in action. According to Christian scripture, all the faithful are saints, not just those officially recognized by the church. Tonight we are going to reflect on the lives of ordinary "saints," living and dead, who have championed justice and peace in our world or who have lived a life of faith in action.

These special people are indeed "saints alive" who inspire us by the way they live.

Perhaps it is Uncle John and Aunt Maria Teresa who work with refugees and migrant workers in south Florida, Uncle Andrew who writes Christian musicals for elementary school children, Fr. Don who organizes college students to serve the people of Appalachia during Thanksgiving break, Mrs. Pierre who visits lonely neighbors, or the Kumat family who does missionary work overseas.

So too, each one of us, adult and child alike, has been given "saintly" qualities. We may not be doing extraordinary deeds, but we can do ordinary deeds in an extraordinary way!

By affirming the unique gifts and talents of one another and acknowledging special people who inspire us to work for peace and justice, our family can nurture a communion of "ordinary saints" right here in our midst!

Reading:
Colossians 1:2, 9-12 *or*
Gandhi quotation

FAMILY RESPONSE

As each person looks at himself or herself in the mirror, have other family members describe the "saintly" qualities of this person, such as compassionate, persevering, creative, or helpful. Then choose one or more of the following options.

YOU WILL NEED . . .

☐ a hand mirror

Option 1:
Myself as a Saint

☐ photocopies of "Myself as a Saint" worksheet in Appendix C: Activities.

Option 3:
All Saints Bingo

☐ a book on the lives of the saints

☐ photocopy of All Saints Bingo Cards, Appendix C

☐ buttons, pennies, or pebbles for markers

READING

Colossians 1:2, 9-12

To the saints and faithful brothers and sisters in Christ in Colossae: Grace to you and peace from God our Father. . . . For this reason, since the day we heard it, we have not ceased praying for you and asking that you may be filled with the knowledge of God's will in all spiritual wisdom and understanding, so that you

(cont.)

may lead lives worthy of the Lord, fully pleasing to him, as you bear fruit in every good work and as you grow in the knowledge of God. May you be made strong with all the strength that comes from his glorious power, and may you be prepared to endure everything with patience, while joyfully giving thanks to the Father, who has enabled you to share in the inheritance of the saints in the light.

———

I claim to be no more than an average person with less than average ability. I have not the shadow of a doubt that any man or woman can achieve what I have, if he or she would make the same effort and cultivate the same hope and faith.

—Gandhi

—Mary Joan Park, Susan Vogt, Ann Marie Witchger Hansen

1. Myself as a Saint

Each family member fills out the worksheet "Myself as a Saint" in Appendix C, Activities. Discuss the responses. Take turns pantomiming what you will do to make the world a better place.

2. A Saint Pantomime

Ask each family member to think of a relative or friend who displays "saintlike" qualities. Take turns pantomiming these special qualities or the specific works of this "ordinary saint" while other members of the family try to guess who it is.

Invite everyone to write letters to their favorite "living saints," naming their saintlike qualities and thanking them for their good example.

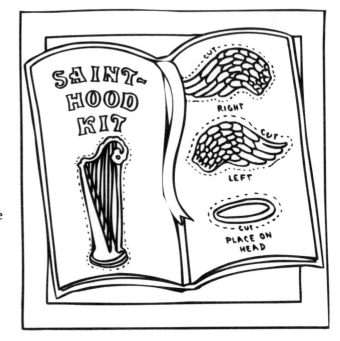

3. All Saints Bingo

Make copies of the bingo card and cut them out (Appendix C, Activities). Have family members look up the saints or heroes in an encyclopedia or a book of saints. Then play All Saints Bingo according to directions.

 **TREAT**

Make an angel food cake and serve it topped with your favorite frozen yogurt or ice cream.

AGE ADAPTATION

Have younger children draw pictures of themselves and talk about what they can do for peace with their arms, hands, feet, and so forth.

BE COUNTED!

OPENING

Gather the family around the kitchen table or other family meeting place. Light a candle in the middle of the table where newspapers and other literature have been gathered. Sing the national anthem or a song about your country.

PRESENTATION OF THEME

Citizenship can be lived out in many ways. Being a citizen is more than obeying laws and respecting the flag; it means caring enough to be informed and to act. Election time is a great time to examine how we show love for our country. Taking part in the political process by voicing our concerns to local, state, and national government officials is just one way of becoming more socially responsible.

Reading:
Acts 1:20b-26 *or*
Nader quotation

FAMILY RESPONSE

Scan newspapers, news magazines, and the newsletters of political action, justice, and peace groups to learn more about issues that affect or interest your family. Discuss your concerns.

Choose one or two issues that are of particular interest. Draw a chart, map, or diagram of how these issues affect you as a family. Try taking the view opposite your own and engage in a lively discussion/debate.

Prepare a family statement that summarizes your views on an issue in preparation for the next family night when you will attend a public meeting.

In addition, have every family member write several opinions on an index card to take with them to the public meeting.

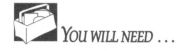

YOU WILL NEED ...

☐ recent newspapers, news magazines, and newsletters from local, state or national government representatives and political action groups

☐ a schedule for the next meeting of the school board, city council, town hall, or other public forum

☐ index cards and pencils

READING

Acts 1:20b-26

"Let another take his position of overseer." So one of the men who have accompanied us during all the time that the Lord Jesus went in and out among us, beginning from the baptism of John until the day when he was taken up from us—one of these must become a witness with us to his resurrection. So they proposed two, Joseph called Barsabbas, who was also known as Justus, and Matthias. Then they prayed and said, "Lord, you know everyone's heart. Show us which one of these two you have chosen to take the place in this ministry and apostleship from which Judas turned aside to go to his own place." And

(cont.)

they cast lots for them, and the lot fell on Matthias; and he was added to the eleven apostles.

———

The challenge is to find activities in our own daily lives that give meaning to our patriotic slogans and that allow us to define our love for our country through civic achievement. Patriotism is a powerful idea and one that should be defined by citizens, not by their rulers alone. For me, the meaning of patriotism lies in working to make America more lovable.... This means working to end poverty, discrimination, corruption, greed and other conditions that weaken the promise and potential of America.... If it is unpatriotic to tear down the flag (which is a symbol of the country), why isn't it more unpatriotic to desecrate the country itself—to pollute, despoil and ravage the air, land and water?

—Ralph Nader, consumer advocate

RELATED READING

Maggie Marmelstein for President by Marjorie Sharmat. Harper Collins Children's Books, 1976.

Soup for President by Robert Peck. Dell, 1986.

———

—Ann Marie Witchger Hansen

TREAT

Serve apple pie and ice cream.

AGE ADAPTATION

For children ages six and under, point out pictures and talk with them simply about issues that may affect or concern your family. Together with the children, draw pictures describing their views of the situations.

HOW TO WRITE AN IMPORTANT LETTER

Should *you* write a letter to the mayor, the governor, a senator, even the president? Of course you should, if you have something to say. Here are some tips to help you get started.

1. Make sure that your letter includes your return address, so your legislator can write back to you.

2. State your purpose in the first sentence. If you're writing to support or oppose a bill, identify it by number and name at the beginning.

3. Stick with one issue per letter. Don't try to wipe out air pollution, improve the budget, start a light-rail transit system, and save the whales all at once.

4. You probably hate writing school assignments that require a certain number of words. Rejoice! Letters to officials should be as short as possible—only a few paragraphs—while still getting your point across.

5. It's okay to disagree with a public official, but do it politely. Never write a rude letter, and never threaten.

6. If possible, be complimentary. It never hurts to include a comment about something good the official has done. There is more willingness to listen to a complaint or suggestion if you start on a positive note.

7. It's not necessary to apologize for taking the official's time. Listening to people—including you—is his or her job. He or she might be surprised to get a letter from a kid, but that could work in your favor.

8. If you write to a legislator other than the one who represents your area, send a copy of your letter to your own representative. That's good manners, and your representative may want to help you, too.

If you are writing a letter to the editor of a newspaper…

◆ Look for any rules or guidelines printed in the magazine or newspaper you plan to write to.

◆ If possible type your letter or write it on a computer. But don't worry if you can't type or don't have access to a computer. You can hand write your letter as long as it's neat and readable. Double-space your letter for easy reading, even if it's handwritten.

◆ Include your return address and signature. Editors won't print your name if you ask them not to, but they probably won't print anonymous letters.

◆ Your subject matter should be something that's "in" or of current interest.

◆ Never accuse anyone without proof or write anything libelous that could get you into trouble.

Power Addresses:

PRESIDENT OF THE U.S.
The President
The White House
Washington, DC 20500

Dear Mr. President:

U.S. SENATOR
The Honorable (name)
United States Senate
Washington, DC 20510

Dear Senator _____:

U.S. REPRESENTATIVE
The Honorable (name)
House of Representatives
Washington, DC 20515

Dear Mr./Ms. _____:

GOVERNOR
The Honorable (name)
Governor of (state)
State Capitol, Rm. __
(City, State, Zip)

Dear Governor _____:

MAYOR
The Honorable Mayor (name)
Office of the Mayor
(Street address)
(City, State, Zip)

Dear Mayor _____:

WORLD LEADER
(Name of World Leader)
(Country) Embassy
United Nations
New York, NY 10017

Dear Mr./Ms. _____:

CANADA—PRIME MINISTER
The Rt. Honorable (name)
House of Commons
Ottawa, Ontario K1A 0A6

Dear Prime Minister _____:

MEMBER OF PARLIAMENT
The Honorable (name)
House of Commons
Ottawa, Ontario K1A 0A6

Dear Mr./Ms. _____:

GET INVOLVED!

Veteran's Day—November 11 (followup to Family Night 52

 ## OPENING

Gather around the kitchen table or other family meeting place. Light a candle and sing "This Land Is Your Land" (Appendix A, Music) or a song about your state, province, or country.

 ## PRESENTATION OF THEME

Citizenship goes beyond understanding the issues that face us as a family and community. Love of our country calls us to speak out for what we believe. Patriotism is the impulse to take an active role in our political process, speaking out on issues that affect or concern us personally. Patriotism is also the impulse to work at addressing what concerns us all, especially what concerns the powerless in our society who cannot speak for themselves, such as children and the illiterate.

 ## FAMILY RESPONSE

Choose one or both of the following activities.

1. Attend a Public Meeting

Review together the local, state, national, or international issues you previously discussed in Family Night 52. Distribute small notebooks, pencils, and index cards on which you made notes on issues. Prepare to attend and participate in a public meeting in your community.

If possible, introduce yourselves to the representative beforehand. These meetings can be lengthy. Ask the representative if your family may present their questions/concerns during the first half hour of the meeting in case you must leave before the meeting concludes.

Sit close to the front so the children can hear and see the speaker, but where they can get out easily to leave the meeting early. Encourage them to note their thoughts or other concerns that emerge from the discussion and to ask questions for clarification as they feel inclined.

 ## YOU WILL NEED . . .

**Option 1:
Attend a Public Meeting**

☐ a schedule of the next public meeting of your city council, town hall, or board of education *or*

☐ an appointment with a representative from local, state, or national government

☐ notebook, pencils, index cards

**Option 2:
Write a Power Letter**

☐ addresses of your city, state, or federal representatives in government to whom you would like to write

☐ stationery, stamps

2. Write a Power Letter

Begin by discussing the following questions. What is the best thing our country has done? What is the worst? How can we change what we don't like?

Ask each family member to write a letter to a legislator or representative about the issues you discussed as a family. Let each share his or her own views and feelings in the letter. Mail the letters, remembering to include your return address so the representative can respond.

 **TREAT**

Have fun with "patriotic sundaes": vanilla ice cream topped with strawberries or cherries (Canadian version). Add blueberries for a U.S. version.

AGE ADAPTATION

This activity works best with young people over the age of five. For younger children, review the issues/concerns in simple terms. Ask them to draw a picture or compose a letter with you about an issue. Add a note of explanation if necessary. Have the child sign it. Send it to your legislator.

With teens, discuss the issue of civil disobedience. Is it ever right to disobey the government? When? Why?

 **RELATED READING**

Arthur Meets the President by Marc Brown. Little, Brown, and Co., 1992.

Children, Let Us Love! Reformed Church Press.

—Ann Marie Witchger Hansen

RITES OF GRATITUDE

Although Native Americans and Native Canadians are often thought of as one group, it is important to remember that we are actually talking about more than 250 different nations (or tribes) that inhabited North America for centuries before the Europeans arrived. Each nation has a distinctive culture, language, and rituals. For the purpose of this family night, however, we will talk about eight groups of nations distinguished by common cultural characteristics. In addition to customs, each of these groups shared geographic location, which affected the type of work they did, their housing, clothing, and food.

> **NOTE:** The term "Native American" is used in this family night in its most popular sense, generally referring to the original people inhabiting southern Canada and the lower forty-eight states. Technically, however, "Native American" could include the Eskimos along with the native people of Alaska, Canada, Central and South America.

1. **Northeast Woodland Cultural Area**—hunters, fishers, some farmers
   Representative nations: Delaware, Iroquois, Huron, Algonquin, Winnebago, Ojibwa (Chippewa)

2. **Southeast Cultural Area**—hunters, fishers, some farmers
   Representative nations: Natchez, Choctaw, Chickasaw, Creek, Cherokee, Seminole, Catawba

3. **Plains and Plateau Cultural Area**—horsemen, buffalo hunters
   Representative nations: Crow, Arapaho, Cheyenne, Comanche, Dakota [Sioux], Pawnee, Shoshoni, Nez Perce, Flathead, Blackfoot, Chinook

4. **Southwest Cultural Area**— "cliff dwellers" (many of these tribes lived in pueblos), farmers, potters, basket weavers
   Representative nations: Taos, Zuni, Hopi, Navajo, Apache, Papago

5. **Northwest Coast Cultural Area**—fishers, woodcarvers, weavers
   Representative nations: Tlingit, Kwakiutl, Nootka

6. **California Cultural Area**—fishers, hunters, gatherers
   Representative nation: Pomo

7. **Basin Cultural Area**—(primarily desert areas) foragers, wanderers, basket weavers
   Representative nations: Ute, Paiute

8. **Subarctic Cultural Area**—fishers, nomadic hunters, fur traders
   Representative nations: Cree, Montagnais-Naskapi, Beaver

Despite the uniqueness of each nation, most Native Americans share some common values, qualities, and characteristics:

◆ Because they all depended on nature for life, they shared a profound knowledge of and respect for the earth.

◆ Native Americans commonly emphasize the *extended family* (or clan) and interdependent community.

◆ Native Americans did not see land as a commodity that could be owned by an individual. Land was seen as communal trust, and in the case of migrating nations, the idea of "owning" land was even more bizarre.

RITES OF GRATITUDE

Thanksgiving

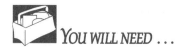 **YOU WILL NEED ...**

- ☐ a real drum or a simple drum made from an oatmeal box

- ☐ a drumstick or mallet made by wrapping a wooden spoon with cloth

- ☐ a recording of Native American music, optional

- ☐ Native American costumes, optional

- ☐ supplies to make simple headbands, strings of beads (craft stores carry inexpensive plastic beads for stringing), or masks

NOTE: Although this theme could be used with any age, it is particularly geared for ages three to ten. See background.

 **OPENING**

Have one child in the family start a simple, slow drum beat. Accent the first of each four beats. With the drum beating softly in the background, the leader or another family member reads Tecumseh's poem:

> When you arise in the morning,
> give thanks for the morning light,
>   for your life and strength.
> Give thanks for your food
>   and the joy of living.
> If you see no reason for giving thanks,
>   the fault lies in yourself.

PRESENTATION OF THEME

As with any distinctive culture, there are several ways of celebrating and remembering important times that carry deep meaning. We call these symbolic actions "rituals." Tonight we will take part in several Native American rituals for Thanksgiving, using the music and dance typical of some Native American groups as they celebrate the harvest.

The drum is important because the sound symbolizes the voice of the Great Spirit or one's own heartbeat. In some cultures a rattle symbolizes the Evil Spirit and bells symbolize humans or the earth. A common drumming rhythm is circular and includes the four directions. Take turns softly drumming and saying the chant we used in Family Night 45. Use a four-count beat with the accent on the first beat.

^My heart speaks to ^your heart. ^May we listen ^to each other.

In order to better understand the Native American's respect for the earth, we will develop a ritual of our own, using some Native American symbols and actions to honor nature that sustains us.

 ## FAMILY RESPONSE

Go outside even if it's rainy or cold. Before modernization, Native Americans didn't have furnaces or air conditioning! Look, listen, and feel the nature around you.

In silence study . . .

◆ The ground

◆ The air (wind or lack of it)

◆ Any water that may be nearby

◆ Any creatures (big, small, flying, crawling, digging, etc.) that you may be able to see or sense

◆ The sun or moon or stars

◆ Others?

After studying each of these elements for a moment, reverently touch the earth, water, air, and reach toward the creatures and heavens, saying something like: "We are thankful for this (<u>element</u>)."

Create a Dance:

Next focus on the theme of harvest, which was important to many Native Americans, especially those for whom agriculture was a way of life. To celebrate an important time or season, some Native Americans would perform a ceremonial dance in festive costume to the beat of a drum and accompanied by a chant. At harvest time, for instance, tribes may have danced, using gestures of reaping and giving thanks for rain and sun. The dance would usually be done in a circle. The step is a simple one:

Tap left toe, drop left heel.
Tap right toe, drop right heel.

Let your family create its own version of a Native American ceremonial harvest dance. Use recorded Native American music from the library or simply have one family member beat the drum and

chant a chant. (Discourage the children from using the stereotypical war cry, patting one's mouth with the palm of the hand. This is not a war dance.) Make up motions that resemble picking corn or wheat, rain falling, and the sun rising and shining.

Dancers would have worn special ceremonial costumes for such a ritual, just as we wear special clothes for religious celebrations such as Easter and Christmas. Try making headbands with real or paper feathers or masks from paper plates. Boys could wear shirts with the tails out. Girls could wear dresses or skirts with the blouses out and belts around their waists.

Although we think of Native Americans as wearing the traditional feathers and beaded leather garments, it is important to remember that *today* Native Americans usually wear clothes that look the same as everyone else's. The dress that we see in pictures is primarily used for occasional ceremonial events.

TREAT

Corn is a food traditionally associated with Native Americans. Maple syrup was also used by Native Americans in the northeast. Make cornbread or corn muffins and drizzle them with maple syrup. For a more authentic treat, try Indian fry bread, a common Native American food that is still eaten by many nations. (See Appendix B, Recipes.)

RELATED READING

I'm in Charge of Celebrations by Byrd Baylor. Macmillan Children's Book Group, 1986.

—Susan Vogt

Watching and Waiting

The Christmas season is loaded (or overloaded) with activity and traditions in most families. Celebrating in itself is not bad, but so much of the festivity seems to begin earlier and earlier every year that Christians often lose sight of the value of Advent—the season of waiting and preparing for the birth of Jesus. Even families who are not Christian, but share the season's hope for peace and good will for the world, yearn for a return to a simpler season. This family night reviews our Christmas activities and tries to recover the original spirit of Advent.

It is our assumption that most families already have a plethora of traditions at Christmas. The need, therefore, is not so much to find additional ways to celebrate the holiday, but rather to prune away burdensome activity and bring the focus back to waiting quietly in the dark of the winter solstice for peace and the light of Christ to be reborn.

Several customs help measure the "waiting time," such as the Advent wreath, Advent calendar, or Advent chain. Even these should be used with discretion, however, since the primary goal is to unclutter this pre-Christmas season in order to reclaim its true meaning.

Some families make a point of writing Christmas cards, decorating the Christmas tree, going to parties, and giving gifts only *on* or *after* December 25. This is a laudable goal, but families should be cautious about tampering with family traditions. It is more important to be happy with each other during this season, if change will cause dissension or tension. Likewise, reducing and simplifying gift giving is also a worthy goal, but you should be sensitive to the feelings of those with whom you exchange gifts.

Symbolism of the Advent wreath:

- ◆ The circle is a reminder of eternity—never ending.

- ◆ The evergreens remind us of life that continues.

- ◆ The four candles stand for the four weeks of Advent. Purple candles are lit the first two weeks. A pink candle is added the third week to symbolize a joyful break in the solemn waiting. The third purple candle is added the final week.

Thus, the family sees the gradual increase in light in the Advent wreath as they move closer to the feast of Christmas.

55 WATCHING AND WAITING

Advent

YOU WILL NEED ...

- [ ] an Advent wreath

- [ ] If the family does not already have an Advent wreath, buy or make one by using three purple candles and one pink candle surrounded by evergreens shaped in a circle—see background.

- [ ] a watch with a second hand

- [ ] a large piece of paper

- [ ] Advent calendar, optional

- [ ] 1x6-inch strips of construction paper, optional

- [ ] figures for a manger scene, optional

READING

Luke 1:26-45

(see Bible for text)

The Cost of Christmas

The 32 billion dollars people in the U.S. spent last year on Christmas gifts does not include the larger costs of Christmas. Christmas has a great impact upon the

(cont.)

Although Advent is clearly a Christian season, a period of preparing for the birth of Jesus, non-Christians may choose to focus on "waiting" as a self-discipline that helps the family appreciate the value of delayed gratification, simplify their lifestyle, and be patient. Jewish families may find many of the concepts below applicable to preparing for Passover.

OPENING

Assuming you are having this family night the first week of Advent, have the oldest child light the first candle of the Advent wreath. All sing the chorus to "O Come, O Come Emmanuel" (Appendix A, Music). If the family does not customarily use the Advent wreath, explain its meaning (see background). Then, without explaining why, wait and do absolutely nothing for exactly one minute.

PRESENTATION OF THEME

First, ask the family what it felt like to have to wait, to do nothing for one minute without knowing why. Was there frustration, anger, silliness? Did people feel "antsy"?

Advent is a time of *active waiting*—for the birth of Jesus. This doesn't mean that we do nothing for four weeks before Christmas; rather, we spend our time quietly preparing for this holy day. This is in stark contrast to our culture that rushes Christmas (and most holidays), celebrating it before its actual time. By the time the actual holiday arrives, we have had many parties, gift exchanges, and shopping trips.

Reading:

Luke 1:26-45 *or*
"The Cost of Christmas"

Tonight we're going to focus on how our family can keep the true spirit of Advent by (1) learning to wait and (2) rethinking our Advent and Christmas customs so that they are in harmony with the Christmas spirit of peace, stewardship, and simplicity.

FAMILY RESPONSE

1. On a large sheet of paper, have the family list all the usual activities and customs of the holiday season (before and after Christmas), for example: get the Christmas tree and decorate it, buy presents, bake cookies, put up lights, send Christmas cards, use the Advent wreath, get out the manger scene, decorate the house, have parties, and exchange gifts.

2. Go through the list and distinguish the activities that truly *prepare* you for Christmas (making and buying presents) and the activities that *celebrate Christmas* (giving gifts and parties). Mark a *P* next to preparing activities and a *C* next to celebrating activities.

3. Go through the list again and assess the *timing* of the activities. Does anyone in the family feel overly busy or pressured during Advent and stressed at Christmas? How can we make Christmas more peaceful?

  a. Consider spacing the *preparation* activities so that they gradually and sensibly build toward Christmas. For example, in the first week set up the Advent wreath; in the second week set up the manger scene; by the third week, get a Christmas tree. Reserve the fourth week for decorating.

  b. Are any of the family activities during Advent truly celebrative? Could we *wait* until Christmas day or the twelve days of Christmas to do them? Are there any preparation activities that could be done closer to Christmas, such as decorating the tree and putting up stockings?

  c. What activities are done out of habit or obligation rather than love, thereby adding undue stress at Christmas? Can we agree to eliminate any of these activities?

4. Go through the list again and note whether any activities serve people in need or contribute to peace in our world. As a way of being faithful to the true spirit of Christmas, discuss how your family can share your resources with those who have less. Consider making a significant donation to a charity, providing gifts for a family in need, or singing Christmas carols at a nursing home. Many churches and organizations offer opportunities for service at this time of year.

5. Is everyone satisfied with the family decisions? Post them in a prominent place in the house. You can make the list more "artful" by putting a big star or Christmas tree in the middle of a large piece of paper with one side labeled "preparing" and the other "cele-

environment. Consider the waste disposal costs of this spending binge or the longterm costs of using irreplaceable natural resources for non-necessity commodities. A drive down the street on the first trash pick-up day after Christmas is a sobering reminder of the amount of waste generated in this celebration. Behind every pound of garbage at curbside, there are approximately twenty pounds of industrial or agricultural waste created in the process of production.

—Milo Thornberry, *Looking Behind the Cost of Christmas*

brating." List appropriate activities on each side. Children could decorate the chart.

6. Choose one or more of the following activities to help the family measure their time of waiting.

a. Light an Advent candle weekly until Christmas.

b. Make or purchase Advent calendar(s).

c. Make an Advent chain of 1x6-inch strips of multicolored construction paper. At dinner every night during Advent, each member of the family writes on a strip the name of a person or cause for which they want to pray. Make a circle with the first slip and staple it; loop the second slip through the first, overlap the ends, and staple. Add a new slip each day. By Christmas the family has a chain of prayers to decorate the tree.

d. Ceremoniously unwrap each manger figure and together set up the manger scene in a place of honor.

e. Invite children to add a piece of straw to the manger each time they do a good deed.

 **TREAT**

Have something easy to prepare—no waiting: cookies, ice cream.

 **RELATED READING**

The Twenty-Four Days Before Christmas by Madeline L'Engle. Dell, 1987.

Who's Birthday Is it Anyway? An Alternative Christmas resource by Alternatives, P.O. Box 429, Ellenwood, GA 30049, 404-961-0102.

—Susan Vogt

Hanukkah, O Hanukkah, come light the menorah.
Let's have a party, we'll all dance the horah.
Gather 'round the table, we'll give you a treat,
Dreidels to play with and latkes to eat.

This popular Hanukkah song captures the spirit of this fun Jewish festival, which occurs between late November and late December. Eight nights and days are filled with songs, stories, games, and foods. Hanukkah is the time to light the *menorah* (a nine-candle candelabrum), to play with *dreidels* (four-sided tops), and to eat *latkes* (fried potato pancakes).

Hanukkah, the Jewish festival of lights, celebrates the victory of a great Jewish leader, Judah the Maccabee, over the Syrian Greeks, who were occupying the ancient homeland of the Jews, now known as Israel. The Syrian Greeks were threatening to eliminate the religious faith and customs of the Jewish people.

A small band of Jews resolved to forfeit their lives, if necessary, to preserve their faith heritage. Thus, Hanukkah also commemorates the struggle for religious freedom. During this season, Jews pledge themselves anew to their beliefs and practices. This is done by lighting the Hanukkah candles or oil lamps and by living with pride in their Jewish identity. These actions "publicize the miracle of rededication" and demonstrate the themes of Hanukkah.

The Story of Hanukkah

In the year 167 B.C.E. (before the common era when Christianity, Islam, and other faiths emerged), the Greek king Antiochus Epiphanes forced all the people under his rule in the land we know today as Israel to adopt Greek culture. Some Jews were intrigued by Greek culture and wanted to blend aspects of Greek culture with their own. These Jews were attracted to Greek life, Greek gods, and the Greek emphasis on beauty and a powerful body.

Other Jews were aghast at the price of this demand. Among other Jewish practices, the observance of Shabbat and the circumcision of eight-day-old boys were forbidden. In addition, the worship of Greek gods and other sacrileges took place in the Jewish temple, the center of Jewish ritual observance, in the holy city of Jerusalem.

One day the Greeks came to Modin, a small hillside village. There they established a Greek religious altar. They ordered Jews to bring a pig as a sacrifice to show obedience to Greek rule. When a Jew was about to do the Greeks' bidding, Mattathias, an old Jewish priest, killed him.

Mattathias's action sparked guerrilla warfare, and he and his five sons led the fight against the Greeks. Before he died, Mattathias named his son

Judah leader of the Jewish army, which was known as the Maccabees, men who were "strong as a hammer."

Because of Judah's superior military strategies, he cleverly defeated the Greeks. Finally he and his followers freed Jerusalem from Greek rule. This victory, on the 25th day of Kislev, 165 B.C.E., allowed the Jews to return to their temple in Jerusalem to worship God.

Legend asserts that the victors wanted to rekindle the eternal light that burned in the temple, but they were only able to find one unopened flask of oil. Although there was enough oil for only one day, it miraculously lasted for eight days until additional oil could be prepared. This is the popular miracle for which Hanukkah is best known and the reason the holiday is celebrated for eight miraculous days.

And the real miracle? The real miracle was the victory of a vision. The miracle was the triumph of religious freedom and the strength of the lesser against the seemingly powerful.

> **NOTE:** How do you spell the holiday for the Jewish festival of lights? You might think that *Hanukkah* is the only way to spell this holiday week. Some variations are: *Chanukah, Channukah, Chanukkah, Hanuka, Hanukah*. Since Hebrew has a different alphabet from English, the sounds can be written in English letters several different ways. There is no one correct way.

 OPENING

Explain to the family: Today we thank God for all the goodness in our lives, for the beauty of nature, for the love we feel for one another, for the Hanukkah tradition. May our celebration increase the light of freedom in the world.

On the first day of Hanukkah, put the ninth candle in the middle of the menorah or in a separate holder. It will always be the first candle lighted and will be used to light the eight candles in the menorah. Also on the first day, place one candle in the menorah on the extreme right and light it with the ninth candle. Each night of Hanukkuh add a new candle, filling the menorah from right to left. Though the candles are placed in the menorah from right to left, they are lighted from left to right. Light the candles after sundown when the whole household is together.

As you light the candles, say these prayers:

Blessed are You, Lord our God, Ruler of the Universe, who has commanded us to light the lights of Hanukkah.

Blessed are You, Lord our God, Ruler of the Universe, who made miracles for our ancestors in times and seasons past.

On the first night of Hanukkah add:

Blessed are You, Lord our God, Ruler of the Universe, who has kept us alive, sustained us, and encouraged us to celebrate this joyful festival.

Sing "Rock of Ages," a traditional Hanukkah song. (See Appendix A, Music.)

 PRESENTATION OF THEME

Summarize for the family the history and meaning of Hanukkah from the background page. Adapt your explanation to the ages and attention span of your children.

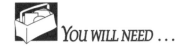 YOU WILL NEED ...

☐ Hanukkah menorah and candles (A menorah is a special candelabrum that holds eight or nine candles. You can buy a menorah, borrow one from Jewish friends, or make one by arranging eight or nine candles in a row. One candle should be higher than the rest.)

**Option 1:
Neighborhood Party**

☐ traditional Hanukkah foods and other festive activities.

**Options 2 and 3:
Dreidels**

☐ a dreidel (pronounced drād l) or materials to make one (see p. 172)

☐ counters such as coins, nuts, buttons

**Option 4:
Cooking Night**

☐ ingredients for latkes (see recipe in Appendix B)

**Option 5:
Decorate Your Home**

☐ construction paper for posters *or*

☐ colored felt and string

FAMILY RESPONSE

Choose one or more of the following, or spread activities over the eight days of Hanukkah.

1. Neighborhood Party

Have a big neighborhood party. Decorate your home and make holiday food "with oil," symbolizing the tiny bit of oil that miraculously burned for eight days in the reclaimed temple. If you are rushed, you may want to buy frozen latkes and serve them with applesauce or sour cream along with ready-made *sufganiot* (jelly donuts). Celebrate with songs, stories, skits, and games.

2. Art Project

You can make dreidels or purchase them. Make a basic dreidel in this way: Make a one-inch cube from construction paper. Using a colorful felt-tip pen, write one of the four Hebrew letters on each side of the cube: *nun, gimmel, hay, shin*. Pierce one point of the cube with a short pencil and spin.

A dreidel could also be made from clay. Shape clay into a one-inch cube. Add a small pyramid or cone shape to one flat side of the cube and a 1x¼-inch stem to the opposite flat side. Let dry for two days, then paint with tempera colors. Paint the four Hebrew letters, one on each remaining square surface. Allow another two days to dry. Paint with a thin layer of white glue to hold the colors. Let dry another two days. Now you're ready to play dreidel.

3. Game Night

Play dreidel. The four-sided top is marked on each side with letters of the Hebrew alphabet that stand for "A Great Miracle Happened There." Gather together nuts or toothpicks or pennies, and divide the counters evenly among two to six players. Each person places one counter in the center of the circle. Take turns spinning the dreidel. If it falls on . . .

- the Hebrew letter *nun*, the player gets nothing;

- the Hebrew letter *gimmel*, the player takes all from the center pot, and all the players must replenish the center pot with one counter each;

- the Hebrew letter *hay*, the player gets half the center pot;
- the Hebrew letter *shin*, the player puts in one counter from his or her stash.

End at any time you wish. The winner is the one who has the most counters at the end of the game.

4. Cooking Night

Potato pancakes, called latkes, are usually eaten at Hanukkah because they are fried in oil, which reminds us of the oil that burned miraculously for eight days in the temple. Everyone can help make the latkes or kugel from scratch. As an alternative, make sugar cookies and cut them out in Hanukkah shapes, such as dreidels and candles.

5. Decorating Your Home

You can make or purchase decorations. Be creative and have fun! Make posters from construction paper. Cut out menorah and dreidel shapes and paste them onto the poster. Or, cut out six-pointed Jewish stars and dreidel shapes from colored felt and string them together into a swag. Hang the swag in your living room and enjoy the homemade spirit of Hanukkah.

6. Giving Gifts

In the United States people also associate Hanukkah with giving gifts. In previous generations, children received Hanukkah *gelt* (money) from all the relatives. Now some families choose to give gifts on some of the evenings. Sometimes the gifts are special and sometimes they are basics.

nun

gimmel

hay

shin

 **TREAT**

Serve latkes or potato kugel (Appendix B, Recipes) with sour cream, yogurt, cottage cheese, or applesauce. At the end of any Hanukkah celebration, give the traditional greeting *Hag Sameach* which means "Happy Holiday."

—Robert and Cheryl Nanberg
and Elizabeth Dowling Sendor

173

Season of Miracles

In the 1500s, when the Spanish missionaries were trying to evangelize the native people of what is now Mexico City, the Virgin Mary appeared to an indigenous man named Juan Diego. Until that moment, the missionaries had not been very successful in converting the thousands of natives to Christianity. The virgin who appeared to Juan Diego, however, was a most significant figure, since her skin and features were somewhat dark, like those of the indigenous people. Her appearance and every article of her clothing had meaning for the native people. She spoke to them in a way the missionaries could not.

Our Lady of Guadalupe asked Juan Diego to go to the bishop and request that a temple be built for her on the mount called Tepeyac. Juan Diego was more afraid than thrilled when he, such a lowly person, saw the Virgin, but he did her bidding and tried to transmit her message to the bishop. But when he went before the bishop, Juan Diego had a very difficult time trying to convince him of Our Lady's message. He tried three times, each time reporting back to Our Lady that he couldn't accomplish the task that she had laid on him. He begged her to find someone else. The Virgin of Guadalupe repeated her request one more time and asked him to fulfill it.

In the meantime, the bishop had insisted that Juan Diego bring him some tangible proof of the Virgin's presence. Our Lady told Juan Diego to go to the bishop once more and unfold his *tilma* (the robe and outer garment). When he did, the bishop saw a picture of the blessed lady on the front of the tilma. Also, a shower of flowers, which were not supposed to be in bloom that time of the year, fell to the floor at his feet. This miracle convinced the bishop to build the shrine. As a result, thousands of the indigenous people were converted to Christianity.

The original tilma is enshrined at the basilica on the site in Mexico City where the Virgin appeared. Many people have studied this painting (made from paints that cannot be identified) and found that the picture on the tilma has remained the same for over 450 years. The tilma itself has escaped several tragedies that have befallen the area.

Perhaps the greatest miracle is the evangelization of an entire people. Our Lady's appearance to Juan Diego served as a bridge from an era of oppression to one of hope and confirmed the dignity of the indigenous people. She is sometimes called The Empress of the Americas.

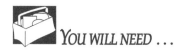 **YOU WILL NEED ...**

- ☐ Our Lady of Guadalupe holy cards from a local religious bookstore (If religious cards are not available, make little bows from red, white, and green ribbons.)

- ☐ the story of Our Lady of Guadalupe from the library (or order from the Mexican-American Cultural Center, 3019 W. French Place, San Antonio, TX 78228)

- ☐ red, white, and green votive candles, optional

 **OPENING**

Hand out holy cards to each member of the family, or pin one of the ribbons on each member of the family. Red, white, and green are the colors associated with Our Lady of Guadalupe. They are also the colors of the flag of Mexico, the country where she appeared. If you have red, white, and green votive candles, arrange them in a centerpiece and light them for the opening. Read together the following poem, which described the feelings of many of the indigenous people of Mexico after they (and their gods) had been overcome by the Europeans.

> Please let us die,
> Let us disappear,
> For our gods have died.

> —Anonymous Mexican poet

PRESENTATION OF THEME

Our Lady of Guadalupe is an important figure for Mexican Americans because she reminds us that the Divine is in a person who is Hispanic. An endearing term for Our Lady of Guadalupe is *La Morenita*, which means "the little one of brown skin." In her honor, the Roman Catholic Church has assigned a special date in the liturgical calendar to her—December 12.

Read the story of Our Lady of Guadalupe from the book you have obtained or the shortened version from the background for this family night.

 **FAMILY RESPONSE**

Symbols express ideas that cannot be conveyed in words. Learning to recognize and understand the image of Our Lady of Guadalupe can be an experience in interpreting symbols. As everyone looks at the picture of Our Lady of Guadalupe, take turns talking about the meaning of each of the following symbols.

1. Her face

Her face told Juan Diego that she was not a Spaniard, but one of his own. Her garments gleamed, and a splendor of light and color

surrounded her. Hers is a young face with mature eyes and a smile of compassion. The "face" for the Mexican is the very identity of the person. It tells who the person is.

2. Red dress

The dress is a pale red color, the color of the spilled blood of sacrifices. It is the color of Huitzilopochtli-Sun, the god who gives and preserves life and was himself nourished with the precious liquid of life—blood.

3. Blue/green mantle

The predominant color of the painting is the blue-green of the mantle. Most importantly, blue-green was the color of Ometeotl, parent of the gods and the origin of all natural forces and of everything that is. This turquoise was the color of the gods and its use was reserved for the deities and royalty. Since the Virgin is dressed in a royal color, she must be of divine or at least royal origin.

4. The stars of the mantle

Ten years before the Spanish conquest of Mexico, a comet appeared. This was interpreted by the native wise men as a sign of the end of their civilization. Just as the stars had signaled the end of their civilization, the Virgin's stars announced the beginning of a new civilization.

5. Angels supporting the Lady

The fact that the Virgin is being carried by angels could mean two different things, or perhaps both.

a. Only very important people were carried on the shoulders of another. The fact that she was carried by heavenly creatures suggests that she came on her own and not with the Spaniards.

b. Time had run out for the previous civilization. The entrance of the Virgin marked the beginning of a new era: the era of Our Lady and everything she stands for.

 **READING**

Luke 1:46-55

And Mary said, "My soul magnifies the Lord, and my spirit rejoices in God my Savior, for he has looked with favor on the lowliness of his servant. Surely, from now on all generations will call me blessed; for the Mighty One has done great things for me, and holy is his name. His mercy is for those who fear him from generation to generation. He has shown strength with his arm; he has scattered the proud in the thoughts of their hearts. He has brought down the powerful from their thrones, and lifted up the lowly; he has filled the hungry with good things, and sent the rich away empty. He has helped his servant Israel, in remembrance of his mercy, according to the promise he made to our ancestors, to Abraham and to his descendants forever."

6. Standing upon the moon and the rays of the sun

The sun god was the principal god in the native religion. Our Lady of Guadalupe does not do away with the sun—the rays of the sun shine as always. But there is now one among the gods who is even greater than the greatest.

Also among the greatest of the Indian divinities was the moon god, the god of night. Although Our Lady stood upon the moon, she did not crush it or destroy it. Because she was greater than the gods of the indigenous people, she was not threatened by their power.

7. Position of the eyes

Even though she is greater than the greatest, she is not prideful or indifferent to the affairs of ordinary people. With downcast eyes, she looks at the people and even allows them to be reflected in her eyes. Her whole face speaks of compassion and understanding.

8. Black band around the waist

The black band around the Virgin's waist is a maternity band. It is a sign that Our Lady was with child, a child she was offering to the New World and to all the peoples of this New World.

9. Indian cross near the navel

This symbol indicates that the new center of the universe is Jesus who lay unborn beneath the cross at Our Lady's navel.

10. Christian cross on the brooch near her neck

Clearly seen on the brooch that Our Lady wears close to her neck, the Christian cross indicates that this Lady, though one of the indigenous people, is both a bearer and a follower of Christ.

From *La Morenita: Evangelizer of the Americas* by Virgilio P. Elizando. Adapted with the permission of the author.

Extending the lesson:

Reading:

Luke 1:46-55 (The Magnificat—Mary's song of faith and justice)

This family night could also be a time to discuss what is known about the Christian's belief in Mary, the mother of Jesus. Did you know that there is only one Virgin Mary, but that she is revered under many different names? What does this say to you about how God has chosen women to do great things? What about the fact that God chooses the poorest people to do great things? Talk about what an important part a "mother" has in doing God's work.

 TREAT

It would be a special treat to find a parish in your city that celebrates the feast of Our Lady of Guadalupe. The traditional celebration is a mass at dawn, usually at 5 or 6 A.M., although some parishes have adopted a later time. "Las Mañanitas," the traditional Mexican "Happy Birthday" song, is sung by a mariachi group. Or you might visit a Lady of Guadalupe parish or any predominantly Hispanic parish that will give your family an opportunity to see a replica of Our Lady of Guadalupe.

If you have your treat at home, sing "Las Mañanitas" (Appendix A, Music) and serve some *repostería* and hot chocolate. Repostería is a variety of Mexican cookies, found in *panaderías* (Mexican bakeries) and many supermarkets. They are crisp, usually brightly decorated cookies.

AGE ADAPTATION

On a deeper level, Our Lady of Guadalupe was important because she encouraged reconciliation between the Spaniards and the indigenous people who hated each other. Her shrine united the two cultures. Teens could discuss other ethnic divisions in the world today and how they might be reconciled.

—Rosemary Piña

LIGHT COMES TO THE WORLD

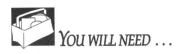

St. Lucia Day—December 13

 YOU WILL NEED . . .

- ☐ four candles

- ☐ evergreen boughs for an Advent wreath

- ☐ a story about St. Lucia (Most collections of stories of the saints will include one about her.)

- ☐ white gown and red sash, optional

- ☐ Lucia crowns and star boy hats:

  - ☐ paper and eight to ten small evergreen boughs for crowns

  - ☐ 12x18-inch construction paper for hats

  - ☐ gold foil

  - ☐ yarn

  - ☐ glue, stapler, scissors

 **OPENING**

Gather the family around the Advent wreath in the dark. Light the appropriate number of candles depending on which week of Advent this date falls. Sing "O Come, O Come Emmanuel" or "Santa Lucia." (See Appendix A, Music.)

PRESENTATION OF THEME

Lucia was an early Christian saint. Depending on which version of her story you read, she was reported to have lived in fourth-century Rome or Sweden. She may never have lived at all. No matter; her story is timeless and universal. Legend has it that as a young teenager, Lucia offered her virginity to God. Later, when pressed to marry a non-Christian, she willingly accepted martyrdom rather than forsake her promise of virginity or her faith.

Today St. Lucia Day is a uniquely Swedish holiday and traditionally marks the beginning of the Christmas season in that country. It is celebrated as the Festival of Light, a celebration of the winter solstice and Advent. Both mark the return of the light. The solstice signals the return of the sun and Advent the approaching birth of the "Light of the World." It is no coincidence that these events fall at the same time or that Lucia's name means "light."

Reading:
Read the story about St. Lucia.

 **FAMILY RESPONSE**

If possible, schedule this family night for December 12 to prepare for the traditional observance of Lucia Day on December 13. Girls can make Lucia crowns. Boys can make star boy hats.

Directions for Lucia crowns:

A Lucia crown traditionally consists of a wreath of evergreen boughs with seven lighted candles mounted on it. An easier (and safer) alternative is to make a basic headband out of stiff paper, about one inch wide and long enough to go all the way around the child's head. Imitate candles by rolling up pieces of white paper. Simulate flames by cutting out pieces of gold foil paper or yellow construction paper. Affix these to the headband with tape. Finally,

staple some small evergreen boughs to the headband, or draw them on with green felt-tip pen.

Directions for star boy hats:

The star boy hat is a simple cone, rolled from a piece of 12x18-inch construction paper and fastened with tape or staples. Trim the lower edge to make it even. Decorate with stars cut from construction paper or foil. Attach yarn ties to the lower edge on either side.

Instruct the children on what to do in the early morning and have them set their alarms. On the morning of December 13, the children will get up before the parents and put on their Lucia crowns or star boy hats. The oldest girl in the family traditionally portrays St. Lucia, donning a white gown with red sash. The other children, Lucia maidens and star boys, are her attendants. Together they will go to wake up their parents, singing "Santa Lucia" (Appendix A, Music) and serving the Lucia buns.

 **TREAT**

All can participate in baking a batch of Lucia buns (Appendix B, Recipes). Or adults may do the baking after the children are in bed to maintain just a little element of surprise for them.

Lucia buns are a traditional treat for this holiday. However, just about any type of sweet roll will do. Coffee is a traditional beverage for adults, and hot cider or cocoa is appropriate for children.

Hint: Set up an automatic coffeemaker the night before, timing it to brew just as the children will be getting up.

AGE ADAPTATION

Teenagers may want to discuss the pressures that peers and society sometimes put on them to become sexually active. Discuss how they feel about sexual abstinence until marriage. Does a decision to be a lifelong virgin for the sake of a religious commitment make any sense? Ask what your teens would be willing to risk to be faithful to their religious beliefs.

—Karen Schneider-Chen

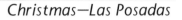

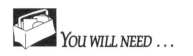

YOU WILL NEED . . .

Option 1:
Las Posadas in the Neigborhood

☐ notes to several neighbors saying that Joseph and Mary will be knocking on their door (be sure to alert them to the appropriate response)

Option 2:
Las Posadas at Home

☐ one child as Mary and one as Joseph (or you can use religious statues of the Holy Family from a creche)

☐ medium-long candles in holders made from small paper plates

☐ invitations to the neighbors to the closing fiesta, optional

☐ a piñata and food for the closing fiesta , optional

NOTE: This family night features a reenactment of Mary and Joseph seeking a room at an inn. You may wish to involve several families in this activity.

PRESENTATION OF THEME

Las Posadas is Spanish for "the inns" and is a reenactment of the journey that Mary and Joseph took to be counted in the census. The journey ended when Mary gave birth to the baby Jesus in a manger because there was no place for them in the inn. Tonight your family will act out the journey. The idea is to remember Mary and Joseph's plight as they tried time after time to find a place to stay and time after time were rejected.

Jesus tries many times to enter into our hearts, and many times we do not give him a place to stay. We still reject him.

Although Las Posadas is clearly a Christian tradition, the plight of people who have been rejected and do not have adequate housing is a universal concern. In our world today, there are many who have no place to stay.

Early missionaries used Las Posadas to show the various indigenous groups a basic Christian belief. In its original form, Las Posadas was done as a novena (a devotion lasting a period of nine nights) from December 16 to December 24. In our busy modern world and especially for the purpose of a family night, Las Posadas can be done all in one evening as a way of preparing for Christ's coming.

FAMILY RESPONSE

Hand out a candle to each participant.

Reading:
Luke 2:1-5 (the story of Mary and Joseph traveling to be counted for the census)

Choose to do one of the following reenactments.

1. Las Posadas in the Neighborhood

Las Posadas can be done around a neighborhood where you have announced you will come to neighbors' doors seeking a *posada*, a place to stay. The folks inside (by prearrangement) will tell you they

have no room for you and you must move along. As pilgrims, you continue to search for a posada until you come to the last place where you are welcomed (by prearrangement) and ushered in with song and joy. You could pick up a few more folks at each home and make this a fun variation of caroling. The special song "Para Pedir Posada" (Appendix A, Music) may be sung by those outdoors alternating verses with those indoors. The song is traditionally in Spanish and should be learned that way; however, the English translation will assure that everyone understands what they are singing.

2. Las Posadas at Home

Mary and Joseph travel from door-to-door outside your own house, carrying the lighted candles in their candleholders. Each time the "pilgrims" knock on a door (at least three) seeking lodging, the family refuses them. The reenactment of the journey can be done inside as well by going to all interior doors of your home where you position some of your family to be "outdoors" and some "indoors."

 *TREAT*

At the last stop (the last home in the neighborhood or the last "door" in your home), Mary and Joseph will be received and given lodging. It is in this home that a big *fiesta* (party) is held. Ideally there would be a piñata filled with candy for the children. Hang a basket of little candies from the ceiling for a makeshift piñata, if a piñata is not possible. The traditional feast for this occasion includes *tamales, buñuelos*, and *champorrado* (Appendix B, Recipes). Hot chocolate may be served in place of champorrado.

READING

Luke 2:1-5

In those days a decree went out from Emperor Augustus that all the world should be registered. This was the first registration and was taken while Quirinius was governor of Syria. All went to their own towns to be registered. Joseph also went from the town of Nazareth in Galilee to Judea, to the city of David called Bethlehem, because he was descended from the house and family of David. He went to be registered with Mary, to whom he was engaged and who was expecting a child.

—Rosemary Piña

Following a 1965 revolt in the Watts section of Los Angeles, a student named Maulana Karenga wanted to help his African American neighbors gain a sense of identity and community. Karenga created a celebration called *Kwanzaa* (Kwanzaa means "first fruits" in Swahili). Though Kwanzaa is based on African tradition, it does not replicate any celebration of continental Africa, and it has no particular religious affiliations. It belongs to everybody. Now more that eighteen million people of African descent all over the world strengthen their own cultural identity through the celebration of Kwanzaa.

Kwanzaa is a seven-day celebration starting December 26 and continuing to January 1. The primary symbol used each day of Kwanzaa is the *kinara*. The Kwanzaa kinara holds three red candles to represent the struggle of the past, three green candles to represent a prosperous future, and one black candle in the middle representing Black unity.

Each evening the family gathers to light the appropriate number of candles (one to seven) and remember the principle the last candle represents. The seven principles (*nguzo saba*), one for each day of the festival, are:

1. Umoja (Unity)
To strive for and maintain unity in the family, community, nation, and race

2. Kujichagulia (Self-determination)
To define ourselves, name ourselves, create for ourselves, and speak for ourselves

3. Ujima (Collective Work and Responsibility)
To build and maintain our community together and make our sisters' and brothers' problems our problems and solve them together

4. Ujamaa (Cooperative Economics)
To build and maintain our own stores, shops, and other businesses and to profit from them together

5. Nia (Purpose)
To make our collective vocation the building of our community, to restore our people to their traditional greatness

6. *Kuumba* (Creativity)
To do as much as we can to leave our community more beautiful and beneficial than we inherited it

7. *Imani* (Faith)
To believe with our heart in our people, our parents, our teachers, our leaders, and the righteousness and victory of our struggle

No matter what color our skin, we can honor the African traditions and the celebration of Kwanzaa as we build community among the peoples of the world.

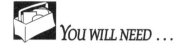

YOU WILL NEED ...

☐ an invitation to a family of another race to celebrate Kwanzaa with you for a multicultural event, optional

☐ a Kwanzaa kinara (3 green candles, 3 red candles, 1 black candle, and a foot-long board or log)

☐ construction paper: 2 black, 1 red, and 1 green piece for each person

☐ scissors

☐ recorded African music, optional

NOTE: Prior to this family night, you may want to make a simple Kwanzaa kinara according to the following instructions:

Drill seven holes in a foot-long board or log to hold candles. Mount the candles on the board or log, either by drilling holes large enough to accommodate the candles or by dripping pools of wax and planting the candles in the warm wax. Place three red candles on one side, three green candles on the other side, and a black candle in the middle. If a black candle is difficult to find, black construction paper or ribbon could be put around a candle of another color.

OPENING

Light the first Kwanzaa candle.

PRESENTATION OF THEME

Briefly explain the origins of Kwanzaa, drawing from information on the Kwanzaa background page. Explain that tonight the family is going to join in solidarity with African-Americans by celebrating the first principle of Kwanzaa, *umoja* or "unity." To do this we will make a placemat that weaves together the three symbolic colors of the kinara: green for a prosperous future, red for the struggles of the past, and black for Black unity. We can then use these placemats at our main meal together for the seven days.

FAMILY RESPONSE

Weave placemats as follows:

1. Fold one sheet of black construction paper in half, the short way. Starting with the fold at the bottom, make the first cut one inch from the left, stopping one inch away from the top. Cut parallel lines at 1-inch intervals until you are almost to the opposite edge. Open the paper and spread it flat.

2. Cut strips of equal width to weave the placemat. You will need one black, three green, and three red strips for each placemat.

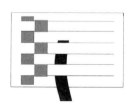

3. Now weave one strip at a time, starting with a red, then green, then red again. Next weave the black strip in the middle. Weave green, red, and finally green.

As the family focuses on the weaving, think about what each color of paper represents and ask:

- What does it mean to you?

- How does it help us understand the way things are today?

- How can we use this knowledge to help make life better for all people?

When your mat is complete, it will serve as a reminder of the dignity and value of all human beings.

While making the mats or upon finishing them, have the family respond to the question for Day 1—Unity: Can our family do anything to improve racial harmony or unity in our community?

Each evening thereafter, the family gathers to light the appropriate number of candles (one to seven) and remember the principle the last candle represents (as described in the background for this family night). During dinner, focus on the question related to the principle of the day.

Day 2—Self-determination: How am I my own person, not a slave to anyone, "boss over my own body"?

Day 3—Collective Work and Responsibility: Is there anyone in our community who needs our family's help?

Day 4—Cooperative Economics: Do we buy any goods or services from Black- or minority-owned enterprises? Could we?

Day 5—Purpose: What is the purpose of my life? I am called to be and do something important in this life.

Day 6—Creativity: What can our family do to beautify our community's environment?

Day 7—Faith: How can I help someone in my family or community have a stronger belief in himself or herself?

RELATED READING

Kwanzaa by A. P. Porter. Carolrhoda Books, Inc., 1991.

Kwanzaa: A Celebration of Culture and Cooking by Eric V. Copage. Morrow, 1991.

TREAT

Red and green striped candy canes for Christmas could take on new meaning when the colors are reinterpreted for Kwanzaa.

—Sue Blythe and Ina Hines

APPENDIX A

SONGBOOK

Rise Up Singing: The Group Singing Songbook by Peter Blood and Annie Patterson, eds. Sing Out Publications (P.O. Box 5253, Bethlehem, PA 18015-0253, 215-865-5366), 1992.
>   If your family likes to sing, this songbook would be well worth the investment. This book of 1200 songs includes most of the songs in this appendix.

TAPES

Bright Morning Star Arisin'. Flying Fish Records (1304 W. Schubert, Chicago, IL 60614, 312-528-5455), 1988.
>   This delightful tape is sometimes difficult to find but well worth the effort of ordering it direct. It includes "Simple Gifts," "Solar Carol," and "Vine and Fig Tree" from this appendix.

Raffi has made numerous children's tapes including: *Singable Songs for the Very Young, More Singable Songs for the Very Young, Music for Little People, The Corner Grocery Store,* and *One Light, One Sun*. Order from: Raffi, P.O. Box 1460, Redway, CA 95560.

Rainbow People. Susan Stark Music (RR 2 Box 927-D, Canaan, NH 10741).
>   This is also available from The Institute for Peace and Justice. In addition to "Simple Gifts" and "Garden Song" (from this appendix), it includes "The Happy Wanderer," "All God's Critters," and more.

Teaching Peace (ages 4-12) by Red Grammer. Smilin' Atcha Music, 1986.
>   This is available from The Institute for Peace and Justice.

Two Good Arms by Charlie King (P.O. Box 6207, Hamden, CT 06517).
>   This includes "Our Life Is More Than Our Work" (from this appendix) and other labor songs and songs for hard times.

Under One Sky (Gentle Wind 1012) by Ruth Pelham. Ruth Pelham Music (P.O. Box 6024, Albany, NY 12206).
>   This tape includes "Under One Sky" and may be ordered for $10.

Songs (in alphabetical order)

NOTE: Music has only been included for less well-known songs and if available. If you want to use a song that is unfamiliar to you, the tapes listed above should be helpful.

Auld Lang Syne

Should auld acquaintance be forgot and never brought to mind?
Should auld acquaintance be forgot and days of auld lang syne?
For auld lang syne, my dear, for auld lang syne,
We'll tak' a cup o' kindness yet, for auld lang syne.

—Robert Burns

Garden Song

Inch by inch, row by row,
Gonna make this garden grow.
All you need is a rake and a hoe
And a piece of fertile ground.
Inch by inch, row by row
Someone bless these seeds I sow.
Someone warm them from below
Til the rains come tumbling down.

Pulling weeds, picking stones
We are made of dreams and bones
Need a place to call my own
for the time is near at hand.
Grain for grain, sun and rain
Find my way thru nature's chain
Tune my body and my brain
to the music of the land.

Plant your rows straight and long
Temper them with prayer and song.
Mother earth will make you strong
if you give her love and care.
An old crow watching hungrily
from his perch in yonder tree
In my garden I'm as free
as that feathered thief up there!

God Bless the Moon

Freely (unaccompanied)

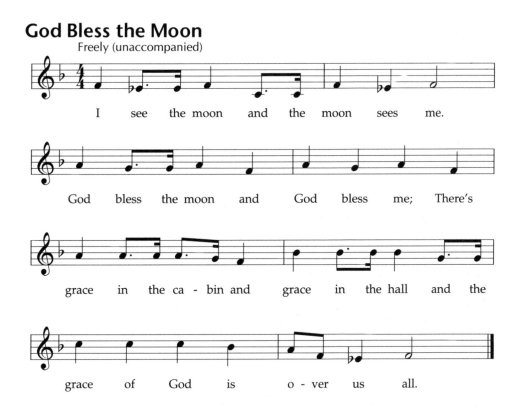

I see the moon and the moon sees me.

God bless the moon and God bless me; There's

grace in the ca - bin and grace in the hall and the

grace of God is o - ver us all.

I see the moon and the moon sees me.
The moon sees the somebody I want to see;
God bless the moon and God bless me
And God bless the somebody I want to see.

I see the moon and the moon sees me.
God bless the moon and God bless me;
There's grace in the cabin and grace in the hall
And the grace of God is over us all.

Grandfather's Clock

My grandfather's clock was too large for the shelf
So it stood ninety years on the floor.
It was taller by half than the old man himself
Tho' it weighed not a penny weight more.
It was bought on the morn of the day that he was born
And was always his treasure and pride.

Refrain:
But it stopped short, never to go again
When the old man died.
Ninety years without slumbering (tic toc, tic toc),
His life seconds numbering (tic toc, tic).
But it stopped short, never to go again
When the old man died.

In watching its pendulum swing to and fro
Many hours had he spent as a boy.
And in childhood and manhood the clock seemed to know
And to share both his grief and his joy.
For it struck twenty-four when he entered at the door
With a blooming and beautiful bride. (Refrain)

Now my grandfather said that of those he could hire
Not a servant so faithful he found.
It wasted not time and it had but one desire
At the end of each week to be wound.
And it stayed in its place, not a frown upon its face
And its hands never hung by its side. (Refrain)

It rang an alarm in the dead of the night,
An alarm that for years had been dumb.
And we knew that his spirit was pluming its flight,
That his hour of departure had come.
Still the clock kept the time, with a soft and muffled chime
As we silently stood by his side. (Refrain)

—Henry Clay Work

I've Been Working on the Railroad

I've been workin' on the railroad all the livelong day.
I've been workin' on the railroad just to pass the time away.
Can't you hear the whistle blowin'? Rise up so early in the morn.
Can't you hear the captain shoutin' "Dinah blow your horn!"

Dinah won't you blow (3x) your horn? (repeat)
Someone's in the kitchen with Dinah,
Someone's in the kitchen I know.
Someone's in the kitchen with Dinah,
Strummin' on the old banjo.

A-playing' fee fi fiddle-y-i-o, Fee fi fiddle-y-i-o-o-o-o
Fee fi fiddle-y-i-o, strummin' on the old banjo.

Itsy Bitsy Spider

The itsy bitsy spider climbed up the water spout.
Down came the rain and washed the spider out.
Out came the sun and dried away the rain,
And the itsy bitsy spider climbed up the spout again.

—Traditional

Las Mañanitas

Es - tas son las Ma - ña - ni - tas que can - ta - ba el Ray Da -

vid y hoy por ser dí - a de tu san - to te can - ta - mos a ti.

ESTRIBILLO:

Des - pier - ta, mi bien des - pier - ta, mi - ra que ya a - ma - ne -

ció, los pa - ja - rill - os ca - tan, la lu - na ya se me - ti - ó.

This is the morning song that King David used to sing
and because it's your birthday we'll sing it for you.
REFRAIN:
Wake up my dear, wake up and see the rising sun,
the birds are singing, the night is gone.

Let Me Call You Sweetheart

Let me call you sweetheart, I'm in love with you.
Let me hear you whisper that you love me too.
Keep the love light glowing in your eyes so true.
Let me call you sweetheart, I'm in love with you!

—*Beth Slater Whitson*

Lift Ev'ry Voice and Sing

1 Lift ev-'ry voice and sing, till earth and heav - en ring,
2 Ston-y the road we trod, bit - ter the chas-t'ning rod,
3 God of our wea - ry years, God of our si - lent tears,

ring with the har - mo - nies of lib - er - ty.
felt in the days when hope un - born had died
thou who hast brought us thus far on the way,

Let our re - joic - ing rise high as the lis-t'ning skies,
yet with a stead - y beat, have not our wea - ry feet
thou who hast by thy might, led us in - to the light,

let it re - sound loud as the roll - ing sea.
come to the place for which our peo - ple sighed.
keep us for - ev - er in the path, we pray.

Sing a song full of the faith that the dark past has taught us.
We have come o - ver a way that with tears has been wa - tered.
Lest our feet stray from the pla - ces, our God, where we met thee,

Sing a song full of the hope that the pres - ent has brought
We have come, tread - ing our path thro' the blood of the slaugh -
lest our hearts, drunk with the wine of the world, we for - get

us. Fac - ing the ris - ing sun of our new day be -
tered, out from the gloom - y past till now we stand at
thee, shad - owed be - neath thy hand, may we for - ev - er

gun, let us march on till vic - to - ry is won.
last where the bright gleam of our bright star is cast.
stand, true to our God, true to our na - tive land.

O Come, O Come Emmanuel

O come, O come, Emmanuel,
And ransom captive Israel,
That mourns in lonely exile here,
Until the Son of God appear.

Refrain:
Rejoice! Rejoice! Emmanuel
Shall come to thee, O Israel.

O come, thou Dayspring, come and cheer
Our spirits by thine advent here.
Disperse the gloomy clouds of night,
And death's dark shadows put to flight. (Refrain)

O come, thou Wisdom from on high,
And order all things, far and nigh.
To us the path of knowledge show,
And cause us in her ways to go. (Refrain)

O come, Desire of nations, bind
All peoples in one heart and mind.
Bid envy, strife and quarrels cease.
Fill the whole world with heaven's peace. (Refrain)

—Anonymous

O Freedom

Refrain:
O freedom, o freedom
O freedom over me!
And before I'd be a slave, I'll be buried in my grave
And go home to my Lord and be free.

1. No more killin's (3x) over me...

2. No more fear...

3. No more hunger...

4. There'll be joy...

5. There'll be singing...

6. There'll be peace...

—Adapted by Student Nonviolent Coordinating Committee

O How Lovely Is the Evening

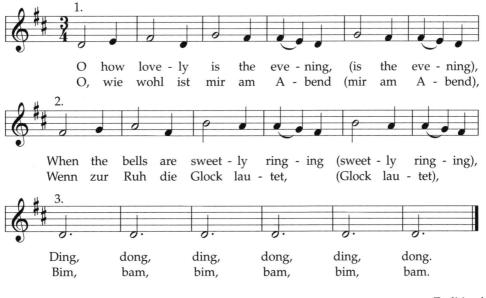

O how love-ly is the eve-ning, (is the eve-ning),
O, wie wohl ist mir am A-bend (mir am A-bend),

When the bells are sweet-ly ring-ing (sweet-ly ring-ing),
Wenn zur Ruh die Glock lau-tet, (Glock lau-tet),

Ding, dong, ding, dong, ding, dong.
Bim, bam, bim, bam, bim, bam.

—Traditional

Our Life Is More Than Our Work

Look all around you, say, look all around you
See all there is just to be alive about
Look all around you, at the people around you
See all there is just to being alive.

>   Refrain:
>   O our life is more than our work,
>   And our work is more than our jobs
>   You know that our life is more than our work,
>   And our work is more than our jobs.

Time clocks and bosses, investments and losses
How can we measure our living in numerals?
Time clocks and bosses, investments and losses
How can we measure our life in this way? (Refrain)

Think how our life could be, feel how our life could flow
If just for once we could get into letting go
Think how our life could be, feel how our life could flow
If just for once we could let ourselves go. (Refrain)

So let go what holds you back, close your eyes, take a dive
We got a universe we got to keep alive
Let go what holds you back, close your eyes, take a dive
We got a universe fighting to live. (Refrain)

By Charlie King. Copyright © 1978
Charlie King/Pied Asp Music (BMI).
Used with permission.

Para Pedir Posada

1 En __ nom - bre __ del cie - lo
3 Ve - ni - mos __ ren - di - dos
5 Po - sa - da __ te pi - do,
7 Mi __ es - po - sa es Ma - rí - a,

Os __ pi - do __ po - sa - da.
Des - de Na - za - ret. _____
A - ma - do __ ca - se - ro.
Es __ la Rei - na del Cie - lo,

Pues __ no pue - de an - dar _____
Yo __ soy car - pin - te - ro
Por só - lo u - na no - che
Y __ ma - dre va a ser _____

Ya mi es - po - sa a - ma - da.
De __ nom - bre Jo - sé. _____
La __ Rei - na del cie - lo.
Del __ Di - vi - no Ver - bo.

198

–Dentro–

2 A — quí - no es me - són. _____
4 No ___ me im - por - ta el nom — bre
6 Pues ___ si es u - na Rei — na
8 ¿E — res tú __ Jo - sé? _____

Si — gan a - de - lan — te.
Dé - jen - me ___ dor - mir, _____
Quien ___ la so - li - ci — ta
¿Tu ___ es - po - sa es Ma - rí — a?

Pues ___ no pue - do a - brir _____
Pues ___ que yo les di — go
¿Có - mo es que de no - che
En - tren pe - re - gri — nos,

No se - a al - gún tu - nan — te.
Que no he - mos de a - brir. _____
An - da tan ___ so - li — ta?
No los co - no - cí — a.

–Entren, Santos Peregrinos–

En - tren, San - tos Pe - re - gri - nos, Pe - re - gri - nos. Re - ci - ban es - te rin-

cón. No de es - ta po - bre mo - ra - da Si - no de mi co - ra - zón.

(See next page for English translation.)

199

The people *outside* sing:

> 1. In the name of heaven
> We seek some room at your inn.
> My beloved wife
> Cannot go any further.
>
> 3. We are so very tired
> We've come a long way from Nazareth.
> I am a carpenter
> Joseph is my name.
>
> 5. A place to rest is all that's requested
> From you dear inn keeper,
> Just for this one night,
> So asks the Queen of Heaven.
>
> 7. My wife is Mary
> She is the Queen of Heaven
> And about to become
> The mother of the Incarnate Word.

The people *inside* sing:

> 2. Sir, this is no inn
> Just move along.
> There's no way I'll open this door,
> You might be a thief.
>
> 4. Your name is of no importance
> Just let me go back to sleep.
> For I have already told you
> That I am not going to open this door.
>
> 6. Well if it is a "queen"
> Who makes this request,
> How is it that on this night
> She's wandering about all alone?
>
> 8. Is that you Joseph?
> And your wife is Mary?
> Please enter dear pilgrims
> I just did not recognize you.

Follow with the song to usher all pilgrims into the home:

> Enter pilgrims, holy pilgrims.
> For I offer you this place.
> I don't mean my humble home,
> But the place here in my heart.

Rock of Ages (Mo-oz Tzur)

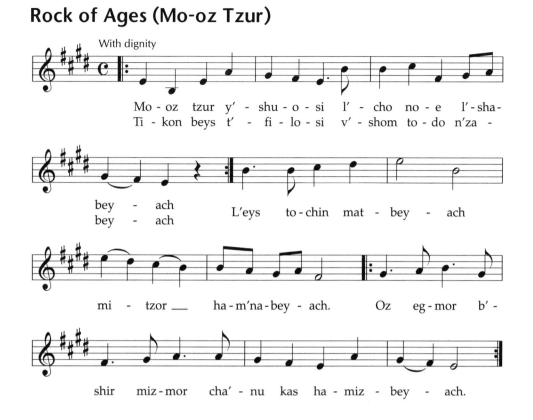

With dignity

Mo - oz tzur y' - shu - o - si l' - cho no - e l' - sha-
Ti - kon beys t' - fi - lo - si v' - shom to - do n'za -

bey - ach
bey - ach L'eys to - chin mat - bey - ach

mi - tzor ___ ha - m'na - bey - ach. Oz eg - mor b' -

shir miz - mor cha' - nu kas ha - miz - bey - ach.

Rock of Ages, let our song praise your saving power.
You, amid the raging foes, were our sheltering tower.
Furious they assailed us, but your arm availed us,
And our word broke their sword
When our own strength failed us.

—*Traditional*

Santa Lucia

Santa Lucia,
Thy light is glowing,
Through darkest winter night,
Comfort bestowing.
Dreams float on wings belight,
Comes then the morning light.
Santa Lucia, Santa Lucia.

—*Traditional Scandanavian Carol*

Simple Gifts

'Tis a gift to be simple, 'tis a gift to be free!
'Tis a gift to come down where we ought to be.
And when we find ourselves in the place just right,
'Twill be in the valley of love and delight.

When true simplicity is gained
To bow and to bend we shan't be ashamed.
To turn, turn will be our delight
'Til by turning, turning we come 'round right.

—Traditional Shaker Hymn

Solar Carol

(Sing to the tune of "Angels We Have Heard on High.")

See the sun how bright it shines on the nations of the earth
All who share this thing called life celebrate each day's rebirth.

   Refrain:
   So-o-olar power, inexpensive energy (2x)

Brother river, so you hear, how the valley calls you down
Send your rushing waters near, let the joyful hills resound. (Refrain)

Sister wind we've heard on high, sweetly singing o'er the plain
And the windmills in reply, echoing their glad refrain. (Refrain)

How we love complexity, when the answer's rather plain
Join the sun in jubilee, sing with us this joyous strain. (Refrain)

*Copyright © 1980 Adam Austill, Court Dorsey,
Charlie King, Marcia Taylor. Used by permission.*

This Land Is Your Land

   Refrain:
   This land is your land, this land is my land
   From California to the New York Island
   From the redwood forest to the Gulf Stream waters
   This land was made for you and me.

As I was walking that ribbon of highway
I saw above me that endless skyway
I saw below me that golden valley
This land was made for you and me. (Refrain)

I've roamed and rambled and I followed my footsteps
To the sparkling sands of her diamond deserts
And all around me, a voice was sounding:
This land was made for you and me. (Refrain)

(cont.)

When the sun came shining and I was strolling
And the wheat fields waving and the dust clouds rolling
As the fog was lifting, a voice was chanting
This land was made for you and me. (Refrain)

As I went walking, I saw a sign there
On the sign, it said "No Trespassing"
But on the other side, it didn't say nothing
That side was made for you and me! (Refrain)

Canadian refrain:
This land is your land, this land is my land
From Bonavista to Vancouver Island
From the Arctic Circle to the Great Lake Waters
This land was made for you and me.

This Little Light

This little light of mine, I'm gonna let it shine (3x)

Refrain:
Let it shine, let it shine, let it shine!

2. All around the town, I'm gonna let it shine (3x) (Refrain)

3. Everywhere that I may go, I'm gonna let it shine (3x) (Refrain)

4. In my daily work, I'm gonna let it shine (3x) (Refrain)

5. For the poor and hungry folk, I'm gonna let it shine (3x) (Refrain)

6. Free of fear and hatred, I'm gonna let it shine (3x) (Refrain)

7. Trustin' in the Lord, I'm gonna let it shine (3x) (Refrain)

8. Building a new world, I'm gonna let it shine (3x) (Refrain)

9. Put it under a bushel - NO!, I'm gonna let it shine (3x) (Refrain)

10. Ain't nobody gonna 'whoof' it out, I'm gonna let it shine (3x) (Refrain)

—Traditional Gospel Song

Under One Sky

We're all a fam - i - ly un - der on sky, we're a
fam - 'ly un - der one sky. We're sky.

Verse

1 Well, we're peo - ple (peo - ple), we're an - i - mals
2 Well, we're sis - ters (sis - ters), we're bro - thers

(an - i - mals), we're flow - ers (flow - ers), and birds in
(bro - thers), we're un - cles (un - cles), and grand - mas

flight (and we're birds in flight). Well we're peo - ple
too (and we're grand - mas too). Well, we're par - ents

(peo - ple), we're an - i - mals (an - i - mals), we're flow - ers
(par - ents), we're chil - dren (chil - dren), all mem - bers of

(flow - ers), and birds in flight (and birds in flight).
(mem - bers of) one fam - i - ly (one fam - i - ly).

3 Well, we're Asian (Asian),
We're African (African),
We're native (native),
and European too (European too).
Well, we're Hispanic (Hispanic),
We're Arab (Arab),
Americans all
in the U.S.A. (the U.S.A.).

4 Well, we're Americans (Americans),
We're Russians (Russians),
We're Italians (Italians),
and Vietnamese (and Vietnamese).
Well, we're Mexican (Mexican),
We're Iraquis (Iraquis),
We're Israelis (Israelis),
and we're Chinese (and we're Chinese).

Vine and Fig Tree

And ev-'ry man 'neath his vine and fig tree shall live in

peace and un-a-fraid. And ev-'ry fraid.

And in-to plow-shares beat their swords, na-tions shall learn

war no more. war no more. Love to your neigh-bor and

love to the spir-it of all life. spir-it of all life. And ev-'ry

1,2,3:
Lo yisa goy el goy cherev
Lo yilmedu od milchama (repeat)

When the Saints Go Marching In

O when the Saints go marching in (2x)

> Refrain:
> O Lord I want to be in that number
> When the Saints go marching in

2. And when the sun begins to shine (Refrain)

3. When the moon turns red with blood (Refrain)

4. On that hallelujah day (Refrain)

5. O when the trumpet sounds the call (Refrain)

Family Night 6

Baked Sweet Potatoes

Wash a medium-sized sweet potato for each family member.

Dry potatoes and grease very lightly with shortening.

Place in a pie pan and bake at 375° approximately 1 hour or until soft when pinched.

To serve, split about half way and insert slice of butter or margarine.

Enjoy!   (Children can help prepare this food.)

Collard Greens

    1 bunch collard greens (about 1½ pounds)
    3 strips bacon (or boiled ham hocks)
    salt to taste
    1 tablespoon sugar

Wash greens under running water; remove large stems and discard.

Roll 3 or 4 leaves into a vertical roll; on cutting board slice in ½-inch slices across roll. Roll and slice all of the greens.

In dutch oven, pot, or heavy kettle, fry bacon strips until crisp. Remove bacon, add sliced greens and 1½ cups water, but do not cover greens. Add salt and sugar. Crumble bacon on top. Cover and bring to a rapid boil. Reduce heat and simmer for 1 to 1½ hours. Greens are done when they are tender. Serve with mashed potatoes or rice and corn bread.

Family Night 7

Gelatin Bars

    9 oz. flavored gelatin (1 large and 1 small box)
    4 packets unflavored gelatin
    4 cups boiling water

Mix dry ingredients; add boiling water. Pour into 9x9-inch cake pan, let cool slightly, and place in refrigerator. Cut into small bars or use cookie cutters for different shapes. No refrigeration is necessary after jelled.

Family Night 26

S'mores

Make a "sandwich" out of 2 graham cracker squares, a piece of chocolate, and a roasted marshmallow.

Family Night 37

Orange Julius

⅓ cup frozen orange juice concentrate
½ cup milk
½ cup water
½ teaspoon vanilla (optional)
5 or 6 ice cubes, crushed

Place all ingredients in a blender and blend to froth.

Smoothies

ice cubes
milk
frozen bananas, peaches, or strawberries

Place all ingredients in a blender and blend to froth.

Family Night 42

Challah

Ingredients:

A. 2 tablespoons yeast
   3 teaspoons salt
   1¾ cups warm water
   ¾ cups honey

B. 2 cups flour

C. 1¼ cups oil
   3 eggs

D. 5 to 6 cups flour

E. Glaze: 1 egg
           poppy seeds

Combine A ingredients in a bowl and stir.

Next, mix in B, followed by stirring in C.

Add enough D to lose stickiness.

Knead in bowl until you have a nice lump of dough. Dump dough onto a board and continue kneading until you have a silky texture. Return to oiled bowl; cover and let rise in a warm spot about an hour. Test for readiness by sticking a finger in the dough (about ½ inch). If the dent your finger makes remains, you're ready to punch the dough down and knead briefly.

Form the dough into three strands (roll it like you would make clay into "worms"). Braid the strands into two loaves. Put on greased baking sheet, cover, and let rise again for about thirty minutes in a warm spot.

For glaze (E):
Mix the final egg and brush it over the loaves. Sprinkle with poppy seeds. Bake at 350° for 50-60 minutes. Check doneness with a toothpick.

Family Night 54

Fry Bread (yield: 8)

Combine in large mixing bowl:

> 3 cups flour
> 1¼ teaspoons baking powder
> 1 teaspoon salt
> 2 tablespoons dry milk powder

Gradually stir in 1⅓ cups warm water.

Mix until dough forms ball and comes clean from edge of bowl. Knead on lightly floured surface until well mixed and elastic. Divide dough into 8 pieces and roll into balls. Using palms of hands, pat into circles about ½-inch thick. Heat ¾ inch of oil to 450° in frying pan.

Carefully slip rounded, flat piece of dough into hot oil. Bread will start to rise to top of hot oil. When underside of bread is brown, turn over and brown other side. Drain well on paper; then place in baking pan in 200° oven and cover with damp towel to keep warm and chewy. Repeat with remaining dough.

From *Extending the Table: A World Community Cookbook* by Joetta Handrich Schlabach. Copyright © 1991 Herald Press. Used by permission.

Family Night 56

Latkes

> 6 medium potatoes
> 1 large onion
> ¼ cup flour
> 2 large eggs, beaten
> 1 teaspoon salt
> ½ teaspoon pepper
> cooking oil
> sour cream or plain yogurt
> applesauce

Peel the potatoes and onion and grate them with a grater or a food processor. Add flour, eggs, salt, and pepper. Heat two tablespoons of oil at medium-high heat in a frying pan. Ladle about ¼ cup of potato mixture into the pan (enough to make 3-inch diameter patties). Let brown on one side, then flip. When they're brown on the other side, dry them on paper towels. Add more oil to the pan before you ladle in each batch of latkes.

Potato Kugel

> 6 tablespoons olive oil
> 1 onion, chopped fine
> 7 raw potatoes, grated and drained
> 3 well-beaten eggs (or six egg whites)
> ½ cup flour
> ½ teaspoon baking powder
> 2 teaspoons salt
> ½ teaspoon pepper

Heat 2 tablespoons of olive oil in skillet and cook the onion. Place potatoes, beaten eggs, flour, baking powder, oil, salt, and pepper into bowl and mix well. Add the cooked onions. Stir. Grease a 9x13-inch baking pan and pour in mixture. Bake at 400° for one hour. Serve immediately or freeze and reheat prior to serving.

Family Night 58

Lucia Buns (yield: eight 4-inch rolls)

¼ cup lukewarm water
1 package dry yeast
¾ cup scalded milk
¼ cup butter
1 egg
¼ cup sugar
1 teaspoon salt
2 teaspoons cardamon
½ cup raisins
3½ cups flour

Dissolve yeast in water. Scald milk, remove from heat, stir in butter, let cool to lukewarm. Add remaining ingredients to yeast. Mix with a spoon until smooth. Knead for five minutes. Cover with a towel, let rise in a warm place (about 85°) for 1½ hours or until doubled in size. Punch down, let rise again for 30 minutes. Break off small chunks of dough and roll into 10-inch long ropes. Slit ends of each stick almost to center, then shape like a cross on a greased cookie sheet. Decorate with raisins. Let rise 15 minutes. Bake at 375° for 12-15 minutes.

Options: Add a pinch of saffron to the dough for color and flavor, or just use a few drops of yellow food coloring for effect. These buns are scrumptious with a drizzle of icing on top. Use your favorite recipe.

Family Night 59

Bunuelos

2 cups flour
1 tablespoon sugar
½ teaspoon baking powder
dash of salt
½ cup sugar mixed with 1 teaspoon cinnamon
1 egg
½ cup milk
2 tablespoons butter (melted)
Oil/shortening for frying

Sift dry ingredients together. In medium bowl, beat egg and milk with fork. Gradually stir in flour mixture, then butter. Turn out on lightly floured surface; knead gently until smooth and elastic. Divide into 12 equal pieces and shape each one into a ball. Cover; let rest for about 20 minutes. Roll out balls to 6-inch circles, like a tortilla, but much thinner. Roll out until almost translucent. In medium skillet, heat 1 inch of oil to 375°. Fry bunuelos, one at a time, turning once, until lightly browned. Drain on paper towels; sprinkle with the sugar/cinnamon mixture.

Champorrado (10-12 small cups)

    1 gallon milk
    1 large can evaporated milk
    1 cup sugar (or sweeten to taste)
    2 sticks cinnamon
    4 tablespoons cocoa
    2 pounds masa (same masa as used to make tamales,
        but more finely ground)

Put all above ingredients, *except masa*, in a large pot. Heat over low heat. In the meantime, dilute/mix the masa with some of the milk from the pot so that it dissolves into a smooth mixture. (Break it up with your hands and then mix small portions with the milk and put it through a strainer. Then work with another small amount until it's all done. You may add a little water at any time.) When the masa is done, pour this mixture into the pot, a little at a time, *stirring constantly*, until thickened but still of drinking consistency (at least ½ hour). *Never bring to a boil.* (This is the difficult, but most important part.) The result is a delicious, warm, soothing, smooth chocolate drink.

APPENDIX C

Family Night 4 | ## World Religion Cards

RELIGION	FOUNDER	HOLY BOOK	SYMBOLS
CHRISTIANITY 1C.E.—30C.E.(approx.)	JESUS CHRIST	THE BIBLE	
JUDAISM 1300B.C.E.	MOSES	THE TORAH (Old Testament)	
HINDUISM 900B.C.E.(approx.)	KRISHNA	BHAGAVADGITA	
BUDDHISM 500B.C.E.(approx.)	BUDDHA	DHAMMAPADA	
ISLAM 622C.E.	MUHAMMAD	THE QUR'AN	
BAHA'I 1844C.E.	THE BAB and BAHA'U'LLAH	THE BAYAN and THE BAHA'I WRITINGS	
ZOROASTRIANISM 600B.C.E.	ZOROASTER	THE GATHAS	

Biographical Sketches of Blacks in History

Frederick Douglass

Douglass was a political leader and orator for the cause of abolition. He spoke extensively in behalf of women's suffrage and was the only man invited to the first Women's Rights Convention. His newspaper, *The North Star*, appeared in 1847 and was one of the most influential and soberly edited abolitionist periodicals of the day.

Senator Blanche Kelso Bruce

Bruce was a United States senator from Mississippi during Reconstruction after the Civil War. He was dedicated to the welfare of all Americans and especially noted for his strong stand regarding the civil rights of non-Black minorities. Bruce spoke out against the proposal to bar Chinese from entering the United States and was equally outspoken in defense of Native American rights.

Dr. Charles Drew

Dr. Drew was a scientist who began the blood bank through his research into the preservation and storage of blood. He pioneered and demonstrated the advisability of shipping blood plasma and serum instead of whole blood to World War II battlefields. He died at age 48 when a hospital exclusively for white people refused to admit him for a blood transfusion following a serious auto accident.

Mme. C. J. Walker

A self-made millionaire, she was an uneducated Black woman who rose from poverty to compete successfully with White men in the international business world. She rose from scrubwoman to rich woman in less than a decade. Mrs. Walker formulated a cosmetic line especially tailored to the needs of African-American women. Her successful manufacturing company employed hundreds of workers and agents. She became a philanthropist, donating large sums to worthy causes.

Dr. Daniel Hale Williams

Performing the world's first successful heart operation on July 9, 1893, Dr. Williams opened the chest of a man stabbed in the heart and sewed up the hole. He was the founder of America's first interracial hospital (Provident Hospital in Chicago) and, at the same location, the nation's first school for the training of African-American nurses. At Freedman's Hospital in Washington, D. C., he established the nation's second school for training of Black nurses.

Richard Allen

Allen was the leader of free Blacks and founder of the African Methodist Episcopal Church. In the summer of 1793, when a plague of yellow fever fell upon Philadelphia, the city was crippled by the epidemic, since preventative measures and a cure were unknown at that time. Officials approached Richard Allen requesting that African-Americans (falsely believed to be immune) assume the burden of caring for the dying and burying the dead. For two months the health of the city was in the hands of its Black citizens. Allen is recognized for his leadership in this crisis and for his work organizing the citizen's militia that defended Philadelphia in the War of 1812.

Dr. Percy Julian

The world's arthritis sufferers owe thanks to this chemist for developing a low-cost arthritis drug—cortisone—vital to the treatment of inflammatory arthritis. As director of soybean research, he made significant discoveries related to the complex chemical makeup of the bean and experimented with new uses for derivatives extracted from the plant. He is also credited with successful development of the drug vital to the treatment of glaucoma, an eye disease.

Mary McLeod Bethune

Bethune was college founder, president, and guiding light of Bethune-Cookman College, which she started in a refuse dump and almost singlehandedly built into one of Florida's most important schools. Mrs. Bethune was widely known as an innovative educator and public speaker. She became a member of Franklin Roosevelt's "Black Cabinet" and served as presidential advisor to Presidents Roosevelt and Truman.

George Washington Carver

Recognized as one of the most productive scientists of any race ever to appear in America, Carver remade the face of agriculture in America, enriching not only the productivity of farmers but our entire economy as well. He promoted crop diversification instead of single crops that depleted the soil. He synthesized new crop-related by-products at an astounding rate: from the peanut he extracted meal, bleach, synthetic coffee, wood filler, metal polish, cooking oils, rubber, linoleum, plastics, and more than three hundred other marketable products. From the sweet potato, pecans, soybeans, wood shavings, and cotton stalks, he produced over one hundred new products each.

William and Ellen Craft

Fleeing slavery in style, this husband-wife team successfully plotted and carried out one of the most daring and ingenious slave escapes. Stealing sets of fine clothing from their respective masters and a luxurious carriage from a third slave holder, they set out in broad daylight. Fair-skinned Ellen passed as the white owner of her dark-skinned husband, who played the role of her coachman and manservant. On their journey from Macon, Georgia, to Philadelphia, they were not stopped or questioned even once. They stayed at the finest "white" hotels and ate at exclusive restaurants on pennies, nickels, and dimes they had saved over the years. After their arrival in the North, they became popular speakers at abolitionist meetings. After the war they returned to Georgia and established an industrial school for Black youth.

> **NOTE:** You may wish to add contemporary names to your hero/heroine index cards.

Thurgood Marshall

Civil rights attorney who initiated civil rights laws, Thurgood Marshall became a Supreme Court justice.

Maya Angelou

A famed author and poetess, Angelou wrote and read a poem for President Clinton's inauguration.

Arthur Ashe

As a tennis pro, Ashe won Wimbledon and the U. S. Open. He was a developer of programs for youth, such as Virginia Heroes Inc.

Jackie Robinson

Robinson was the first black major-league baseball player.

If there are "detectives" in the group, they may enjoy finding out why the following lesser-known names are important to know.

Josephine Matthews
Leontyne Price
E. M. Bannister
Hiram Revels
Carter Woodson

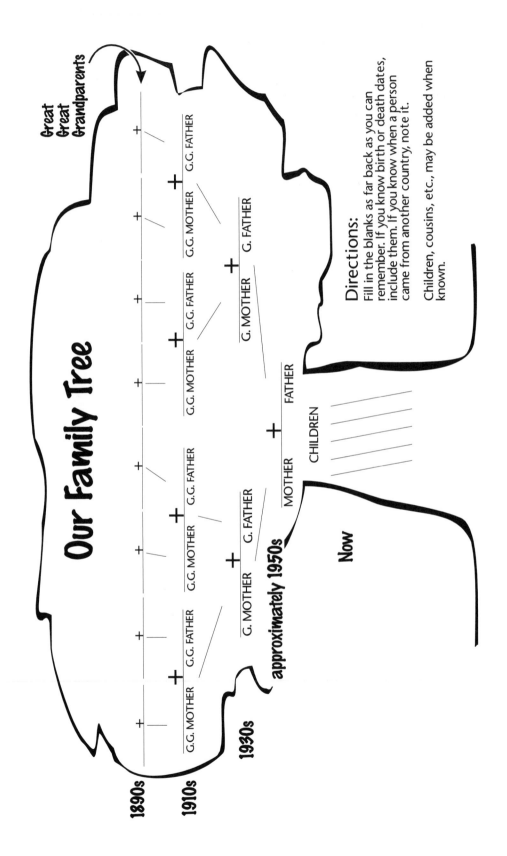

Our Family Tree

Great Great Grandparents

1890s
1910s
1930s
approximately 1950s

G.G. MOTHER | G.G. FATHER | G.G. MOTHER | G.G. FATHER | G.G. MOTHER | G.G. FATHER | G.G. MOTHER | G.G. FATHER

G. MOTHER | G. FATHER | G. MOTHER | G. FATHER

MOTHER | FATHER

CHILDREN

Now

Directions:

Fill in the blanks as far back as you can remember. If you know birth or death dates, include them. If you know when a person came from another country, note it.

Children, cousins, etc., may be added when known.

Videos and Values Worksheet

PART 1

	Passive/Weak		Nurturing		Aggressive
Male images:	1	2	3	4	5
Female images:	1	2	3	4	5

	Prudish		Healthy sexual awareness	Seductive/Sex object	
Male images:	1	2	3	4	5
Female images:	1	2	3	4	5

	Dumb/Silly		Smart		Dominating
Male images:	1	2	3	4	5
Female images:	1	2	3	4	5

	Not pictured		Mildly pictured		Strongly pictured
Violent images:					
Toward objects	1	2	3	4	5
Toward self	1	2	3	4	5
Toward women	1	2	3	4	5
Toward men	1	2	3	4	5

	Boring		Very funny		Ridiculing
Humor:	1	2	3	4	5

	Only one race		Realistic mixture		Negative stereotype
Racism:	1	2	3	4	5

Content:
❑ Superficial   Example: _____
❑ Social issues addressed:
   ❑ war   ❑ pregnancy   ❑ homophobia
   ❑ drugs   ❑ other_____

Religious/Moral Values:
❑ Denigrated   Example: _____
❑ Respected   Example: _____

Language:
   ❑ childish/repetitive   ❑ respectful   ❑ funny
   ❑ racial/ethnic slurs   ❑ intelligent   ❑ gross
   ❑ unnecessary profanity   ❑ inclusive   ❑ slang

(continued on next page)

PART 2

1. What emotions did this video leave you with? (happiness, anger, sadness, fear...)

2. Were video images presented in a distorted way? (use of blurred lens, rapid images, zombie-like expressions...)

3. What did the video say about relationships?

4. What did you like about the video?

5. What didn't you like about the video?

THE FOX
Compromise—Manipulation
Illustrated by Frances Gregory

THE OWL
Fighting Fair—Collaboration
Illustrated by Frances Gregory

THE TEDDY BEAR
Accommodation
Illustrated by Frances Gregory

THE SHARK
Aggression—Competition
Illustrated by Frances Gregory

OUR FAMILY'S ANIMAL

THE TURTLE
Avoidance—Passivity
Illustrated by Frances Gregory

THE OWL

- Uses "I" language when talking about feelings
    "I don't feel good about the way this is going."
- Separates the problem from the people
    "I care about how you are feeling."
- Listens attentively and with care
    "Sounds like you're pretty angry."
- Confronts openly, honestly, fairly
    "I don't like it when you … "
- Cooperates to find solutions, problem solver
    "Let's think up some other possible solutions."

THE FOX

- Looks you right in the eye
- Promises a quick fix
    "I know you're upset, so I'll treat you to an ice cream cone."
- Uses negotiation talk
    "Let's split the difference and forget it."
- Wheels and deals
    "Can we make a deal?"
- Trades off for quick solutions
    "If you stop being mad at me, I'll let you play with my skateboard."
- Puts getting something ahead of principle
    "I'm going to get that no matter what. I'll beg, borrow, or steal."

THE SHARK

- Invades other people's space
- Accuses others, calls people names
    "You're so stupid!"
- Uses "YOU" language
    "You always mess things up."
- Uses sarcasm, putdowns
    "Get out of my way, slowpoke."
- Uses words like *should* and *must*
    "I don't care what you say. The flowers should be planted right there."
- Uses rigid arguments, won't listen to others
    "You dare come across this line, I'll beat you up."
- My way is the only right way
    "We'll do it my way or no way at all."
- Destroys relationships
    "So? Go home. I don't care."

THE TEDDY BEAR

- Looks down or away rather than into the eyes
- Hides feelings
    "What's wrong? Nothing."
- Agrees with everything
    "Okay, whatever you want."
- Goes along with the crowd
    "Well, if you think it's okay."
    "If you don't think anyone will mind."
- Smooths over issues to keep friendship
    "I'll do anything you want if you'll just be my friend."
- Ignores own needs
    "What I want isn't important."
- Pretends everything is okay

THE TURTLE

- Fidgets uncomfortably, looks away
- Avoids conflict situations
    "Please don't ask me."
- Tries not to get involved
    "I don't know anything about it."
- Believes the situation is hopeless, feels helpless
    "I'll never understand that."
- Changes the subject
    "I'd rather do anything but talk about that."
- Cries
    "Boo-hoo-hoo, I really don't want to talk about it."

OUR FAMILY'S ANIMAL

- How would this animal typify the way someone in your family deals with conflict?

Example: THE PARROT—talk, talk, talk

(source unknown)

220

Conflict situations to resolve:

(G—girl; B—boy)

G—age 10: Your brother just brought in some food and spilled it on the table. How will you handle it?

B—age 8: Your sister accidently knocked over your bike, but you don't know that it was accidental. You hear the bike fall over, you go outside, and you see your sister standing by the bike.

G—age 13: Your sister borrowed your blouse and gave it back with a big stain on the front.

B—age 15: Your teacher gave you a grade lower than you thought you deserved on a test. When you add up the points, you find that you should have a higher grade.

Mom: Your son just came in half an hour late for dinner.

G—age 8: Your older brother accuses you of taking his portable stereo from his room when you're not supposed to be in his room at all, but you didn't really do it.

Dad: You look into your daughter's room and see a wall-to-wall, helter-skelter mess.

Mom: You walk into the bathroom and see toothpaste blobs splattered all over the mirror, and you just cleaned it this morning.

Mom: You've told the children not to leave roller skates in the hallway. After you fall on the roller skates in the hallway, how do you react?

B—age 11: You stay in bed until twenty minutes before the bus. As you're on your way out the door, your mother calls you back to put on a jacket. You miss the bus. What do you say or do?

B or G: Your best friend spent the night with a new classmate. You feel jealous. What do you say to your friend?

B—age 9: You know your bedtime is at 9:00. At 8:55 you realize you didn't do your book report, which is due tomorrow. How do you feel? What do you do?

B—age 12: Someone calls you a nerd because you wear glasses and you're smart in school. You don't like it. What do you do?

G—age 11: You get hit in the cheek with a soccer ball while playing soccer. The person who kicked the ball is not your favorite person. What do you do?

B—age 10: You come home hungry from school, hoping for hamburgers and french fries for supper. You find out your sister has just made a new vegetarian dish for the meal. What do you do?

G—age 9: Your favorite TV show is on tonight. You've already seen your TV quota for today. What do you do?

Myself as a Saint

My greatest strengths as a person are:

_____

_____

_____

_____

_____

_____

_____

_____

_____

```
┌─────────────────┐
│                 │
│                 │
│      Paste       │
│   a photo        │
│  of yourself     │
│     here         │
│                 │
│                 │
│                 │
└─────────────────┘
```

If I were to describe myself in one word it would be…

_____

People can count on me to…

_____

_____

_____

I make the world a better place by…

_____

_____

_____

I would most want to be remembered for…

_____

_____

_____

From *Saints Alive!* by Judith Bisignano and Corine Sanders.
Copyright © 1987 Sheed & Ward. Used by permission.

All Saints Bingo

Directions:

1. Make copies of the bingo card and list of names for everyone.

2. Using the list of names, have one person put the names on separate pieces of paper and mix them up in a small box or paper bag. Feel free to substitute other favorite saints or peace and justice heroes.

3. Have everyone write the same names at random on their playing cards. As you write the name on the card, talk about that saint/hero.

4. To play the game, have one member draw the names from the bag or box and call them out, while others mark their cards. The first person to complete a horizontal, vertical or diagonal line wins the game. **To vary the game so that everyone wins,** put the names in the same arrangement on all cards.

All Saints Bingo

		FREE	

SAINT JOHN
SAINT JOSEPH
MOSES
NELSON MANDELA
GANDHI
ABRAHAM LINCOLN
DAU AUNG SAN SUU KYI*
SAINT PAUL
MICAH
MOTHER TERESA
SAINT MICHAEL
SAINT PATRICK

SAINT ELIZABETH
HARRIET TUBMAN
SAINT LUCY
SAINT ANN
SAINT ROSE
SAINT CATHERINE
WOODROW WILSON
RALPH NADER
SAINT LUKE
ABRAHAM
SAINT RITA
AARON

* Dau Aung San Suu Kyi (Burmese woman who uses nonviolent means to resist government violence in Burma; Nobel Peace Prize winner, 1991). A list of other Nobel Peace Prize winners may be found in *The World Almanac* under "Awards." Feel free to substitute other favorite saints or justice and peace heroes.

Appendix D

Parenting for Peace and Justice Resources

All Parenting for Peace and Justice resources can be obtained from:
    The Institute for Peace and Justice
    4144 Lindell Blvd. #124
    St. Louis, MO 63108
    314-533-4445

Resources can also be obtained from the publishers listed with each work and at some bookstores.

Educating for Peace and Justice: Religious Dimensions (Grades K-6) by James McGinnis, 1993.

Educating for Peace and Justice: Religious Dimensions (Grades 7-12) by James McGinnis, 1993.

Educating for Peace and Justice: Global Dimensions (Graces 7-12) by James McGinnis, 1992.

Helping Families Care by James McGinnis, 1989.
    Offers a wide range of family activities on the themes of peacemaking, diversity, consumerism and stewardship, ecumenism and worship.

Helping Teens Care. James McGinnis, ed., Crossroads, 1991.
    A helpful resource for parents, teachers, youth ministers, and others who work with teens.

Parenting for Peace and Justice: 10 Years Later, Revised Edition, by Kathleen and James McGinnis. Orbis Books, 1990.

Parenting for Peace and Justice Network Newsletter.
    This resource is included in P.P.J.N membership of $25.00. It is published six times a year and includes practical ideas to further peace and justice in the home. Recent issues have dealt with Loving the Earth, Racism and Sexism, Media and Domestic Violence, Parents and Teens, Single Parenting, Family Systems, Family Stress.

Starting Out Right: Nurturing Young Children as Peacemakers by Kathy McGinnis and Barbara Oehlberg, 1988.
    Adapts the original P.P.J. book to families with pre-school age children.

Books That Deal with the Family Night Concept

Family Time: A Revolutionary Old Idea by Grady Nutt. Prepared and published by the FamilyTime Committee of the Million Dollar Round Table. 1977 Million Dollar Round Table, 2340 River Toad, Des Plaines, IL 60018.

Prime Time for Families by Michael G. Pappas. Winston Press, 430 Oak Grove, Minneapolis, MN 55403, 1980.
> Over 50 activities, games, and exercises for personal and family growth.

Seasonal Stories for Family Festivals by Armandine Kelly. Resource Publications, Inc., 160 E. Virginia St. #290, San Jose, CA 95112, 1987.

To Celebrate: Reshaping Holidays and Rites of Passage, 6th ed., by Eugenia Smith-Durland. Alternatives, 1990. P.O. Box 429, Ellenwood, GA 30049.

The Virtues Guide: A Handbook for Parents Teaching Virtues by Linda Kavelin Popov, Dan Popov, Ph.D., and John Kavelin. The Virtues Project, Inc., 192 Sun Eagle Drive, R.R. 1, Ganges, B.C. Canada, 604-537-1978.
> A collection of family activities on virtues such as compassion, creativity, honesty, service.

AUTHORS

Editor

Susan Vogt

Susan is married to Jim Vogt, P.P.J.N. administrator. They have four children, Brian, Heidi, Dacian, and Aaron. They have been doing family nights for about fifteen years. Jim and Susan share the job of co-director of Family Ministry for the Catholic Diocese of Covington, Kentucky. They are founding board members of P.P.J.N., contributing authors to *Helping Teens Care*, lead workshops, and belong to a family support group.

Contributors

Sue Blythe

Sue is single and co-parents three girls, Jill, Susanna, and Keri, between their dad's house and her own. She has been doing family nights for about eight years. As a consultant for peace education, Sue teaches, does parent education, and is a volunteer coordinator. She is a P.P.J.N. board member and workshop leader in Gainesville, Florida.

Joseph Ceja

Joe is married and a retired civil engineer. He consults with the Hispanic caucus of the Catholic Diocese of Fresno, California, in the area of Hispanics and other minorities. He and his wife do catechist training and teach natural family planning.

Jean Chapman

Jean is a single parent with joint custody of two children, Sandy and Joyce. She has been doing family nights since the girls were small and has led P.P.J.N. workshops which have "had a *major* influence on my family." Jean is a pediatrician in North Carolina with the Hillsborough County Public Health Department.

Nancy Corindia

Nancy is married to Tom and they have four children: Nicholas, Emily, and twins, Alex and Francis. Nancy is a Quaker and has a doctorate in elementary science education. She often collaborates with Patricia Higgins in joint P.P.J.N. projects in Hanover, New Hampshire.

Louise Bates Evans

Louise is a divorced mother of three grown children, Myrtle, Bill, and Louis, and has two grandchildren. She lives in Indianapolis, Indiana, and is retired as director of Family Ministry for the Christian Church (Disciples of Christ). Louise is a P.P.J.N. board member and director of the Black Family Ministries Project of the National Council of Churches.

Jim Ford

Jim and his wife, Nanette, have three children, Aaron, Amy, and Melissa. They have been doing family nights "forever." Jim is a campus minister, high school teacher, and professional musician. He is co-editor of the *P.P.J.N. Newsletter*, workshop leader, and member of a family support group in St. Louis, Missouri.

Janet Fraser

Janet is married to Glen Kruck and they have two children, Heidi and Adam. Janet has held a variety of social work jobs ranging from working with infants, to teens, to senior citizens. She also leads workshops on family choices, nonviolent toys, cooperative games, and garbage crafts in Manitoba, Canada.

James Goodman

Jim and his wife, Susan Talve, are both rabbis. They have three children, Jacob, Sarika, and Adina, and live in St. Louis, Missouri. In addition to caring for their children, working with the temple and P.P.J.N., Jim plays the guitar. Their greatest fear? "To have my children say, 'You were out saving the world and forgot about us.' "

Ann Marie Witchger Hansen

Ann Marie and her husband, John, have eight children, Elizabeth, Erik, Teresa, John Robert, Mary Frances, Rebekah, Matthew, and Anna Kateri. They have been doing family nights for about eight years. Ann Marie is a freelance speaker and writer on parenting, global education, and peacemaking. Since Ann Marie and John have returned from overseas missionary work, she has given P.P.J.N. workshops and organized a peace camp near Pittsburgh, Pennsylvania.

Peggy Haupt

Peggy is married to Joe and they have a blended family of four children, Adam, Joey, John, and Sara. She is coordinator for religious education at Mother of God Catholic Church in Covington, Kentucky. Peggy also coordinates and leads, with her husband, a marriage preparation program for couples entering a second marriage.

Patricia Higgins

Patricia is married to Scot Drysdale and they have two children, Helen and Carol. She is an organizational consultant in Hanover, New Hampshire. Until recently, she was a P.P.J.N. board member and has led numerous P.P.J.N. programs at local churches. "Being a Quaker, the themes were a natural extension of my spiritual journey."

Ina Hines

Ina is a single mother of one daughter. In addition to her work in the African-American community, she is active in Junior Achievement and works with a variety of church, community, and peacemaking groups. She frequently collaborates with Sue Blythe on projects in Gainesville, Florida.

Tom Kruer and Karen Zerhusen

Karen and Tom are married and have two children, Adriane and Nathan. Tom is an engineering consultant and works out of his home in Edgewood, Kentucky. Karen is a lawyer and mediator in private practice. They are members of a family support group in the Greater Cincinnati (Ohio) area.

Mike Magrath

Mike and his wife, Linda Holtzman, have a blended family of five children, Pat, Sheila, Bernadette, Dora, and Alex. Mike is co-director of National Louis University's Interdisciplinary Studies program. He has long been involved with peace, justice, and parenting issues in St. Louis, Missouri.

Robert and Cheryl Nanberg

Bob and Cheryl have two grown children, Jon and Joshua. Bob is Jewish and Cheryl is Catholic, and over the years they have made a point to celebrate both religious traditions with their children. Bob works in women's retailing and Cheryl is a homemaker. They reside in Avon, Connecticut.

Wendy Bauers Northup

Wendy and her husband, Steve, have four children, Chhun, Adam, Maris, and Kathleen. They have done a lot of family nights over the years. Wendy works as a consultant in conflict resolution and violence prevention in the Ashland, Virginia, area. She is a founding P.P.J.N. board member, has been a workshop leader for over twelve years, and is a member of a family support group.

Mary Joan Park

Mary Joan and husband, Jerry, are natural and adoptive parents of six children, Sarah, Jonathan, PJ, Jimmy, Tommy, and Timmy. Mary Joan is a teacher and, with her husband, founded Little Friends For Peace in the Mount Rainier, Maryland, area. They lead workshops and retreats on peacemaking and other P.P.J.N. themes.

Nina Phipps

Nina and husband, John, live in Huntsville, Alabama, and have three grown children, Terri, Karen, and John. She is the office manager for a doctor's office and is active in Christian education, camps, and youth groups of the Church Street Cumberland Presbyterian Church. She has worked extensively in the African-American community.

Rosemary Piña

Rosie is married to Roberto and they have two grown children, Cristina and Leticia, and two grandchildren. She works as an administrator in health services for the army. Rosie also is adjunct staff at the Mexican-American Cultural Center in San Antonio, Texas. She leads workshops on Hispanic family life and is a former P.P.J.N. board member.

Karen Schneider-Chen

Karen and her husband, Ming, are the parents of three children, Emily, Suzanna, and Stephanie. They have been doing family nights for about eight years. Karen is a folk dance instructor and is a local P.P.J.N. leader in Seattle, Washington.

Elizabeth Dowling Sendor

Liz is married to Ben Sendor and they have three children, Julia, and twins, William and Adam. She is a journalist and an intern for Holy Orders in the Episcopal Diocese of North Carolina.

Colleen Aalsburg Wiessner

Colleen is married to Rev. Dr. Charles Allen Wiessner and they have two sons, Nathaniel and Benjamin. It seems like they have been doing family nights "always." Colleen is associate for Christian Nurture for the Synod of the Mid-Atlantics (Reformed Church in America). She is the author of many books and articles and treasures doing creative things as a family in Harrington Park, New Jersey.

Evelyn P. Wilson

Evelyn and her husband have four children, Charles IV, Gina, Adrienne, and Wyatt. She is an educator and former P.P.J.N. board member from the Church of God. She lives in Gilbert, Arizona, where she is also involved in the African-American community.

Arthur and Marian Wirth

Art and Marian have three grown children and two grandchildren. Art is a professor at Washington University in St. Louis, and Marian is an author and educator in the area of early childhood education. They are founding members of Parents and Friends of Lesbians and Gays (P-FLAG) in the St. Louis area. Marian and Art are former P.P.J.N. board members.

Linda Lapp Young

Linda and husband, Jim, have three children, Zeb, Zura, and Zion. Linda is an elementary school teacher. She leads workshops, is a P.P.J.N. board member, and belongs to a family support group. "Over the years, we've experimented with a variety of family nights. When the children were small, it was very modest with perhaps the biggest discussion being what flavor of ice cream to have at the next gathering."